Private Terror / Public Life

Private Terror/ Public Life

PSYCHOSIS AND THE POLITICS OF COMMUNITY

James M. Glass

CORNELL UNIVERSITY PRESS

ITHACA AND LONDON

First published 1989 by Cornell University Press.

International Standard Book Number 0-8014-2300-7
Library of Congress Catalog Card Number 89-31059

Printed in the United States of America

*Librarians: Library of Congress cataloging information
appears on the last page of the book.*

*The paper in this book is acid-free and meets the guidelines for
permanence and durability of the Committee on Production
Guidelines for Book Longevity of the Council on Library Resources.*

For Cyndi and Jeremy

In Kafka, long before the sentence is executed, even long before the malign legal process is ever instituted, something terrible has been done to the accused. We all know what that is—he has been stripped of all that is becoming to a man except his abstract humanity, which, like his skeleton, never is quite becoming to a man. He is without parents, home, wife, child, commitment, or appetite; he has no connection with power, beauty, love, wit, courage, loyalty, or fame, and the pride that may be taken in these. So that we may say that Kafka's knowledge of evil exists without the contradictory knowledge of the self in its health and validity.

LIONEL TRILLING, 1955

Contents

Acknowledgments   xi

Introduction   1

PART I   DISINTEGRATION AND STRUGGLE

1 Metaphor as Political Knowledge   11

2 The Struggle between Delusion and Intersubjectivity   26

3 Psychotic Terror: The Imaginary Unleashed   40

4 Withdrawal from the Public World: Nightmares and
   Histories   56

5 The Destruction of Mind   72

6 Return to the Human Text   86

7 The Wish for Nonbeing   103

PART II   EFFORTS AT RESOLUTION

8 "Mama, Make Me Dead": The Power of Depression   125

9 Spring Lake Ranch and the Rousseauian Bases of
   Community   148

10 Boundaries of a Public Selfhood: Labor and Work   167

11 The Politics of Exclusion and the Concept of Place   193

Notes   221
References   237
Index   243

Acknowledgments

I am grateful to the Sheppard and Enoch Pratt Hospital in Towson, Maryland, and to its director of inpatient services, Dr. Wolfe Adler, and the chairman of the hospital's institutional review board, Dr. Gerald Whitmarsh, for their continued support of this project. Many on the nursing staff have been extremely helpful: Rosalie Alsop, Joe Bass, Jane Cole, Jane Goldsborough, Debbie Kennard, Siobhan Powers, and Ruby Oster, to name only a few. Art therapists Christie Bergland and Rosanna Moore-Gonzalez consistently demonstrated to me the power of images and symbols in elaborating the linguistic productions of the self. Among doctors and other staff who were generous of their time and conversation, I especially thank David Cowie, Denise Fort, David Gonzalez, Rachel Hamilton, Mayer Liebman, Charlie McCormick, Joan Naess, Charles Peters, Miles Quaytman, and Sally Winston.

This book and its predecessor, *Delusion* (1985), would not have been written without the inspiration and guidance of Drs. Maria Klement, Roger Lewin, and Clarence Schulz. In large measure my interpretations of psychotic and borderline states and their linguistic frameworks have been inspired by these therapists' sensitivity, their broad practical and theoretical knowledge, and their work with patients at Sheppard-Pratt. I have been fortunate to learn from them.

I also thank Michael Wells, director of Spring Lake Ranch in Cuttingsville, Vermont, for his hospitality and for providing me access to Spring Lake and its residents.

For their insightful comments on the political and philosophical context in which this research was undertaken and for their continuing encouragement, I am indebted to Fred Alford, Fred Dallmayr, Michael Weinstein, and Victor Wolfenstein. My understanding of connections between the clinical and political worlds has benefited from discussions with Benjamin Barber, Eugene Brody, Alfonso D'Amico, Michael Diamond, Jean Elshtain, Richard Flathman, Ralph Hummell, Seymour Rubenfeld, and Vamik Volkan.

I would like to acknowledge the General Research Board of the Graduate School of the University of Maryland for its generous and ongoing support of this project.

I am grateful to my typist, Flora Paoli, for her detailed and careful work on the manuscript throughout its development.

To the patients of the Sheppard and Enoch Pratt Hospital and the residents of Spring Lake Ranch, I owe a special thanks. Without their cooperation and willingness to share their inner worlds, an activity frequently filled with intense struggle, this project could never have been realized. It is their experience that lies at the heart of this book.

JAMES M. GLASS

College Park, Maryland

Private Terror / Public Life

Introduction

This book is concerned with the politics of the self as that politics appears in the utterances of persons whom society considers to be psychically estranged, mental patients who experience their human selves as nonexistent, dead, worthless, thinglike, and in some instances animallike. Symbolic narrative as commentary on the self's inner transformation guides the discussion. The presence of voices, hallucinations, delusions, immobilizing depressions, and uncontrollable manias affects the self's position in the world, its capacity to act, to be, to make decisions, to participate in collective environments. These internal states seriously alter one's sense of freedom, one's scope of participatory citizenship; they interfere with the psychological conditions necessary even to begin to perceive oneself as a political being, a citizen.

My intent is to look at the basic conditions of an internal imprisonment, to examine the relation between delusional presences in the self and the equally compelling desire to find one's way back to a communal attachment. It is a dilemma often phrased by patients as "Where shall I live? In my delusional world with its familiar and busy action or in agonizing and despairing association with other persons?"

If Aristotle's view of the self as essentially or naturally political—more accurately, communal or social—is demonstrable (I elaborate on

1

the Aristotelian view in Chapter 7), then at least some of the proof lies in accounts of persons who find themselves both outside and inside the walls of the *polis* (community), who discover their humanness because of a breaking-down of delusional defenses and a subsequent integration into shared and reciprocal experiences. Proof of the unnatural state of delusion, its denial of the historical self, may be found in persons who remain psychotic, who never find their way back—the tragedy, for example, of chronic schizophrenics. To be in the consensual world is not only to establish a trusting relationship with another human being; it is also to participate in a communal setting that transcends private need, preoccupation, and fantasy. What patients and former patients say testifies to the importance of community and the role of public space in guiding the self toward a sense of its own humanity. It is specific evidence of how important the sense of place, a connection to the public world, is to those who find themselves excluded from it.

Persons who experience themselves as inhuman, as things or objects, as pieces of dead matter, as merging with spaceships or spirits, live in unfree states of being. Nothing in a world of community or association—none of the benefits of a participatory citizenship—lies within their frame of reference. It is a condition radically alienated from civilized values; it is a tragedy, a withdrawal from shared public realities, from being and working in common. Narratives and reflections by persons who have endured considerable psychological anguish demonstrate the extent to which such individuals feel themselves driven from a common humanity and a common history. Their experience shows a retreat to private inner worlds whose meaning is obscure, whose function lies in defending the self from fear, annihilation, and fragmentation.

In the Aristotelian view, the issue regarding the self's citizenship is not whether one is a human being, whether the self considers itself to be a person or not. Aristotle assumed that these questions had been resolved for the citizen and the "good man"; any others lived as either beasts or gods and were peripheral to the concerns of the *polis*. From a modern perspective, however, the question of the self's habitat is considerably more complex, because to be borderline or manic-depressive (the major diagnostic clusters covered in the narratives) is to be not a beast or a god—although delusion may define the self in those terms—

but a human being whose internal world projects identifications of overwhelming dehumanization and worthlessness. Even more fundamental than whether or not one has the skills necessary to be a citizen in public and administrative environments is the knowledge of whether one is or is not a human being. Even to begin to practice citizenship, the self requires a sense of its humanness, its existence in a social world. Delusion blocks that recognition; community encourages it.

The center of this study of the relation between self and community is the experience, the phenomenology, of human beings who see themselves as less than human, whose inner worlds force them outside the human community, who face the unequal distribution of power coming from delusion (the internal frame) and the encounter with others, who find themselves tormented and frightened by what consensual reality offers as participation, community, and belief. As David (all names and any other identifying material have of course been changed), who is described in Chapters 2 and 3, puts it: "When I was crazy, I wanted to be a particle flying over the face of the earth; I hated the idea of leaving my world, of having to deal with persons, with life on the Hall [ward]. I had been designated by God to be in a special place; and I fought coming back to a world that had caused me so much pain."

Unfree inner states affect the way the self perceives others, the way it interprets events in the consensual world. If consensual reality impinges on consciousness, if it implodes on the self, if truth and meaning lie in symbols shot through the heaven by God's angels, if the present is really 1943 and not 1983 (as it was for Ruth, described in Chapters 4 and 5), if razor blades become teddy bears (as they did for Julia, Chapter 7), then what sense does it make to speak of citizenship and participation, governing and self-governing? Before the self engages in relations with others, much less in complex communal interaction, it is first necessary to dismantle the domination of internal images and their peculiar power to terrorize and to enforce hermetic withdrawal. For the person living inside a delusional system, the external world matters little; it is, in any event, understood through what delusion projects as interpretation. The politics of the inner world, therefore, the internal enchainment, speaks to different concerns than does the politics of either an institutional or an elective setting. But it is a politics nonetheless; since the delusional self comes up against the constraints of public and consensual definition, it finds itself subject to the politics of exclusion. In withdrawing from the power and structure of the external world, from society and history, consciousness finds itself forced to confront the power exercised by its internal constructions.

This is the position I argued in *Delusion* (Glass 1985). What I want to convey in this book is the power of the drive for community as a response to the delusional introject, and the concrete efforts of individuals—the participants in communities who speak with and listen to the narratives of the mentally ill—who are actively engaged in diminishing the impact of these internal forms of enchainment. Part I addresses the content of the narratives themselves, their storytelling, the phenomenology of the fragmented self and its existential presence. Part II examines environments that respond to these stories of deprivation and disintegration with counternarratives of community and association.

In describing the politics of the self and the communities that surround the very special situation of fragmented selves, I am not speaking of freedom, equality, power, authority, rights, and justice as I might in describing a political regime, a revolutionary movement, or a group conflict within unstable organizational environments. I am, however, speaking of *feelings* of freedom, equality, power, authority, rights, and justice, since these political objects, in both their delusional and their consensual representations, appear in the self's experience. The transformation, which I see as a politics, from an inner deadness or anarchy (hidden in a private language) to participation among other selves (acknowledgment of being as a social process) is a recurring theme in the narratives. Further, to be free psychically becomes from the patient's perspective a vital, social good, since the psychically displaced find themselves afflicted and dominated by knowledge that maintains the self in varying degrees of unfreedom, knowledge that imprisons and victimizes through the imposition of pain. Delusion is not a place of happiness or security; the narratives describe the discovery of community as a refuge from delusional uncertainty, as a place where momentarily dependent relations allow the self to discover some measure of social connection. Delusion is a universe of mythic proportions, of endless anarchic eruptions, of eternal torment; the schizophrenic, for example, might be thought of as a modern variation of Sisyphus.

To be entrapped by delusion is to experience extreme injustice; and this politics, while not conventional, depends on internal psychological realities that are as "there" and as compelling as the politics of the external world. What happens inside the self is a politics because psychological transformation conveys meaning about need and desire, the structure of domination, the process of freedom, the experience of equality and inequality, the difference between being a subject and being a participant in community. It is a politics because survival depends on the capacity of the self to reach beyond its own internal imprisonment, to break down emotional isolation, and to forge relations of trust and attachment. To argue that what the psychotic or delusional self faces is not a politics is to deny the facticity of the internal world, the thought of persons whose knowledge systems revolve around delusion and the social and political values repudiated by this massive inversion of the consensual framework.

In contrast, a therapeutic community such as Spring Lake Ranch (described in Chapters 9 and 10) presents an image of possibility both in language and action which seeks to dispel the determinism and futility of a myth like that of Sisyphus. It is as if the narrative structure of such a place as Spring Lake Ranch stands in direct competition to the languages of the inner world which push the self into isolation.

To be delusional, to understand oneself as dead or as an object to be destroyed, to be fascinated (like Julia, Chapter 7) by methods of cutting and slicing veins and arteries or to conduct research on the rate of blood flow through different arterial systems in order to speed up the time it takes to die is to exist in a psychically horrifying state. It is an internal domination as deadly as any external tyranny. Except that its source lies in hidden, obscure, and split-off areas of the self's developmental past, it is a tyranny resembling that under which a political prisoner faces the actions of a radically disrupted political and cultural history. In both cases, the being of victimization carries with it a political meaning and significance; in both instances, the self suffers a loss of place and context; it experiences confusion, misunderstanding, and strange and unfamiliar environments. For the psychically displaced, these environments appear in the language and images of delusion.

The status of the mentally ill is an event in the public life of the culture; it is therefore political. And for the self that lives emotionally and in many cases physically on the borders (or beyond them) of civilization, for the schizophrenic whose psychological habitat has absolutely no connection with consensual reality, public life offers little in the way of refuge or comfort. Afflicted by terrifying internal images, facing the exclusionary dynamics of the economic and social universe, the self in these narratives constructs a statement about community and its loss, shared fellowship and its absence, reciprocity and its lack.

Several themes recur in the narrative presentations: the critical importance of language in establishing contact with the external world; what the setting defines as participation; the recovery of the self's public being, its relatedness, in the Aristotelian sense of living inside the walls of the *polis*; the importance of that process in convincing the self of its essential and natural humanity; the relation between association and broader social processes of exclusion and banishment; and the idea of the self as a psychic refugee and the role of community in diminishing psychic pain and in responding to the political status of refugeehood. Each of these themes points to the larger issue of the relation between the private concerns of the internal world and the capacity of the withdrawn self to establish some sense of personhood and attachment to a public space.

The major focus of Part I is the voice of mental patients. I rely heavily on narrative to convey a sense of this inner world, its terror, its sense of shut-up-ness and futility. I introduce theoretical perspectives, periodically, but it is primarily the patients' *imagos,* their presence in language, that I wish to convey. What these patients say is often unpleasant and quite painful. It is therefore essential for the reader to understand that these transcribed narratives are efforts to reveal and describe an inner terrain, a world that oscillates between the borders of civil society and what lies beyond those borders. In this respect the language of madness—and the value that lies behind its narrative—is not a pathology, a description of an isolated sickness, but commentary on patterns of relatedness and their interruptions, on the fantasies and defenses that define the human project as an interpenetration of what Jacques Lacan (1968) calls the Imaginary with the Real.

Further, particularly in Part II, I pursue the following objectives in addressing the relation between the status of the self and its presence in community: (1) to think about the concept of the public realm in the context of environments not normally considered political—namely, the mental ward and the therapeutic community; (2) to demonstrate the drive for community and its strength in persons whom the society classifies as seriously mentally ill (or, to put it another way, the primacy of an Aristotelian/Rousseauian commitment to association over the more divisive and egoistic dynamic of the Hobbesian aggregation of wills); (3) to suggest that the phenomena Aristotle consigns to the household may, because of their effect on the self, be fitting objects for political study (I refer here to the legacies of infancy and childhood and their accompanying feeling-states). I argue that the narratives of mental patients and former patients, when refracted in concrete efforts to build counterenvironments, contain a set of facts that shed light on such political concepts as community, citizenship, participation, action, and transformation.

The loneliness of mental illness intensifies the wish for or fantasy of community. That wish preoccupies consciousness; it is a powerful drive that involves the desire to be a person, the desperate effort to overcome debilitating internal images in the form of delusion, and the very real need to establish reciprocal exchanges with other human beings. Mental patients strive, in often stumbling ways, to establish relations that might be considered public or associational. It is a movement toward finding oneself as a citizen among others, even though that citizenship involves a frightening encounter with internal images that pull consciousness away from its rootedness in consensual reality.

PART I

DISINTEGRATION
AND STRUGGLE

1 /

Metaphor as
Political Knowledge

To listen to and transcribe the self as a form of oral history, as history of the self, is to be moved and disturbed; it is to enter a world filled with nightmare and horror; it is to become involved in a process of recollection that traverses the deepest layers of conscious and unconscious reality. It is to find oneself aware of a level of suffering that often provokes unsettling and frightening feelings. I frequently walked away from these dialogues wondering how consciousness could survive such morbid and deadly preoccupation, how imminent was Freud's (1920) concept of the "death instinct" refracted in a symbolism obsessed with annihilation and disintegration.

Even the act of reconstructing the dialogues brought back the emotional intensity of their original description. It is difficult to convey in prose how intense, how overwhelming, those inner worlds are, how deeply they reach into the Other, how the process of listening becomes a dialectic, constructing its own special field and structure, and how these patients struggled to reveal thoughts they live with every minute of every day. To listen to and reflect on thoughts of death, annihilation, self-mutilation, hopelessness, and despair becomes itself a process of transformation and change, a movement inward toward untouched spaces in the self, my self, which even now I find troubling. To encounter images that place consciousness on the "edges"—or what Jacques Lacan (1977) calls the rim—of a common humanity is to experience those edges as real, as empirically present, almost tangible. It is to be in the presence of a peculiar form of immanence, with no possibility of transcendence, to feel a despair that often takes the form of nihilism, unbounded rage, and physical mutilation.

To cite Lacan's celebrated observation, the unconscious may be thought of as "structured like a language," as a "concrete discourse" (1968: 32); or *"the unconscious is the discourse of the Other"* (1978a: 131). To be caught up in this discourse and its imaginative figures was to find myself in the midst of intense emotional and psychological contradictions, a flow of experience that acted as a commentary on the self's peculiar and often disguised history. It meant witnessing the transformation and annihilation of being, as well as its reappearance and resiliency; it meant encountering an alienation that impelled patients to carve messages into their flesh, to ruminate on the most successful ways of physically killing and mutilating the body, to contemplate external experience as a continuing journey into some murderous Hell, a continuing reenactment of Dante's Inferno. A strikingly macabre form of this alienation occurred in one patient who for her Christmas decorations made papier-mâché snowflakes look like double-edged razor blades.

I entered a psychological field surrounded by a discourse whose origins were obscure, a field composed of images reflecting on the tragedy of desire, on the deathlike qualities of human existence, on the anguish of the self in its exclusion from relatedness and association. In this respect, I took seriously Lacan's view (1977: 106) that "the psychoanalytic experience has rediscovered in man the imperative of the Word as the law that has formed him in its image." Language could be understood as a form of action, since the inner world appeared to these patients as felt and lived experience. To speak was to find oneself literally engaged with the *action* of speech. Lacan continues: the psychoanalytic experience "manipulates the poetic function of language to give to [the self's] desire its symbolic mediation." What these patients spoke was their being, its "symbolic mediation" in the form of language. Language, being, and metaphor became totally bound up in one another, and the speech act itself took on a lived, vital quality. It was as if the symbols spoken, the images described, were real and alive in consciousness, filling completely the dialogic field.

Each narrative arose from a "concrete history where a dialogue is engaged, in a register where no sort of truth can be found in the form of a knowledge which is generalizable and always true" (Lacan 1978b: 1049). In this sense, language became an activity joining me to the Other in a shared excursion through meditations on the tragedy of desire, on the failures of relatedness and community. No absolutes or universal truths appear in these reflections; each contains its own special commentary on the history of the self and its nightmare world of terror and disintegration. David's reflections on becoming a "particle" and flying through the skies on his way to war (Chapters 2 and 3), Ruth's on Auschwitz and the world as 1943 (Chapters 4, 5, and 6), Julia's on cutting and the use of razor blades as teddy bears (Chapter 7): each of these meditations, these frames enclosing reality, describes something of being and the origins and the destruction of desire. Because "the reality of each human being is in the being of the other" (Lacan 1978b: 933), it is impossible for me to say or maintain that my reaction to these stories remains separate from the being that speaks the language. And my interpretation of the stories finds itself deeply affected by the sheer presence of the persons narrating them.

To have been objective, then, in whatever terms—whether through coding responses, or devising questionnaires, or setting up scales, or somehow systematizing the language—would have been a distortion on two counts. First, it would have entailed an alteration of the symbol relations themselves, breaking them down according to a formalized criterion, damaging the existential context of what was being uttered. And second, it would have distorted the field established between the speaker and me. Each of these commentaries is a story being told to an Other; and it seems to me that the presence of the Other is a central element in what the story speaks, in what its symbolizations convey as forms of meaning.

The narrative of the self may be thought of as a form of storytelling, as tales transmitted by a spoken language that reflects on the relation between the self and its surrounding culture and history. Paul Ricoeur (1970) speaks about storytelling—particularly in its use in psychoanalysis as a way to reveal the self's history in discourse—as part of an "oral tradition" that has its origins, at least in the West, in the spoken epic.[1] Claude Lévi-Strauss (1969, 1973) uses storytelling quite extensively in his analysis of the role of myth and metaphor in building an epistemological framework. Storytelling provides a unique perspective in the social sciences; it delineates meaning and content through its power as symbolization and lived experience. It relies on metaphor as commentary on patterns of mind and desire.

In these storytellings each patient struggles toward association, what Rousseau calls an *interdependent* existence, but each is caught up in the flows of an internal nature that leaves the self isolated, sometimes psychotic, and withdrawn from consensual relationship. The delusional self is separated from culture, from association; it is precisely this *separation* that becomes life threatening, that keeps the person outside or on the borders of those moral and personal interdependencies that distinguish culture from nature in the Rousseauian sense. Each narrative, then, posits—indirectly and through the use of symbolic reflection—the essential opposition between what is psychotic (or the noncivil in the political sense) and what is "associational" (or the interdependencies of culture, community, and intersubjectivity). And each reflects on the view that existence in association or community becomes itself a civilizing and humanizing dynamic. It is paradoxical that tormented individuals in the midst of nihilistic despair, locked into themselves, so *alone,* construct eloquent testimony to the importance of community.

None of the patients I spoke with desires, at least consciously, to remain bounded in an isolated emotional universe (although Julia, for example, believes that isolation defines the contextual environment of the self in the world). None willingly chooses to be psychotic or delusional; none wishes to remain forever tied into what Lacan calls the Imaginary as a form of imprisonment.[2] Rather, the patients' language suggests the opposite: the natural movement of the self toward association—with the caveat that the external world often presents such threat that association may be subverted by a corrosive entropy that lies both inside and outside the self. Many, particularly the "borderline" patients (see Chapter 4), would agree that delusional and psychotic states constitute regressions, unwanted movements away from social reality, terrifying descents into boundless worlds that shatter ego functions and social relationships. As an aberration provoking great torment, delusion or a susceptibility to delusional regression brings an unbearable loneliness.

Metaphor and Truth: On the
Importance of Symbolization

What follows in these storytellings is not a sociological treatise or a cultural epidemiology. Nor is it an effort to prove any causal theory or method of treatment. I look at etiology only as it explains or illuminates specific events in the narratives. Biological and chemical factors enter into an analysis of the causes, for example, of schizophrenic states, although this study utilizes the patient's voice as evidence for analysis in addition to observations made by therapists, nurses, and mental health workers. No matter how biological or chemical the origins of severe mental illnesses may be (and it is not at all clear that borderline states have a biological etiology; the evidence is more persuasive with schizophrenia and manic-depression), what exists beyond brain chemistry or genetics are persons who express feeling, who assimilate experience, and who live among other persons. It is that realm of being, in addition to the meaning of community as a *political* event in the life of the self, that lies at the center of this book. It is commentary from persons who experience their human selves as dead or in Searles's sense (1960) nonhuman, who feel that existence in civil society has become an intolerable, oppressive burden.[3]

Two orders of symbolization appear in the narratives. First, there is the concrete, in which the symbol is experienced as real and metaphors have an action component, in which the schizophrenic or psychotic self believes that the icepick actually picks at the brain (cf. Giovacchini 1986). Second, there are the symbol formations of civil society, in which the self understands speech acts to be in fact symbolic and not real, is able to say, for example, that the sun is "burning me up" without holding to the belief that the sun sends its rays down to ignite the flesh; there is some distance between the utterance and the recognition of its symbolic component. In delusional or psychotic states the symbol is experienced as real, not *as if* it were real but as reality itself. Illusion—what Nietzsche (1956) called the "Apollonian"—can be considered symbolization that lies more on the side of culture; it involves what he saw as "dream images," or the reflections of culture, art, sensibility, and aesthetic.

Illusions provide a more cultural and social frame; in contrast, delusion and psychosis can be understood as phenomena that take the self closer to an unbounded, frenetic nature, a Dionysian universe that has lost the ameliorating effects of Apollonian imagery. Illusions exist within a set of social expectations; they may even be encouraged and fostered by cultural aspirations or ideals. Delusion, however, removes the self from culture, from the Apollonian world. Delusion is an attack on ideals, cultures, histories, and, most important, on consensually validated patterns of meaning.

This difference between delusion and illusion might also be thought of in terms of Winnicott's notion (1965) of the "transitional space" and the "transitional object," the "illusions" that for the infant occupy that "intermediate" area between "inside" and "outside." Delusions belong more to the inside, the autistic and withdrawn. Illusions, because of their capacity to be shared, because of their presence in art, constitute critical, participatory structures in the beliefs that bind communities. The shared, the public, the dramatic as artistic *form* moves outward in contrast to the solipsistic, isolated realm of the interior monologue, the delusion without any shared component or audience.

In using as evidence the narratives of mental patients, I argue that states of mind represented in symbol should be thought of as a form of discourse illuminating political life. To cast the argument in more theoretical terms, I look for a moment at Plato's critique of poetry and the poet in *The Republic*. Plato raises important questions regarding speech and its form which apply with some force to the kind of imagery regarded as appropriate or right knowledge. For him, the indeterminate and volatile speech of poetry constitutes a critical danger to the polity. In effect, I argue that the language of madness possesses the same kind of volatility, is a nonrational speech that stirs up emotion and feeling.

Plato (1964) banishes the poet from his "city of speech"; poetry, he argues, not only acts as a competing source of power and influence but induces states of mind that disrupt order and reason. The poets conceal themselves behind their characters; and they speak, elliptically, not the truth but a pale imitation of what might be understood as the truth. Their verses detract from the pursuit of the Good. Poetry disturbs and

falsifies reality. It has no significance in delineating the relation between the self and the public world that surrounds it. It dwells in the
realm of appearance; it lacks form, pattern; it imitates. "The creator of
the phantom, the imitator, we say, knows nothing of the reality but
only the appearance" (10.601c). It is a seductive influence that speaks
to the inferior part of the soul, to feelings of pleasure and pain; it is a
mode of discourse not concerned with knowledge; it imitates in that it
is speech that refuses to address the "truth," the "forms" behind appearance, but stands at "three removes from reality," a sly but dangerous apparition.

According to Plato, poetry should not be allowed into a "well ordered state because [the poet] stimulates and fosters this [inferior]
element in the soul and by strengthening it, tends to destroy the rational part" (10.605b). Philosophy, on the other hand, the method of
reason that teaches and guides the guardians, is not imitative; it relies
on logic; it speaks directly to the mind, not the passions. It refuses to
inflame or pull the audience toward images of failure, tragedy, disillusionment, and human frailty. If the Guardians are to imitate anything,
"they should from childhood up imitate what is appropriate to them—
men, that is, who are brave, sober, pious, free." But the images of the
poet, "things unbecoming the free man," they should avoid, "nor be
clever at imitating, nor yet any other shameful thing, lest from the
imitation they imbide the reality" (5.395c). It is the imitative basis of
art that Plato finds dangerous and corrupt: "The more debased [the
speaker] is, the less will he shrink from imitating anything and everything" (3.397ab). Poetry, as a "kind of art," provokes a "corruption of
the mind of all listeners who do not possess as an antidote a knowledge
of its real nature" (10.595b).

If in transcribing the narratives of mental patients I engage in what
Plato calls "imitation," transcribing thoughts and images "at three removes from reality," it is because I believe that such imitation (if it can
even be called that) contains its own kind of commentary from which
much can be learned. Consider that such reflections may reveal fractures in human experience and sensibility not subject to rational explanation or scientific understanding as these are normally conceived. It is
possible, indeed probable, that metaphor and poetry address levels of
reality which escape reason. This is not to say that science or reason is
unimportant in studying the kinds of questions raised in these reflec-

tions; rather, it is to suggest that imitation or metaphoric imagery speaks to aspects of human nature in a language that contains a significance and resonance absent in, for example, an inquiry into the chemical or genetic or epidemiological origins of mental disorders. That kind of scientific language (and its use) portrays a different area of reality, a different sense of the internal than does the symbolic reflection or the poetical statement.

Or to put it another way: the tragedies of Sophocles offer messages or insights into human society beyond the analytic power of reason and philosophy to provide, beyond what Plato reveals through his philosophic dialectic. The playwright or poet moves to enclose worlds of emotion and feeling in symbols that, because of their sheer dramatic presence, pull an audience closer to the turbulence of the human self and its effect on action. What is an audience to make of a Medea, an Oedipus, a Clytemnestra? Are these figures, who have violated the most profound sensitivities of civilization, insignificant or negative in describing "truths" about human nature? Are such imitations worthless? Are these statements, in Plato's words, examples of human "cowardice"? "And shall we not say that the part of us that leads us to dwell in memory on our suffering and impels us to lamentation, and cannot get enough of that sort of thing is the irrational and idle part of us, the associate of cowardice?" (10.604d).

Yet why should the description and admission of human weakness as frailty be seen as "cowardice"? Or are lamentations and ravings—the madness of Oedipus at both Thebes and Colonus, the plottings of Clytemnestra, Medea caught in murderous rage and grief—commentaries on the extent to which passion and tragedy govern the self and the polity? Are such figures not symbolic representations that possess the power to instruct? Notice how Lacan (1978b: 1025) describes this relation between speech and the unconscious: "Oedipus' unconscious is nothing other than this fundamental discourse whereby, long since, for all time, Oedipus' history is out there—written, and we know it, but Oedipus is ignorant of it, even as he is played out by it since the beginning. This goes far back—remember how the Oracle frightens his parents, and how he is consequently exposed, rejected. Everything takes place in function of the Oracle and of the fact that Oedipus is truly other than what he realizes as his history—he is the son of Laius and Jocasta, and he starts out his life ignorant of this fact. The whole pulsation of the drama of his destiny, from the beginning to the end, hinges on the veiling of this discourse, which is his reality without his knowing it."

Another consideration is inherent in the use of symbolic narrative: the metaphoric content represents the internal self in a language more attuned to a description of the emotional than of the rational. Plato criticizes poetry in the interests of establishing philosophy's dominance and in asserting philosophy or reason's claim as the right knowledge informing political judgment and rule: given the nature of the poet's position, the poet's imagery turns into a disruptive and corrupting, not to mention competing, influence; it dilutes philosophy's claim to explanation and regulation. It may be something of this dynamic that stands behind Plato's attack on imitation and the worthlessness of what he calls the imitative arts as sources of reliable knowledge.[4]

Plato fears the power of the poet to inflame (which, given Lacan's interpretation, is precisely what Sophocles accomplishes), to stir up passions, to draw attention away from philosophy and its projection of control and definition. Plato therefore argues that imitation has nothing to teach; it should be disregarded; it should neither be part of the Guardians' instruction nor act as inspiration in the polity. To argue that poetry is not knowledge is, however, to regard it as useless, an alien presence to be cast out, banished. "Imitation is a form of play, not to be taken seriously"; "it is phantoms, not realities, that [the poets] produce" (10.602b, 599a).

Similarly, to argue that the reflections of mental patients have no place or role in understanding self and community is to dismiss the role of a *special* symbolism, the play of images, which addresses the relation between nature and culture, and of the dynamics that push individuals away from community and bring them back to it. Metaphor encloses the self with an immediacy and immanence that is lacking in philosophic reason and science: the horror of a Medea requires the poet to dramatize an act that violates the very foundations of humanity and civilization; the crime of Oedipus and its impact on the polity, his guilt and banishment, the horror and transcendence of Oedipus at Colonus become living, vivid commentaries on the force of desire and its connection with the public realm.[5] In Lacan's terms (1978b: 1031), "It is natural that everything would fall on Oedipus, since Oedipus embodies the central knot of speech." Jacques Derrida (1982) makes a distinction between "live metaphors" and "dead metaphors." "Live" metaphors have not lost their capacity to highlight, to dramatize. "Dead" metaphors, assimilated into discourse, have been depleted of numinosity, their power to shock and surprise. From this perspective, Plato, in his attack on tragic poetry, confronts very *live* metaphors: "In regard to the emotions of sex and anger, and all the appetites and pains and pleasures of the soul which we say accompany all our actions, the effect of poetic imitation is the same. For it waters and fosters these feelings when what we ought to do is dry them up" (10.606d). But why "dry them up"? Should not the metaphoric commentaries in the form of symbolic reflection make claims regarding political matters?

Plato's criticisms were directed largely at the tragic poets, since tragedy revealed weakness in the polity's structure (the infusion of politics with desire) and demonstrated the role of the irrational in defining action and community. However, to exclude the evidence of the irrational or nonrational (as such phenomena are named by society or—for Plato—by philosophy), to refuse it legitimacy, is to eliminate from discourse specific commentary on human nature, *no matter how idiosyncratic*. Poetry and metaphor ask disturbing questions of reason; in the form of tragedy, suffering, and despair they tend to remind the audience that politics is not always ennobling and that human motive, its baseness and violence, may bring down the most "rational" constructs of human ingenuity: hence Plato's strong wish to keep poetry out of the ideal "city of speech." The poet argues that passion—or, in Lacan's word, desire—is stronger than artifice or reason; that blindness, culpability, stupidity, and frailty inform both private and public life. The language of the poet, therefore, with its peculiar forms, unsettles rational perception and asks perplexing questions of the public order. In this sense psychotic or delusional speech, because of its metaphoric content, may be thought of as more akin to the world of the poet than that of the philosopher. And like the poetic utterance, this discourse may run up against conventional languages and concepts and may reveal fractures in the very structure of being itself.

I suggest that reflections of mental patients may be thought of as sources of political knowledge. It may be an unusual way to think about language that society for the most part ignores, but I hope to show that such utterances contain a meaning beyond their classification as pathology or illness. I regard this speech as evidence of and an aid to understanding the dynamic behind such political concepts as community, participation, and citizenship. It certainly is evidence for an empirical base that rests on the concreteness of human suffering and alienation. And should not the experience of suffering be included in theorizing about politics and political life? Why should thinking about political theory be governed only by the assumption that rationality or rational theories of self are the exclusive source for the foundations of political knowledge? If these narratives suggest anything, it is the fragility of the rational process and the insufficiency of reason or calculation alone to explain why people feel and act as they do.

Perhaps discourse that is not austere, formal, or technical, discourse that overwhelms and invades the senses, is necessary to reveal connections between the private and public which more mediated forms of rational or scientific discourse obscure. Scientific language denudes the interpretive landscape of metaphor; it substitutes an often strained objectivity for overpowering human facts. Is it not equally important to let these human facts speak for themselves? And might not such expressions, with their symbolic and metaphoric content, open up the epistemological field in a way foreclosed to a rationalist language? I am arguing not against reason but only for more sensitivity to utterances that enclose a poetic, allusive speech lacking a strict design. The language of madness requires a different kind of listening than do the languages of science and of institutional power. It is a listening that does not benefit from the safety provided by technical or formal thought, the certainty of *category*, but rather accepts the indeterminacy of an internal nature that appears in often frightening, even grotesque, forms. Or to put it in another way: the social desire *not* to listen to such languages, to hide them away, to wrap them in scientific category, may indicate a deep fear of their meaning, of their potentially anarchic effect. The language of madness erodes what Machiavelli called the fortresses of power.

Self as Narrative Text: The Language of Metaphor

Paul Ricoeur (1977: 7) argues that "metaphor is the rhetorical process by which discourse unleashes the power that certain fictions have to redescribe reality." In this sense, the figure or images lying at the heart of these narratives (since they are a product of the imagination, although that imagination is very real for the self) bring to consciousness a vision of reality that is neither ordinary, normal, nor instrumental. It is a vision that represents what the unconscious is structuring through speech, and this is precisely why the normal methods of social science lack that peculiar sensitivity to penetrate and interpret what the unconscious projects as symbol. Further, the function of the metaphoric is not to prove anything, or to set out to discover pattern or truth in a Platonic sense (although the narratives do make claims about reality and its organization). Its aim, rather, is "to compose an essential representation of human actions; its appropriate method is to speak the truth by means of fiction, fable and tragic *mythos*" (Ricoeur 1977: 13).

Narrative filled with metaphor, then, is not discourse that relies on the ordering of concepts or the rigors of conventional logic. It rejects formalization, what Ricoeur calls "distanciation"; it may break through syntactic rules; it does, however, forge a communication that reaches beneath the surface of a conventional or descriptive logic. The informative capacity of metaphor lies in its immanence, its "thereness," its capacity to expand the sense of what is present to consciousness. "In service to the poetic function," writes Ricoeur (1977: 247), "metaphor is that strategy of discourse by which language divests itself of its function of direct description in order to reach the mythic level where its function of discovery is set free."

I am not arguing that these narratives constitute in any historical sense true poetry, nor would the patients consider themselves to be representing any poetical tradition, style, or "mythos"; nor is it my purpose to raise technical philosophical problems regarding metaphor. I am arguing that the patients' use of language, their reliance on narrative, expresses historically recurrent themes that comment on the relation of self to community and that metaphor is the key to understanding both their inner states of mind and outer experiences of reality. No matter how bizarre the language or imagery, it still implies a connection to and observation of the world. It is *knowledge* available to us as observers, even though that knowledge may be phrased in unusual or striking metaphor. Further, the act (or action) of language is far preferable to the disavowal of language altogether, to the mute self lost in an isolated, cutoff nature.

I regard the first-order experiences of the self as texts whose content is a valuable contribution to political knowledge. Though the texts used here come from persons whom society considers mentally ill, they remain commentary that relies on metaphor, parable, Ricoeur's *mythos*. The intellectual task is to discovery how to read these texts, how to understand the role of metaphor in that reading, and how to apprehend the forms by which symbolic reflection becomes a commentary on the order of consensual reality. The self is a compilation of metaphor; it represents itself in speech; discourse is "worked upon" by the metaphoric (an image Ricoeur borrows from Jacques Derrida). The self is broken up, smashed, scattered, reconstructed in the presence (and refraction) of metaphor.

Ricoeur (1977: 302) writes: "*Imaginatio* is a level and an order of discourse. *Intellectio* is another level and order." Precisely so: *imaginatio* is not a better or superior level but another "order"; it may enhance what *intellectio* discovers in language. For example, a patient says: "When I was psychotic, the Christmas tree bulbs turned into shrunken human heads"; to listen to what that means, to approach that utterance as metaphoric commentary, constitutes an act of *imaginatio*. To argue that the patient hallucinates shrunken human heads because of dopamine levels, abnormal vascular structures, brain viruses, or pathological genetic structure transforms the utterance and radically alters what it means. My point is that to ignore either *imaginatio* or *intellectio* has its interpretive costs; unfortunately, in the modern search for certainty and the suspicion and often downright hostility toward inner forms of experience, *imaginatio* finds itself neglected in those discourses that define and control power.

Ricoeur, citing Heidegger, argues that metaphor opens the "largest view"; it certainly contributes a view of experience that is wanting in rationality. This is not to say that interpretation should be either reason *or* metaphor, the rational or the nonrational; however, Ricoeur does make a strenuous argument for the importance of the nonrational in reflecting on the origins of concepts and conceptual thought. Further, he suggests that it may very well be nonrational psychological dynamics, what he calls the "precategorical" self, the underlying *affective* structures, that determine the uses to which rationality is put. In psychoanalytic terms, his argument appears to be that early developmental and psychological history affects not only the capacity for attachment, intimacy, and relationship but the very process of thinking itself. Thinking involves *feeling* as well as cognition or ratiocination, and precisely these precategorical or prelinguistic emotional factors, the unconscious or split-off self, may have tremendous influence on how the adult self reasons and how the rational human being thinks. Ricoeur in this respect assumes an anti-Cartesian position.

Metaphor enriches the world; it creates a sensibility that invokes different images than does rational analysis. "Metaphor is living," Ricoeur (1977: 303) argues, "not only to the extent that it vivifies a constituted language" but also by virtue of the fact that it introduces the spark of imagination into a "thinking more" at the "conceptual level." Metaphor may even enhance the aims of interpretation or reason but *only* if the rational listens to the metaphoric, if it is open to this level or order of reality. One of the criticisms of biological psychiatry, for example, is that it refuses to listen to the brain that speaks, to the speech acts of its subjects. This struggle to "think more," to infuse reason with the vividness of metaphor, Ricoeur continues, is the "soul of interpretation."

This argument echoes the importance that William James assigns to noncategorical or figurative thought and the dependence of thought on disconnected flows of experience (the world as it is, as it strikes consciousness directly). Ricoeur and James share a distaste for the notion of truth as a categorical representation, as a thing, an object, or a pattern.[6] Even to conceive of form or patterns (in the Platonic sense) behind experience falsifies, in James's view (1971: 120), both the nature of consciousness and phenomena: "The relationship we call knowledge is often only a series of intermediate experiences easily described in concrete terms. It is not at all the transcendent mystery in which so many philosophers have taken pleasure."

Finally, Ricoeur, like James, moves to break down the artificial distinction between inside and outside. Metaphor accomplishes this; it speaks to the interpenetration of the self with the world, the Imaginary with the Real, internal perceptual structure (including emotion) with the phenomena of experience.[7] "Is it not the very distinction between 'outside' and 'inside' that is shaken along with that between representation and feeling?" Is this not the function of the poetic or metaphoric in discourse? "Poetic discourse brings to language a pre-objective world in which we find ourselves already rooted, but in which we also project our innermost possibilities," and of which we are often unaware (Ricoeur 1977: 306).

To listen to madness, then, is literally to witness this interpenetration of the Imaginary and the Real. It is not to take craziness as the norm, nor is it to place oneself in the position of experiencing insanity as one's own experience—although that may indeed happen. It is rather to see the Imaginary revealed for what it is: a powerful, determining, and elemental force in human life. "Feeling is no less ontological than representation" (Ricoeur 1977: 305).

It is in this spirit that I approach the storytelling of extreme psychological alienation as a means of understanding the relation between the inner self in its most estranged position and the languages of political life. The stories that follow, though not directly political, nonetheless possess a symbolic dimension that highlights the importance of community in human aspiration and the capacity of the human psyche to survive powerful countervailing tendencies toward withdrawal and hermeticism.

2 /

The Struggle between
Delusion and
Intersubjectivity

In this chapter I offer as a hypothesis the notion that the public dimension of the self—its existence-in-common, its intersubjectivity as a form of metaphor—may have a great deal to do with the dismantling of delusion and the emergence of a coherent self-connection with community. I do not suggest that this is the whole picture, or that the self that resists delusion does so only because of its refraction in the metaphor of discourse. But I do argue that intersubjectivity and its presence as metaphor and symbolization may be an important factor, that the discourse between the self and its public field may constitute experience of considerable benefit for a consciousness desperately fighting the entropic pull of tyrannical inner images.

The public space, as an antidote to the seduction of the inner, continually unfolds and transforms. It is not static. It takes into itself and metabolizes shared activity; it draws on the self's organizing and intersubjective capacities. It creates a common set of purposes; it coalesces interest *in a collaborative universe that the participants define as political*. At the hospital where I conducted my research, the "Hall" or ward did sometimes constitute such a political space, a community where relations involving patients, staff, and therapists developed in an intensely conflictual environment with participation on all levels. From this perspective, the Hall functioned as a laboratory for a limited yet real concept of citizenship. The politics of intersubjectivity worked itself out through a persistent, collective examination of the individual, the group, the distribution of power among patients and staff, the expressions of justice and injustice as matters of public discourse, and the persistent *public* mediation of private hells and inner conflicts. The clinical environment is by no means a democracy; it is, however, a place that values participation and collaboration as forms of treatment.[1]

The Sheppard and Enoch Pratt Hospital is a nonprofit, multipurpose mental institution located on several acres in Towson, Maryland. Founded by Moses Sheppard through a bequest in his will, the hospital first opened its doors in the last decade of the nineteenth century. Sheppard, heavily influenced by the ideals of his Quaker faith, envisioned it as a humane, caring environment, not a prison or dungeon but a place where the afflicted could find some relief and hope. Today, the hospital offers a number of in- and outpatient services; in its long-term units where I conducted my research, patients are routinely given psychotherapy in addition to medication. They are treated with dignity and care; in addition, many therapists and staff members, contrary to prevailing tendencies in modern psychiatry, devote considerable attention to the status of the patient's inner self, to the content of the language and the interpersonal environment that surrounds the patient.

Hence, I found myself associated with a part of the institution where philosophical, theoretical, and epistemological issues were, at least indirectly, of some interest to practitioners. Yet I was persistently aware of my role as a theorist rather than a practitioner, particularly as a political theorist, which frequently led me to raise questions that were tangential to the hospital's primary therapeutic concerns. The only requirements placed on me as a researcher were to obtain the required legal consent of the patient and the consent to the project of the patient's therapist, to keep in touch with the persons involved in the patient's care and therapy, and to submit periodic reports on the status of my research to the hospital's institutional review board. Over the years I also attended case study analyses, Hall meetings, hospital lectures, and conferences, as well as providing some feedback to the staff through periodic grand rounds lectures. To be a political theorist (particularly when I was reading Michel Foucault) in an environment where madness found itself contained by the walls and theories of an institutional psychiatry was often a strange and perplexing experience. Yet even though my views sometimes conflicted with those of staff, I was treated with respect and encouraged to continue a research project that would haunt me even when I was miles away from the hospital.

The Public and Private Selves

The ability to negotiate, to express viewpoints, to make alliances, to sustain relationships, to manipulate and handle imbalances in power, to acknowledge and confront authority, to internalize a reciprocal sense of responsibility and obligation, to transform empathy into regulation and governance: all these *actions* take place in language, in a public, intersubjective field. It is difficult enough for persons not experiencing delusion to engage in this kind of activity. For the delusional self, such connections—becoming aware of existence as an interactive process, taking participatory risks in the very public environment of the ward, forging identity in relationship with others, expressing dissatisfaction—all assume therapeutic properties in moving consciousness away from its enchainment by delusion.[2]

In its therapeutic function the public realm returns the self to the world of concrete experience, to historical time, reciprocal obligation, and community. It demystifies the language of delusion and helps to break up the kind of metaphor that imprisons the self: that is, the Imaginary as the embodiment of the "phenomenon of dying, of disappearing, or of being kidnapped" (Grotstein 1986: 43). The public realm encourages collaboration and debate; it brackets the unboundedness of the inner self and its imaginary monologue. It has a great deal to do with the ultimate ideal of self-governance. Further, the public realm heals character by fostering the development of moral relations and enhancing feelings of mutuality and reciprocity. I do not attribute to community or the public space the power to "cure," but I do argue that the politics of persons and their intersubjective nexus may have something to do with diminishing the force of delusional states of mind, with reversing a way of life and a knowledge system that revolves around what Grotstein calls the "assimilation of terror."

To elaborate on the effects of the public space on the images of intersubjectivity, I turn to a case analysis that illustrates the power of relationship and reciprocity in confronting the pull of the private, the inner, the delusional. David grew up in an upper-middle-class world; his father, a corporate executive with a major multinational company, shifted posts constantly. The family (mother, sister, and younger brother) found themselves over the years living in several different places. David had attended a university for two years; he presented himself as a highly articulate, intelligent young man. But he had been in and out of hospitals since the age of seventeen and came to Sheppard-Pratt at twenty-four with a diagnosis of "manic-depression";[3] his prognosis, poor. His manic episodes, lasting anywhere from a few days to several weeks, immobilized him, and delusion swept him off to other worlds.[4] Yet he managed, always, to come back to reality, "settling out" (as one of his psychiatrists put it) of his psychotic states.

Over a period of fifteen months I met with David on an average of twice a week. His treatment depended in large measure on his persistent struggle with actions designed to engage the public aspects of being and on a continuing scrutiny of the emotional and psychological reasons for his massive regressions. That David managed to emerge from his delusional world and to leave its more pernicious effects behind demonstrated in my view not only the effectiveness of his treatment but his own engagement with the *civitas,* the public space of his life, which for almost three years centered on the life in his Hall. And since David's public world evolved from the place where he lived, it was in that environment that his basic sense of self, as a participant in a community of shared ends, was forged.

By the time David arrived at Sheppard-Pratt in the fall of 1983, he had lived as a solitary wanderer, isolated from all human contact and shared experience. Not only had he withdrawn from the public world; he also felt less than human, a shell, dead and inert.

> I felt as if I had ceased to be, as if a part of me, my core, lay buried in those cemeteries I used to visit years ago. I envied the dead; nothing could disturb them locked silently into their graves. Why couldn't I be there, I thought, with them, in that peacefulness, in the coolness of their earth?

He believed himself to be fundamentally base, poisonous, corrupted, and filthy; extended contact over any period of time, he felt, might bring harm, corrosion, filthiness, and pain to the Other. But he also believed himself to be an extraordinarily gifted poet, capable of writing verse to rival any of the greats of the past (a central feature of his grandiose self). Nevertheless, because of his extraordinary fear of closeness, he developed the mental facility to wipe out relationships, to expunge them by thinking the past out of existence, dissolving it into nothingness. From his therapist:

An example of David's lack of connection to the past is found in his remarks about a visit that he made home. Upon his return, he described the visit as "like a package apart and separate in time." He described himself as mentally "wiping the person out" at the end of a day or the end of an interaction.

David frequently attributed malevolent motives to others; he reacted strongly to any expression of negative feeling toward what he did or said. Negative reactions threw him into intense despair, and "he feared any verbal expression of negative affect," his therapist noted, "thinking this would result in [his being excluded] from his family and in his being discharged from the hospital." Further, "his sensitivity to criticism sometimes led him to engage in misdirected and poorly planned efforts to demonstrate a hyper-independence." He became obsessive about what other persons wanted of him and spent a considerable amount of time scrutinizing their remarks, facial expressions, and body movements.

David's relationships during the early part of his hospitalization involved misattributions, miscues, and misunderstandings. Because he was so preoccupied with what others were thinking of him, any realistically based intersubjectivity became an impossibility constantly distorted by his own fears and projections. Memories of community, too, were disrupted by his state of mind, and he "would have difficulty remembering even simple events which transpired in [his family] because he would invariably be preoccupied with his own ruminations and anxieties" (from therapist's notes). Any real connection that felt too close threatened David's fragile sense of self, although he often constructed fantasies about relationships which he kept to himself and refused to reveal to anyone until much later.[5]

David's treatment confronted enormous psychological obstacles: his pathological dread of separation and loss; hidden romantic fantasies obstructing the outward flow of desire; periodic bouts with an immobilizing depression; an inner chaos and disorganization during his manias which totally disrupted perception; the absence of any constancy in his relation with others; intense self-hatred and rage; a sense of futility, worthlessness, hopelessness; and, when he was psychotic, terrifying delusions that isolated him from the human community.

That David was ultimately able to confront his terror of intersubjectivity, to acknowledge and talk about it, testified to a will to live that he referred to as his "Ph.D. in life." Further, his struggle with psychosis and the Imaginary involved not only desperate efforts to overcome serious fractures in his self-concept and self-organization but also the very real effort to find an attachment to a shared reality, to discover a sense of place that he could call his own, that would be real and not fantasized, that required collaboration with real, embodied others and not delusional images wandering about in his imagination.

How David acted on the Hall, how he responded to his therapist's absences, how he performed in various therapies (art, dance, occupational), how he perceived other patients and staff, how he dealt with his rage: all this composed an intricate tapestry that held clues to fundamental motifs in his mind. Though he had great difficulty in establishing shared realities, in forging relationships grounded in real (not delusional) perceptions, it was nonetheless his active engagement of a public world, his need to move out of himself, that became a central dynamic in his therapy.[6] It was this focus on the intersubjective world and its meaning which *in part* enabled David to encounter and transcend the delusional core of his manias.

Narrative Reality: Isolation and Being

David's description of his inner world covered three phases: the loneliness and isolation, the descent into mania (the fever of the madness itself), and the return to what David called his "civil world." First I turn to reflections, in David's own voice, on his feelings of isolation. Again, let me emphasize that presenting these extended narratives is an effort to define the relation of the linguistic self to its symbolic world; to demonstrate, as a kind of oral history (a phenomenology of the self), the importance of the metaphoric in illuminating the self's relation to both inner and outer realities. As David made quite clear, what motivated his preoccupation with internally derived and therefore autonomous images was his pathological fear of community and his felt sense of the loss of family. What he experienced as loss in his historical family connection he replaced with delusional imaginings populating an inner and disconnected perceptual environment.

> Before coming to Sheppard, I ran long marathons by myself to escape the loneliness. The deeper I ran into the forest, the crazier I became. It was particularly bad when it stormed. I lost direction: paths disappeared. I lost sight of familiar landscapes. Everything moved so quickly. I found myself caught in the sheer force of my madness, running through trees into branches, scraping my skin, feeling sharp edges cut into my flesh, not caring where I fell or what obstacles careened off me. Yet I paid no attention to the welts on my body, the bleeding, the branches cutting into my face. I saw my rage; I stood in the middle of atrocities playing in my mind like a movie reel gone off its tracks. It's impossible to imagine what your mind does with reality, the horrors it commits, the worlds it desecrates, what you do with yourself in the midst of all this violence. You commit unmentionable crimes, and your madness carries you as if your body had no weight at all.
>
> When I'm psychotic, reality disappears and my mind moves away from ordinary experience. I find myself in places no one understands, worlds that bear no resemblance to this one. But I always manage to return; I find my way back and store up the experience. It sits there until I feel the need to express it. But to even talk about what I see and feel, I need a place, a settledness making the fear endurable. . . .
>
> It's still now, here, talking together; what could be more tranquil? The world seems safe, certain. It's May and everything is bright. The hardness of the chair, the immobility of those trees, the quiet in the air, the heaviness of its moisture: nothing can disturb this moment. It surrounds us; it defines you and me; and the madness seems far away. But when I leave this place and return to the Hall, it all starts up again. And when the chaos returns, my memory of this place, these few minutes, will disappear. I'll feel like Ulysses strapped to the mast, listening to the

Sirens, rushing toward them.[7] I have to listen, because unless I let myself be with their voice, unless I see their visions and open myself to their melody, I'll never be free of their power; they'll always be out there, taunting me, waiting. At least here, I'm protected from their seduction; and if staff are careful and watch me, I probably won't hurt myself.

There are times when I feel like a continuum of "its," just particles, no identity, nothing substantial inside, everything floating haphazardly around in my mind. The world shifts when you're crazy. It pushes you in a thousand directions; the compass spins frantically, the Sirens work their way into your soul. I think of myself sometimes as a kiwi bird or an eagle flying out of the fire or a great hawk circling the Mojave. Or I might see myself as a wild animal, free in nature, to create my own destruction or escape from it, however it goes. And then I might look at myself shaving; my face slowly peels off and I stand there, above it, watching my eyes, nose, cheeks, and lips slide into the drain. And then I dissolve into nothing, a faceless being becoming particles, molecules, atoms, and then finally, air. Who I am becomes smaller and smaller until even my consciousness floats off into the universe.

Place is important to me; it's a feeling I've never had, something everyone takes for granted, a home protected by walls and love, a place you call your own. I try to find it when I'm not crazy. I imagine I'm a mountaineer looking to nature's basic certainties to take me through the day. The sun rises in the east, sets in the west; its pathway through the sky creates a continuity, a thread tying things together. I know it will always be there, in the same *place,* in the morning and evening, even if I can't see it. Its presence brings warmth and heat; its absence brings cold and darkness. The sun's rising and setting, the stream's movement, the water's iciness, the murmur of the wind: that much in the world I trust. Or as I put it in one of my poems, "In the meadow and forest of nature there is solace, a monastery for those who left."

Even in the midst of this wilderness, no matter how painful, it's impossible to escape the effects of civilization, its graveyard shifts and rootless fear, its gray-black dawns. It's there, even if only in your mind, and you see the greed, mistakes, and jealousy of people.

I hear this voice sometimes. I call it the "maelstrom of manufac-
tured criticism" because it always tears away at me, rips my identity into shreds, and slices away at everything I am. It's like being in
the midst of the straits of the Sirens with a ferocious storm over-
head, no sun, just black clouds that turn the world into night.
Sometimes the voice booms in my ears; other times, it sounds like
a song, a melody, but the lyrics, even though the singing is sweet,
are filled with criticism and attack.[8] The verbal abuse never lets
up. It goes on and on for hours. Nothing outside touches me
when it's there: I refuse to talk to anyone; I sit, stare, smoke
cigarettes until the voice leaves.

Language, David believed, brought him back into history, time,
continuity, and action. In Foucault's terms (1954: 47): "Consciousness of the illness arises from within the illness; it is anchored in it, and
at the moment the consciousness perceives the illness, it expresses it."
To speak, to embody in linguistic imagery the variations in pain and
terror, particularly in exchanges with staff, allowed David to "resist the
Sirens." To make himself known, then, to feel tied to the Other
through a dialectical and shared symbolism, enabled him to feel a sense
of place, to express terror yet at the same time to understand, almost
intuitively, that he was safe. When he was psychotic, however—when
he kept language within, held private monologues, uttered cryptic and
indecipherable statements meant for a delusional audience—David
thought of himself as a "gigantic cipher for experience." It was as if
nothing held "here" (consensual reality) and "there" (the phantasms of
the imagination) together. Psychosis destroyed moral and linguistic
connections; it projected its own form of knowledge; it massacred the
intersubjective and historical self and transformed human existence
into a grotesque play involving inanimate, nonhuman, and sometimes
part-human figures. It was a process that in its action (delusion as
action) radically disoriented and broke up conventional meaning structures. In dissolving boundaries, psychosis (in Lacan's terms [1968])
made the Imaginary into the Real. It abolished fixed, external points of
reference and led to a mammoth confusion over the relation between
identity and reality.

On Going Psychotic: The Descent into Nothingness

Leaving the civil world, the world of community, and entering one of his manic phases involved a process that David saw as "reality slowly slipping away." He spoke of it in one of his poems as "yet another season missed . . . too late salvation, [it] cannot be made." The shift was not a sudden one but a withdrawal that intensified over a few days as he gradually lost his capacity to distinguish reality from delusion, his "other world." Slipping into psychosis constituted a threat not only to his connection with his own historical identity but to the very integrity of his being, which became, as David put it, "particles floating in the universe, abandoned in space."

> Psychosis is like being cornered and I just let myself go. I give in to it. I strap myself to the mast and let the Sirens take my mind.[9] You figure, why fight it? Why resist the flood of images and the strange visions? Just let it happen; let it all fly apart. And, of course, it does. It explodes and the whole world begins to shatter and you see yourself lit up like a thousand-watt light bulb traveling a million miles an hour. You're moving fast, nothing stops you. Soon the mundane becomes meaningless. It's no longer a problem of whether to wear a shirt or wash your jeans. It never occurs to you to wear anything, since in the world you travel everything happens so quickly that to take time out to even put on clothes might cause untold disaster and destruction. You fly into your world and all else diminishes in importance.

The concrete evaporates. The self loses sight of necessity; time and history disappear. Hyperawareness increases, and delusion replaces consensual reference and collective value. In the inner world, identity comes to be defined through an intensifying series of images.

> Someone holds a gun to your head, and the trigger is about to be pulled. You don't know if you're going to be alive the next second or hurled into outer space or sliced into a thousand pieces by some berserk person slinging an ax. To sleep is to lose control of the simultaneous plans revving up in your mind. Everything I do,

everything I am, becomes caught in the persistent flow of images; my mind separates, completely, from mundane considerations happening all around me.

Nothing really stops the madness. I rarely change clothes; hygiene and meals become too much. And I have more important things to do than be bothered with my nutrition or cleanliness. Contact with people seems closed off; I lose interest in what happens on the Hall. I forget what day it is; I lose track of mealtimes and Hall meetings. Something as simple as selecting a shirt paralyzes me. That's what begins my psychotic episodes, little things, nothing more dramatic than trying to find a shirt. It's like this huge problem overtakes you: moving toward the closet, opening the door, searching through the rack. Each step of the process is like climbing Mount Everest, so you say to yourself, "Why bother, let it be, stay with the one on your back." Little things are magnified a thousand times, and what happens inside your mind takes on much greater importance than your own hygiene or appearance.

In psychosis, routine has no existence, no place:

You find yourself everywhere, and all your energy is spent trying to keep from dying. Psychosis creeps up on you; it's a hollowness, an emptiness. I described it once in a poem as "ritual unrestrained, from mat to mattress; in wake, from stupor's coil to coffee lost to cigarettes, to cycles lost in concordances. At night the rain does not hit the sidewalk or the street light."

Psychosis leaves you with fear; you lose all sense of yourself as a person among other persons. You feel yourself dissipating; your distinctiveness vanishes. No voice in the universe sounds like yours; yet all voices sound like yours. You see yourself as a vast multitude; and these millions in the multitude become you. This voice, this multitude that is me, has a detached quality to it, without substance or body. The multitude drowns me; it swallows me up. With its persistent hollowness, the voice blots out any sense of an I and this hollow sound, like drums beating in a huge cavern, encircles me and paralyzes my thoughts.

The "hollow sound" took David away from himself; it removed him from his body; it drowned out the presence of staff, therapist, and other patients. It absorbed his being; it killed reality. It made him see food as poisonous, the care of staff as unwanted interruptions of his journey, the concern of other patients as unwelcome intrusions on a private world beyond their understanding.

> It's like all my cells are exploded over the universe, and I live in each of those millions and millions of nuclei shooting in every direction. In the midst of all this, how could I possibly deal with the concrete, even tie my shoelaces, much less find my shoes?

Psychosis not only breaks identity into fragments; it thoroughly destroys memory:

> It spews people and events outward; you fly away and lose sight of the earth. It blasts everything into a million bits, and you're left trying to find yourself amidst this infinity of particles.

Coming out of this universe takes a considerable time; it requires relearning the laws of cause and effect, discovering how to organize sequences, how to see things in a series. Think of a self so shattered, David said, that to rebuild identity is a task as monumental as weaving a million disconnected pieces of thread. It takes an enormous amount of energy to relearn sequence, time, cause and effect; to climb out of the inner hollowness; to dismantle the voices and live in a familiar world bounded by historical time. Madness is a great enemy to historical continuity, to the integrity and resiliency of community, to metaphors grounded in consensual reality.

Connections in psychosis take on unusual and unpredictable meaning. Something as ordinary as a cigarette, for example, becomes for David a connection to life:

> I know life exists because I sit and smoke a cigarette to its end. Nothing could be more certain: the cigarette will not run from me. It will not refuse me its attention; it will not make demands. I control its destiny. I trust it completely. It will not ask me to

change my shirt; it will not insist that I take a shower or talk or go to the cafeteria or eat my dinner. It will not inquire about my feelings. The cigarette and I establish an alliance, an understanding. It's there for me and no one else. It knows I'm here; I place it in my mouth; I draw smoke. My lungs fill up. It's an event which shows me I'm alive, which justifies my existence. At that moment in time my identity, who I am, lies in my connection with the cigarette. Nothing else matters. It's reliable. It goes away when I say it should. The cigarette is much more reliable than people. When you touch it, it won't hurt you.

David's most frightening moments in the hospital were spent living on the border between sanity and insanity, not knowing where he was or in what condition he might wake up each morning. Even though he sensed what was happening, he felt powerless to stop it; he was incapable of grabbing hold of anything familiar. It was as if the world became so slippery that nothing would stay still.

I convinced myself several things were happening; unrecognizable voices invaded my ears; transmitters had been planted in the ceiling; everyone on the Hall spoke about me; my behavior was watched and discussed by staff; nursing reports, patients' journals, were filled with hundreds of pages describing my appearance and movements; spies were sent into the Hall exclusively to keep track of me, and to report any suspicious behavior to the hospital administration; therapists ignored their own patients and spent hours in endless discussion, looking at the ramifications of my case; TV cameras, hooked into the walls, taped my facial expressions; every morning, around 3 A.M., three thousand spotlights aimed directly into my eyes; staff prepared elaborate strategies to humiliate me, to expose me and leave me naked in front of the Hall; killers hid behind closed doors and waited until night to sneak into my room; food poisoned my insides and rotted out my intestines. Lying down, my body became so brittle I felt it cracking into a thousand pieces; at night, my roommate fed on my blood. Not exactly sane thoughts. In my frame of mind, if I were to stay alive, I had to be attuned to every movement on the Hall.

David lost his sense of place and community in madness. He found himself surrounded by demons, spirits, devils, and armies that threatened, cajoled, and even at times killed. His physical coordinates and sensibility disappeared; he experienced a universe of pure imagination transforming nature into weird shapes and forces, into twisted bodies, unnatural mutants, and outlandish situations. It was in the midst of his psychosis that David encountered pure, unmediated terror.

3 /

Psychotic Terror: The Imaginary Unleashed

As David moved into psychosis, his behavior and perception had noticeable effects on those around him. The impact of these effects and their course or pattern frequently appeared in the Hall's nursing notes. Typical entries detailing David's movements on the Hall are valuable as a kind of phenomenological record, a counterpoint to David's internality, which at this point was still quite hidden and inaccessible.

—David was quite preoccupied with his clothing, ruminating excessively on the idea that his pants did not fit properly and that other individuals would make a sexual interpretation about the way his clothes fit.
—David continues to express paranoid ideas; he felt people looked at him because his shoelaces were weird. David said that it all started last week when he got a "weird" haircut. He feels that the barber saw his weird shoelaces and so she gave him a weird haircut.
—The wish of self-death is still a common theme . . . states that he does not deserve to eat . . . thinks that others are thinking bad thoughts about him, and that he is evil.
—Pt. [patient] became agitated when staff told him this was his evening for showering. Pt. finally did shower after much stalling and bargaining, but came out complaining that someone had walked into the shower while

he was in there. [David believed that showering or bathing would burn his skin off, that the showerheads actually were conduits to an acid pool; showering felt like "acid being sprayed all over my body." He also believed that the dirt on him was part of his skin; therefore, to be clean, to be without dirt, was to be without skin. So a shower was the most horrible torture imaginable, but he could not express this to staff.]

—David felt he was never rooted and never felt a sense of belonging to anyone or anything and would attempt to cling to an "anchor" out there, sometimes in the form of a female relationship. [David's construction of these relationships, including sex, was largely a function of fantasy; see Chapter 2.]

—Patient said that on the surface he looks o.k. but "feels in a thousand pieces on the inside."

Even though he felt reality slipping away, David could still witness or observe the disintegrative impact of his psychosis. He stood between two worlds, aware—if only for a brief moment—of both.

> I knew it at the time; I could feel it coming on. Staff knew; they saw it in my face, in my pacing and smoking. I couldn't sleep; and the world outside me started to disintegrate. Showers became acid baths; conversations on the Hall turned into derogatory comments made about me behind my back. I began to see staff as fools and no one could be as smart or witty as I. I entered arenas of greatness and power. Everyone should leave me alone.

Or, as David described his increasing isolation in a poem:

> Nothing.
> Wheels, ground in,
> Rumble
> Silence, a soul unknown.
>
> Nightmare's entrails of fear
> Wound in bizarre accoutrements
> Light wakes to light.
>
> Coffee and cigarettes
> Perpetual, in cycles of

Ingestion and motion
Action taken, and with
Movement, process
And so a soul
Dimly seen

To rebuild a culture
Of my own
Hopes of a jigsaw contest
Come together.

Locked Door Seclusion: The Space of the Imaginary Unleashed

Every Hall at Sheppard-Pratt has a "quiet room" set aside for patients who experience terrible anxiety or who, for whatever reason, strike out at other patients and staff. It is a room kept immaculately clean; it has a window and an adjoining bathroom; it is furnished with a mattress, nothing else. Sometimes patients request quiet room; sometimes staff feel that it is necessary for a patient to spend time there, that the patient needs space away from the common areas of the Hall. The quiet-room door remains open; staff periodically look in and ask whether the patient needs anything. The patient may come out whenever he or she feels capable of being outside quiet room. Occasionally certain conditions will be imposed: no visits from other patients or quiet periods lasting from fifteen to twenty minutes. But quiet-room time is fairly flexible and rarely lasts for more than an evening or a few hours during the day. It is a place where patients work through (alone) particularly unsettling or shaky moments.

"Locked-door seclusion" (LDS), however, is another matter. A patient who must stay in the quiet room with the door closed and locked is experiencing such intense anxiety, confusion, and terror that continual monitoring is essential, not only for the patient's welfare but for the sake of staff and other patients who might otherwise find themselves within range of that person's fury. It is a space where the patient (in David's mind, like Ulysses strapped to the mast) may express madness as fully and completely as possible without fear that his or her rage will hurt anyone else; where the demons, terrors, and what David called "crimes" of madness receive their fullest expression. To listen to a patient in LDS is to experience the extent to which psychosis drives the self out of the human community. It is a chilling and often frightening phenomenon, a descent into a delusional terror distinguished by its despair, violence, and chaos.

Staff closely watch patients in LDS. An intercom in the nursing station remains on throughout the patient's stay; every fifteen minutes the patient is observed through a small window in the door, and notes are made. There are periodic breaks for meals and personal needs. Only when the delusional chaos becomes more organized, when the self recedes somewhat from its terror, when consciousness shows signs of returning to consensual reality, is the door unlocked and opened and the rules of quiet room instituted.

Nursing notes give some indication of David's state of mind in and out of quiet room.

—David continues to give his belongings away. . . . "I don't see an end to this," he exclaims. David has appeared confused, coming on the Hall naked, not making much sense verbally. . . . David continues to be psychotic, expectorating in his hand, flipping ashes in his hand, and ripping up cups. . . . David remains in a manic state, loud, grandiose, with psychotic behavior. David has been talking about being an actor and the historical [stage] is his theater. He continues to ask staff if it's time for intermission. [David believed he had been chosen to act out great events in the universe.]

—David was in quiet room until 7:30 A.M., sitting, talking to himself, and yelling out to peers incoherently (after a while he quieted down) but kept himself naked and urinated on the floor. . . . David has talked to himself and others about things that are not really happening. In conversation he goes off on tangents, picking certain words and using their "sound alikes" that have other meanings [hear, here; there, their; hare, hair; dear, deer]. David has spoken of spirits in his bedroom and in the quiet room which will "beat me up if I go in there."

—David is very agitated today. . . . This morning he was singing a song about suicide and hanging in a noose. . . . David tore up two sheets and also disrobed and went on the Hall naked and exposed himself from within the quiet room.

—David spent part of the shift dressed as a leaf for Halloween; continues to speak rapidly about a variety of unconnected subjects.

From David's own perspective, quiet room and seclusion transformed into a succession of intensifying delusional symbologies:

> I was like a wind in the mountains, a blade of grass trampled on by hikers, a stanza of Walt Whitman's rubbed out by smokestacks. Quiet room was where life began, where it died. I saw myself being born, came out into the Hall and felt like a new person, but after a few minutes I died again. Birth happened several times a day. Quiet room became a womb, and I a naked body entering life. When I sat in the living room on the Hall, I felt myself going through life rapidly, and when death seemed imminent, I returned to quiet room to die and wait for rebirth. I was born a thousand times; I died a thousand times. In that tiny room, with no one else around, the play expanded; the entire universe became a stage. And I became the greatest actor of all time. I could be whoever or whatever appeared in the script. I could be the emptiness that I am.

It was after these events—David defecating and urinating on the quiet-room floor, coming naked onto the Hall, screaming epithets at other patients and staff—that the door was locked and David placed in locked-door seclusion. The following narrative provides only a glimpse into what David experienced during such phases, the most intense and disorganized moments of his psychotic or delusional state.

> LDS became a temple where I performed ritual penance, relieved myself of evil and the stinking badness attached to my flesh. It became my sacred fortress, and I the High Priest took care of God's will. I was overwhelmed with feelings of devotion; I prostrated myself before Him. I determined to show God this sinner could redeem himself; that in my temple, filled with *my* dirtiness, *my* filth, and *my* scum, I might sacrifice to His welfare. Inside His glory, I bathed myself. I purified my soul, I sanctified my being. Only in my Temple would such an offering be made. LDS turned into an altar where I ran after God's forgiveness and His retribution.
>
> Justifying my temple, living in it, took several forms. First, I believed I had to be married; and I built a marriage canopy. I

asked God to deliver me a bride, to mark her with a symbol of His greatness and His love. I waited patiently; brides came and went, never getting too close, always retreating before entering the canopy. At times, I thought *I* had been transformed into the bride; and I saw myself with veils, flowing gauze, a gleaming translucent train, a sign of God's favor and trust. Grooms came toward me, large men with huge hands, laughing and kicking at the air, violent thrusts of their feet, huge biceps with muscles that stretched their jacket seams. . . . But they disappeared, and the canopy remained empty, just myself staring at the seclusion room walls. I asked God why he played with me like this; hadn't I proved myself? Hadn't I been His faithful servant? But He only smiled, the kind of smile that sends chills up and down your spine.

My father stood back in all of this, watching, saying nothing, just staring, his eyes turning into great caverns of blackness, nothing there, just a gigantic emptiness. I could not see my mother.

LDS turned into an endless series of adventures. I traveled over the world, demonstrated my worthiness to God. I hardly had time to eat; I lost twenty pounds. I made myself light, lighter than air. I dissolved my physical being so I could leave the seclusion room and travel with the rangers. I told myself I was borne along; I was light as air. Therefore I became an airborne ranger appointed by God to be with the "special forces" and to range over the world completing missions. In my mind I traveled everywhere, to foreign countries: as an ambassador, as a fixer for international conflict, as an emissary for the CIA, as an agent for army intelligence. I constructed maps of all kinds, ferreted out secret weapons plans, acted as spy for the rangers, sat in on presidential briefings, directed communications from the White House. Everything I did brought me closer to the centers of power, and it all started in LDS. That was Command Central. God wished it that way, and since I was His servant, I tried to please Him. What better gift for God than to do His bidding.

An emissary of the "special forces" came to visit me, a big guy, all decked out in uniform, tough, weather-beaten face, the eyes of a killer, someone who specialized in death. He informed me I had been chosen out of hundreds for a delicate mission that involved considerable courage. I was to accompany the emissary on a mission of great importance, whose purpose lay in upholding the honor of the nation. It would be a signal to our enemies of our military resolve and the superior power of our special forces.

I was ecstatic; finally I had the opportunity to prove my worthiness. So airborne we went. We crossed continents and oceans. It was an exhilarating journey, and I felt part of a force vastly greater than myself. Our mission required us to lay waste to Iran, kill three hundred thousand Iranians as an object lesson in the costs of revolution, and seek out and assassinate the Ayatollah. We accomplished all of it: massacred populations, leveled towns and villages, destroyed half the country, polluted the water supply, spread poison gas over cities, burned down mosques and holy shrines, and killed the Ayatollah. It exhausted me, and after it was all over the ranger congratulated me on a job well done and told me if I were needed again, I would be called.

At times in seclusion I listened to my heartbeat; it was like a single theme of life, a rhythmic certainty, an identical repetition of the preceding moment. I fixed on that rhythm, on its sound, ta *da,* ta *da,* ta *da.* When everything seemed lost and I doubted even if I was alive, I found my existence through that sound. It was my justification, my being, the person I am, my irreducible self; in my heartbeat I kept track of my identity. Physical sensations would often be the only connection I had to myself. I knew I was David because my flesh touched the tiled floor, my hand felt cold against the bare wall; I screamed and heard myself; I tied nooses around my neck and felt the air supply cutting off. I went full circle in seclusion, from life to death and back to life again.

You recall the symbol of the serpent who ate his tail? That's what I mean by full circle. I consumed myself in my madness, and then brought myself back, a complete cycle. I began to have doubts; projects wouldn't come together. My efforts to attain grace with God were failing. He refused to reward me for my efforts to please Him. It was time, I decided, to rejoin the world. It was a lonely and difficult decision complicated by the fact that to reach the world I had to navigate through what I believed were twenty-one levels reaching high above the seclusion room ceiling. LDS lay deep beneath the earth, perhaps a million miles, and to climb to the surface required moving up through levels each of which contained its own special reality. I had no idea what awaited me on each level, but I had to endure the journey. Like Ulysses, I had to chance it, since I wanted to return home.

But I sat, overwhelmed by the enormity of it, discouraged, feeling like a particle light enough to float off with the winds. I needed to make myself more substantial, heavier, bigger, before I had the strength to begin the journey back, the long climb upward. I had to find my body again; physical energy had been dissipated in my airborne travels across the earth and into the universe. I needed *weight* to resist the winds and sustain the long hike and endure whatever trials I might face on the way back. I struggled to develop a frame of mind which refused to believe such a journey was futile, since I thought I might get lost or find myself caught in the midst of wars that would take centuries to resolve. I feared my skeleton might be found, in a thousand years, lying in a field of calcified human waste.

In madness you construct your own universe; you make yourself appear and disappear. You create your own audience. I had set up God as my audience, and I did everything in His service. He watched over me, and I saw myself through His eyes. I never thought of God in any religious sense; He had no doctrine or truth, only His presence encircling me in His light and His glory. He gave me strength and command, and what God asked me to do, I did. All my attention focused on His will; my life depended on His approval, guidance and sanction. Even though he tortured me with His demands, He stayed. He never left; He never went away; He watched over me.

I hated to fall asleep in LDS. It was not the fear I might die of a heart attack or someone might murder me in my sleep, nothing like that; I felt that if I allowed myself to sleep, to drift off, I would lose touch with the continuity of things, with the thread of life. And I would awake to utter chaos and confusion. *Nothing would be the same.* My heartbeat would change; earth would be turned upside down; strangers would wander around the Hall; bodies would be distorted and twisted up into different shapes. It was a terrible fear of losing what is familiar and constant. Each day then involved refinding the thread, the continuity, making sure everything was as it was the night before, looking out the window to see if Nat or Sherry [nursing staff] were still there, trying to figure out where I was. In Sheppard-Pratt? In a spaceship? In a hole deep in the earth? And then spending a good part of the morning putting it all back together, searching for the thread, the thin lifeline of your identity. Imagine going to bed at night with the fear that the following morning all continuity, all certainty in life, may disappear, that you may find yourself in a spaceship going to Mars or in a torture press in China or drowning off the coast of Nigeria. That's something of what it's like to be in LDS, to be mad.

As I climbed up through the twenty-one levels, reality became more confused; yet my delusions seemed less certain, less defined. I lost the rangers; God seemed more remote; I forgot how to make myself small and light. I no longer flew. God one moment tormented me and the next praised me. I found myself moving from scenes of massive destruction to peaceful settings and then back again. At times I saw the Hall as a lending library, a civilized place where people came to chat, pick out books, talk about important issues, and drink tea. Yet just as quickly that lending library turned into a shooting gallery, with people picking me up as if I were a book, peeling off my flesh like pages in a volume, and then spiking the book to a target board with my fellow patients firing twelve-gauge shot at the cover. Or I thought the Hall, with staff as chief torturers, became a chamber of horrors; and I had been chosen as a subject to test the reliability of new instruments designed to cause slow, burning death.

I wondered if my climb back would take centuries; where was I going? Was my will being tested? Had I been chosen to endure this pain and degradation because of a secret purpose God hid from me? And if my trials were to be timeless, if I had been condemned to pain lasting into eternity, would God, please, give me a weekend off every century from such demanding work?

I felt like I stood in the middle of a vise that kept closing. It was an impossible situation. But there I was, standing on "impossible" and wondering why? Why does this happen to me? How am I going to resolve "impossible" if I'm on top of it? "Impossible" had no anchor, no stability; it slid around, back and forth. I edged myself into a corner of the seclusion room as if it were a mast on a huge sailing ship, and I remember feeling very seasick, not knowing where to stand or what to grab onto. "Impossible" was slippery and unpredictable. It sank into the ocean, forced me to stay afloat in twenty-foot waves. It shifted me all over the place; I careened from wall to wall, corner to corner, trying to find a place that wouldn't *move*. I could only wait it out.

Psychosis for David was a lonely battle without awards, or congratulations.[1] There were no medals or testimonial dinners, no one to toast his struggle, no spotlights. It was a lost world, a subterranean universe that had forged a desperate isolation and left him without friends, a job, or a place to stay, wandering in his own inner wilderness until the mania repeated itself. At least the efforts of persons living within consensual reality (the world of normal persons) have an audience, a context in a given history or society, a *dialectical* frame with others. The struggles of psychosis, however, are silent, unwitnessed battles, nondialectical and therefore not part of any history. Toward the end of his hospitalization David wrote:

> It has been a long season; nine years of scholarship and overriding bewilderment in rooms Lincoln floored, obliterating medications and attachments to those I did not know. Finally, the opportunity to make some sense of it. . . . There is no triumph here or vanquish; only cross country—the long distance through the worst terrain. The Marines never knew what this half was like. But there were people there and they seemed to know. And so, on being discharged this year, my memory comes with me. The anguish and suffering of those years will stay as any long struggle cannot be forgotten. I only hope for the best and pray not for recurrence but independence and attachment.

Citizenship as Discovery of the Public Space

David's discharge came thirty months after his admission to Sheppard-Pratt. During this period he established a public identity with others in a shared context—a difficult task, given his struggle with delusion and his pathological fear of intimacy. David's political being was circumscribed, but it was political nonetheless. His public space, no matter how narrow, how focused on specific relationships, involved the obligations of being a citizen *within the framework of his treatment environ-*

ment; it involved the recognition of reciprocal rights, acceptance of responsibility beyond the needs of the self, and acknowledgment of a public realm (containing purpose and meaning) which could exist simultaneously with inner belief structures.

David's discovery of his intersubjective presence in a human and not delusional community contributed enormously to the dismantling of his private language and preoccupations. His participation in Hall meetings and in activity therapies, his discussions with other patients on the Hall, his enlistment of staff in the shared venture of exploring the structure of relationship itself: all this enabled him to acknowledge the reality of rights, power, obligation, authority, and reciprocity. It was in this way that David exercised at different times his citizenship within the limited but very real sociality of the Hall environment. Again, it is vital to understand the importance that the community of the ward has for such patients. It initiates the beginning of some idea of citizenship or responsibility attached to collective decision-making within the circumscribed limits of an institution. It is not a complete, juristic citizenship in the Aristotelian sense; nor is it the ideal environment of citizenship in the broad sense of that term. But for those who have experienced most of their lives in an isolation and loneliness so overbearing as to make the intersubjective world one of tremendous threat, the very capacity to interact, to be autonomous, is a significant gain.

It was difficult for David after a manic phase; he would have to rediscover his being-in-public all over again and literally relearn the arts of social life. He would struggle with his therapist and nursing staff. But David was quite clear on this point: his capacity to live, his *will* to live, depended in large measure on the ability to metabolize his terror in an environment that contained his rage and fear and yet made it possible for him to participate. For David a manic phase possessed compelling qualities. It was a state of being that induced a tremendous amount of contained energy: nothing lay still; everything moved; all life was transformed into motion. In the words of Ning-Pie Pao (1971: 794–95): the self in a manic state "neither allows himself to rest nor takes time out to eat or sleep. The need to be on the go amounts to a compulsion. If interrupted during his swing of action, he becomes enraged." Or the self may turn to strangers who become the recipient of "boundless love," thus warding off the threatening effects of intimacy and closeness (as in the romantic fantasies that David kept silent and internal, never sharing them with the Other, fantasies distinguished by their private interior monologue). The manic defense also appears, Pao argues, "in the face of a loss or disappointment. They serve to cope with the disappointment, as well as with the aggressive-destructive impulses." External reality becomes unbearable; the consequence is a flight into mania and the hermetically sealed world of delusional identification. Yet "the sadness following the mania is actually an expression of mourning over the loss of all the glories experienced in the manic fantasies."

It took time for David to assimilate the images of reciprocity, the position of the Other, negotiation, and so on. But the more engaged he felt—with staff, Hall meetings, discussions about Hall projects, the hospital's poetry magazine, arguments with other patients—the more real, in the sense of being in an embodied world, he believed himself to be. He had to retrace, after his manias, the simple acts of association, the initial steps in the return to the civil world, toward culture and away from the deadly isolation of his own inner nature. What normal people take for granted, David had to struggle toward; he had to study what relationship meant, how to cooperate. As he began to experience his connection to the community of the ward, his delusional thought became less compelling, a less competing influence. Anything having to do with cooperation or the consensual use of language gave him the opportunity to see himself as others saw him and contributed to the delineation of his interpersonal field and the corresponding decline of the power of his delusional field. The process, then, of developing *moral relations* as a function of his acceptance of a shared symbolism underlay the more complex construction of his citizenship as a participant in community.

The important issue here is the use of intersubjectivity in the service of self-transformation, in the search for shared meanings, in the public discussion of treatment, need, and collaboration. Is not such activity— the sheer process of talking, sharing, and being in a bounded, identifiable public space—political? Is this not public action filled with symbolic commentary?

In David's delusional world, human interaction possessed no permanence; delusion destroyed relationship, shattered human contact, substituted perfect idealized connections for the real messiness of human experience. It projected an endless variety of dramas with always the same ending: separation and extinction. In psychosis, David's leaping beyond cause and effect, his inversions of physical reality, his masochistic and sadistic symbologies all derived from an inner self-representation obsessed with annihilation and imminence. His sense of chaotic disintegration, his images of grandiosity, his symbolic representations of vast power altering the structure of matter: all these thoughts filled out an inner world that because of its utter fragmentation lost contact with history, time, and community. Relationship could be whatever imagination created; it had no boundedness in time, in the physical imperfections and mistakes of history. It was not dependent on the vicissitudes of the Other, on the flows of desire, on the effect of chance in human interaction but derived from what Jacques Lacan (1977: 69–70) calls the self's "imprisoned meaning," its "hermetic elements," its "primary language of symbols." In delusion, relationship appeared as the denial of intimacy and of shared symbols, as an attack on reciprocity and desire, and as the representation of horror, terror, fear, and a grandiosity thoroughly removed from the physical constraints and limitations of consensual reality. David's delusional consciousness, then, found itself populated with the images of a life-threatening despair, a persistent unraveling of brutal and vicious contact, a denial of everything human.

All human life for David revolved around disappointment, loss, and suffering; he experienced his own humanness as filled with coldness and emptiness; pleasure lay outside his field of human possibility. What better defense than delusion in his refusal to risk the embodied foundations of desire? Delusion substituted for an intimacy grounded in desire; its defensive functions preserved the remnants of the self's integrity, of its shattered thread of being. Delusion's elaborate inner scenarios destroyed the human foundations of action; its seeming perfection protected the self from acknowledging deep-seated feelings of worthlessness and badness. Delusion kept David from encountering reality as imperfect, messy, and indeterminate; it prevented the human Other from being polluted, corrupted, even destroyed by what David felt to be his own poisonousness. If all feeling could remain blocked by the grandiosity produced by delusion, it would be unnecessary for him to seek gratification or contact in the human world, in community. In delusion, then, not only was the real Other safe from David's poison, but David himself could escape the terrifying pain, dread, and loss inevitably waiting for him in the human environment. He could protect himself from the dialectic of subjectivity. It was not delusion that threatened his self-concept; rather, it was the reality of closeness and intimacy that brought the risk of disintegration, annihilation, death, and the eternal pain of Sisyphus. Yet in the chaos of his dematerialized, dissociated inner universe, David still struggled to maintain the thread of being; and it was this resilience, this will-to-be, that eventually led him out of his nightmare.

To conclude: the more appreciation David had of the politics of human relationship (both in his therapy and on his Hall), the less prominent was delusion in his consciousness. As his *participatory* and intersubjective connections became stronger, his delusional ones receded; as his tolerance for ambiguity and ambivalence intensified, his need for "all or nothing" solutions and visions diminished. The more integrated David became in the community of his Hall, the less powerful was the entropy working its way through his self-system. The more aware he became of the needs of others, the less preoccupied he was with delusions or hallucinated symbologies. The more conscious he became of his own past and its relation to the present, the less volatile were his moods and self-perceptions. The more attention he gave to the public dimension of his life, to personhood as a function of participation and collaboration, the less likely he was to withdraw into the privacy of his own internal conflicts. Both elements, then, in David's treatment—his education in self-governance (his public being) and his self-reflection in psychotherapy (his private being)—brought coherence to a self whose organization had been shattered: the more enhanced his intersubjectivity, the more stable his self.

Success in David's treatment could not have occurred without an integration of the private and public: the private, conflictual self (his split-off pain and rage, the fears and grandiosity represented in delusion), and the public self (struggling with others' perceptions, desperately trying to construct relationships, working to engage others realistically, negotiating with staff, observing, reflecting, and fighting with the ever present tendency to withdraw into delusion). To attain self-coherence, to heal his fragmented being, he required a treatment sensitive not only to his bizarre inner constructions but also to the public, intersubjective world involving the desires and needs of others, their perceptions and views, and the inevitable disagreements of imperfect human beings.

To be in a *polis* is as much a state of mind as it is a historical fact; and to be a citizen of a city, no matter where it is or what form it takes, involves energy and activity, the acknowledgment and sharing of common ends and aims. I consider David's Hall or his unit or his current halfway house to be a city—one not obviously like a Greek *polis,* certainly not a city in any modern republican sense, but simply a public space bringing people together, generating common meanings, mediating serious conflict, and forging shared understandings. That kind of community creates a politics, a consciousness of what it means to live together, to share and express a common *civitas,* to dwell in what David called his "civil world." Mediating what happens in that city, in that community, requires political being, an awareness of phenomena that historically have been called political.

That David is not a member of a legislature or any deliberative body constituted and regulated by the state has little or no bearing on the practice (or *praxis*) of his citizenship or his meaning as a person living within a definable *civitas.* David constructed his own citizenship. He was not born into it; he fought for it, both in his own mind and in the extremely tense and often painful public environments of his living arrangements. He discovered much of his identity through that public space and its effect on his self-concept and self-organization; the process was intensified by his interaction with staff and other patients during the most painful moments of his withdrawal. David won the right to his public being; in large measure he survived because of his efforts to make contact with others. In the universe of delusion, in the dominion of the Sirens, citizenship had no existence, participation no meaning, reciprocity no function or purpose. And that kind of world David was (and is) determined to reject.

I have been concerned in David's case not about the specific psychodynamic or developmental factors delineating the frame of his illness (I have more to say about these in the discussions of Ruth and Julia, Chapters 4–7); rather, my primary purpose has been to describe, as a phenomenology, the process of psychotic disintegration and the language of madness as experienced both by David and by the staff surrounding him. Further, David's case highlights the importance and role of intersubjectivity in pulling the self out of its solipsistic inwardness. In this respect David's capacity to *be* had a great deal to do with the political relations of participation that became for him, particularly after his manias, lifesaving connections to the world. Too often this *political* side of emergence from psychosis—the self as agent in its own curative process, its struggle with the rudiments of civil society—is ignored in case analyses. At the risk of ignoring other important aspects of David's treatment and history, I have chosen to emphasize the singularity of his struggle with delusion and his hard-won achievements in establishing a civil relation with the community in which he lived.

4 /

Withdrawal from the
Public World:
Nightmares and Histories

Persons the society names as schizophrenic or those, like David, caught up in the manic phases of bipolar illness exist or live beyond the psychological borders. To be psychotic is to be outside the sphere of social rationality; it is to be trapped in the frenzy of the Imaginary. Delusion replaces consensual reality as the focus of being. Meaning, orientation, and reference for psychotic states lie in the command of voices, hallucinations, and delusions; the concerns and tasks of everyday life, the skills and assumptions of consensual reality, recede from consciousness. Schizophrenics, for example, find themselves psychically outside the social forms of identification. The self may inhabit alien universes, the bodies of animals, other planets, machines, subterranean caves, computers, and so on. Logic, thought, and association proceed according to delusional premises, and the linear and serial logics of civil society possess little or no significance.

This is not the case, however, for the self who lives and survives not *beyond* but *on* the borders of society. For such persons, although peculiar thoughts and hallucinations may be very real and immobilizing, language and linguistic production appear functional and comprehensible, and time orientations are not distorted. Intellectual and cognitive operations consistent with social norms and prevailing communication patterns remain largely intact; and the borderline person, capable of normal conversation, possesses a sense of time that corresponds with the assumptions of the existent social world. Cognitively, the intactness of the borderline patient may seem quite striking and impressive. In addition, appearance often seems quite normal.[1]

For the schizophrenic, both cognition and emotional structure have disintegrated; the structures of civil society have been assimilated into a delusional logic or system. For the borderline, however, it is the affective world that has sustained extraordinary injury. Cognitive functions, often operating at high levels, disguise a radically disordered inner world that persistently threatens the self with dissolution and annihilation. What Heinz Kohut (1977) ascribes to narcissistic patients applies with equal force to the borderline state of mind: fragmentation, disintegration anxiety, the use of fantasy as defense, the periodic loss of contact with reality, and the struggle with early infantile injuries to the self.

I have more to say about this psychiatric diagnostic category and its phenomenology in a later chapter;[2] here, I introduce a borderline narrative by turning to the experience of Ruth. Her case illustrates how fragile the membrane is between psychosis and reality, how permeable are the structures of consensual reality, and how easy it is for the borderline self to move into psychosis. But what distinguished Ruth from schizophrenic patients and, to some extent, the persistent immobilizing manias of a David was her capacity to resymbolize her experience and to speak about it in a language that acknowledges an existent social and historical world. Ruth might periodically become psychotic, but unlike the schizophrenic she did not dwell within an unyielding and ritualized delusional epistemology. To that extent she was freer than a schizophrenic who remains trapped within a complex delusional system that is rigid and often impermeable. Though Ruth experienced several days and weeks of psychosis, her state of being was not permanently psychotic. Nor did she suffer the illness that frequently kept David struggling throughout his adolescence and early adulthood with the *presence* and *actuality* of delusion. David faced the continual prospect of epistemological inversions coming from his bipolar oscillations. For Ruth, the struggle, with some few striking exceptions, was primarily on the level of affect. Her entire emotional universe as far back as she could remember had been a Kafkaesque nightmare of dread, hate, and the fight to avoid psychological disintegration, which often manifested itself in suicide attempts.

To be borderline is precisely to live on the *borders* of society; it is to feel so alienated, so extruded from the social world, that consciousness finds it impossible to find or locate a sense of place. Psychological placelessness, a horrifying experience of aloneness and disconnectedness, becomes the norm, close to the pull and nearness of delusional identification. In the hospital, delusion came to threaten Ruth's life; the resymbolizing properties of a language rooted in intersubjectivity pulled her out. Following Ruth's narrative, a phenomenological account that includes the perceptions of her treatment environment, I look at the meaning of her experience within an interpretive framework that is both political and psychoanalytic: political in the sense that her phenomenological world possesses properties that shed light on Rousseauist assumptions regarding community, and psychoanalytic in the sense that Ruth's illness and therapy illustrate psychodynamic principles in the theory of Heinz Kohut. In addition, many of Kohut's ideas, particularly his understanding of empathy, constitute a fascinating commentary on the Rousseauist notion of *pitié*.

Background: The Torment of the Past

Ruth, an attractive woman of thirty and the mother of three children, highly regarded in her orthodox Jewish community, understood herself to be on the outskirts of life and society, on the far edge of what political philosophers have considered civil or political, *polis*-like. She found herself preoccupied with the will not to be, with meditations on extreme alienation, with intense and unrelenting feelings of being less than human, of being hated, reviled, and rejected by a persecuting and treacherous community. Her emotional world revolved around periodic feelings of terror, emptiness, and depersonalization; she experienced herself as empty, her body as dead; care and empathy, she believed, are deceits that disguise the deviousness of human intent and the malevolence of human motive. Self-destructive acts, including five suicide attempts within three months of coming to the hospital, run through her history. Yet Ruth was not considered *clinically* psychotic.

When I began to meet with Ruth, she had been at Sheppard-Pratt for seven months. Our conversations took place over an eight-month period. We spoke in a small room on her Hall without the benefit of a tape recorder, which she refused to permit: her project at the hospital was to "disappear," she said, to kill all forms of human connection; if I taped her words, it would make her "bigger" and more "noticeable." Nor would she allow me to take notes during our meetings. I reconstructed her narrative immediately afterward.

According to psychiatric records, Ruth

attended a private high school in Cleveland, where she graduated in 1969. She was quite modest about her achievements in high school, and only after some prodding did she admit that she was valedictorian of her class as well as the editor of the school newspaper. She stated that she often found herself in situations and roles where she did not feel particularly comfortable with her skills (i.e., leadership, writing, public speaking). However, she worked hard to develop these skills, although she did not particularly enjoy using them.

After graduation (according to social workers' and psychologists' reports), she enrolled at a local Jewish college that was

devoted primarily to functional or vocational skills, at which time she married and did not complete the two-year program. . . . As a child the patient has apparently been quite patently anxious. Thus mother would reproach her for her "nervousness," which probably was a reference to agitation, tension, outbursts of screaming temper, a general fearfulness, a constant worry to the point of dread that something catastrophic was likely to strike at almost any moment. . . . [Ruth's relationship to her mother was characterized as] screaming outbursts . . . a sense of approaching the brink, of going to pieces . . . fearful possibilities. [She complained of] being misunderstood; [she has] hypersensitivity with the consequence of readily feeling mistreated and hurt, a constant readiness to feel that others have disappointed her. . . . In these attributes she emulates mother's masochistic sense of martyrdom, a trait she recognizes readily in mother but not in herself. . . . Without any handle at all on her own angry feelings, she avoids self-recognition in this area by rigidly adhering to an image of herself as a virtuous person, whose first reaction to any criticism is to act out the role of a good girl with a masochistic intensity. To accommodate this type of reaction to the opinions of others, she becomes self-abasing and suggestible to a self-demeaning degree. . . . Ruth's over-doses [of over-the-counter sleep medications], she said, were not related to wanting to die but were out of anger and wanting to sleep because she felt that there was no way out. . . . Ruth demonstrated little feeling as she described her overdoses.

In the hospital Ruth continued to try to kill herself. A month after her admission she ran away. Six hours later she returned, complaining of "weakness, dizziness, and . . . some difficulty with ambulation," having taken a massive dose of over-the-counter medication, "includ-ing Sominex and Comtrex." Three weeks later she ran away again and took an overdose of an over-the-counter analgesic. She was found soon afterward in the washroom of a local motel and treated at a local hospital.

Entries in the nursing notes for June–September 1982 give an in-dication, early in her hospitalization at Sheppard-Pratt, of what Ruth felt and how she responded to the hospital environment.

June 12: She came out and spoke with the writer; she stated that she dislikes the image that others have of her as being competent and bright and organized. She wants to be "impulsive," "rebel," "test" the waters, find out if she can be bad and still be loved. To find out if she wants to be bright, competent, organized for herself, not because others want or ex-pect it of her. She states she's been pressured to excel from birth and doesn't like it. She wants and expects the doctors to see past her bright, competent, organized side. Stated: "I hate being told I have a strong ego and am organized."

July 17 [from art therapist's notes]: Ruth drew a circular saw covered in blood; explained that this image shows the dangerousness of her fears about her abilities as a parent.

August 7: She feels a lot of anger inside her but doesn't want to give it up because then she wouldn't have anything. . . . She says she's developing an affinity for pain . . . [she] describes a frightening nightmare . . . a dream she has had for the past three nights. It involves the police and her rabbi putting her in jail for not keeping a "kosher house," and her husband not helping her but agreeing with [the police]. . . . She says that lately she has been doubting her religious beliefs and feels the religious laws are too strict for her to follow [this part of Ruth's identity, her orthodox Judaism, figures prominently both in her delusional identifications and, several months later, in her rebellion against any form of orthodoxy]. . . . She states that she used to fantasize about her husband and children dying. "I finally decided that rather than killing them, I should die."

September 14: She feels she will die at home but will not try to commit suicide. . . . refers to husband as a "corpse" . . . says "my life is now fallen or is falling apart" . . . going home will be a death sentence. . . . Also reported feeling as if she were an observer to her own conversations several times during the day. "I felt as if I was listening to what I said from the outside of me." She says she can't eat because she has a bitter taste in her mouth.

September 26 [the day before Ruth again ran away from the hospital with the express purpose of committing suicide]: Ruth has been observed sitting and lying in a fetal-like position. . . . a peer informed staff that Ruth had scratched her wrist. Staff found superficial scratches on her wrist. Pt. is to be placed on special observation, scratches cleaned with water. Pt. seems confused, hopeless, and desperate. Stated only that something terrible happened today that convinced her that there is no hope of her being able to live without pain. . . . [It was, however, a pain that persistently drove her to suicidal actions; later, Ruth discovered inside herself ways of handling pain that did not threaten her physically.] Ruth stated to writer: "How do I feel right now? I would take anything to try to kill myself." She also complains of not being able to sleep in the past 72 hours.

Ruth's Narrative: The Disintegrating Self

Ever since I've been in the hospital, I have this need to kill myself. It seems to follow me around wherever I go, to activities, therapy, on walks, at meals. Sometimes I imagine the food should be poisoned and then I won't have to do it; or I fantasize a bomb will be dropped on the hospital, and later the rescue squads will find me smashed underneath a thousand tons of stone and brick. Everywhere I look, I see futility . . . I hate my husband; he's a monster who refuses to understand me; he treats me like garbage, but then, why not? I *am* garbage, a piece of dirt, a nothing . . . suicide is the best way. And what's wrong with that? Why shouldn't I die? No one will miss me; my children will be happy that finally their crazy mother has left them. My husband will have a celebration and invite his friends over. They'll dance and proclaim to

God I'm better off with Him than on earth. My children will hug their father and tell him how good it is I'm gone and why didn't I do it earlier. The Rabbi will spit on my grave . . . and my parents won't even notice I'm dead. . . . Papa will probably think it's better for the grandchildren not to have their *meshuggeneh* [crazy] mother around. . . .

I bring chaos to other people's lives . . . it's all worthless, a mess, a great big zero. . . . Why do you think I try to commit suicide, why I want to escape from here and take whatever I can to put me to sleep forever? It's mechanical; I have no feeling when I do it. Suicide is like taking an action, any action. It has no significance other than what it is. I feel, right before, no sadness, just relief I've finally found a place where I can do it, where the job can get finished, done. It's the only way to relieve the emptiness . . . like the possibility of dying fills me up. The whole thing is mechanical. I find the pills, a place to do it, I put them in my mouth, swallow, no feeling or fear, no regrets, but a sense I've finally accomplished something good and meaningful.

It's incredible. They want to keep me in here! Staff tells me they won't give me a sign-out [a brief leave from the hospital, from a few hours to a day or two; the sign-out requires the approval of the patient's therapist, and all sign-outs are discussed in staff meetings] because they know I'll try and kill myself. So is it any of their business what I do? Why should they dictate my life? I'm an adult; and if I want to die, then they should let me do it! It makes me so angry when they refuse. I feel like cracking open everything in the Hall, driving the nurses through an open window. It's maddening, their arrogance, to want to keep me alive! Yesterday, I felt like exploding into a million pieces. Staff told me they wouldn't let me have a sign-out; other patients agreed it "wouldn't be good for me." I wanted to strangle them! I remember looking at the window and thinking, let me put my fist right through it. It'll break and then I can jump, and it'll be over. But I just sat there, burning. And I spent the rest of the day talking with Pearl [Ruth's closest friend on the Hall] about the best ways to kill ourselves, whether it was better to use a razor blade or a knife. Maybe it would be more painless with pills, less messy. You think I'm joking? That's the chief topic of conversation around here; what else is there to talk about? Pearl and I have a suicide pact; whoever does it first, the other follows. We understand each other.

Staff really should give up on me . . . I don't think I should be here; a better place would be a crematorium. Or maybe if they won't do that, put me in a kennel, at best a state hospital for the criminally insane. . . . I don't deserve to be human. . . . Yesterday I didn't want Dr. —— [Ruth's psychotherapist] to see my face. I kept it covered during the entire session. . . . If he saw my face, he would see me for who I am . . . a monster . . . a cockroach. . . . My anger disgusts me; it brings up all the helplessness, all the horror. I turn it on myself; it makes me feel terrible. I'm a nothing . . . dirt to be manipulated. I hate myself, everyone, you.

Evidence for Ruth's delusional preoccupation, her traversing the border toward the psychotic side, emerged slowly. A nursing note in October stated that she felt "greatly misunderstood . . . says she regretted being born a Jew. Because of historic Jewish suffering, she must live a holy, productive life in order to decrease the suffering of others now." Firmly convinced that God demanded perfection from her, Ruth saw piety as a form of atonement for the historic causes of Jewish suffering: the more perfect she was as wife, mother, devout Jew, the more glory she would bring to God. Obedience to ritual and belief became devotional penance. The feeling was closely tied up however, in Ruth's identification with her parents' experience as concentration-camp inmates during World War II. It was this connection that served as the foundation for her conviction that the Nazis were as much a presence in her life as they had been in her parents' lives.

Psychiatric and psychological evaluations during this phase reflect Ruth's anger and confusion.

November 19: Within the individual psychotherapeutic session, she has spoken in detail about the enormous anger she has felt from childhood with respect to her family members. At one point following a weekly therapy meeting with her husband which included her children for the first time, she became upset. The next day she found relief by hitting her hands against the wall. There were rather large hematomas on the surfaces of both.

December 14 [a staff psychologist's review]: Borderline personality would seem to be the best diagnostic fit. Ruth continues to harbor a myth of a . . . perfect world which she is reticent to release. She is an intelligent individual who somehow feels justified at this point in egocentrically exploring the world and satisfying her wishes to undo felt restrictions of the past. Ruth is definitely going through a reexamining of her identity, which remains blurred and unclear at this point. In a positive sense, she feels on a symbolic level as if there is a rebirth process under way. Yet one must be concerned that she does not act this out in a distorted, concrete fashion through further overdoses. Getting involved and close to others is still highly problematic and for the time being she will maintain a pushing away while continuing to be dependent and insecure.

Ruth:

> When I was growing up, my parents constantly harped on how horrible I was, what a bad, unresponsive child I had been. Everything I did, from getting dressed, tying my shoes, how I ate, the friends I played with, hobbies I tried to share with them, all of it was bad, and they complained I never listened or wanted to please. Every effort I made to do for them, to make them happy, they ignored, throwing my overtures away like spoiled pieces of garbage. Of course, now they deny it; they tell the social worker and my therapist how good I was, what a sweet child Ruthie was, how she did everything right. . . . They just don't understand why I want to kill myself, and they deny it by saying it must be a phase I'm going through. But even when I was little they never knew the truth; they were so busy, so preoccupied, they never took the time to look inside me, to really find out exactly what was happening with their child. . . .
>
> It made me so mad; I remember the anger when I was a teenager, but it had been there all the time. It's hard bringing it back. Sometimes entire years escape me . . . it's like swimming around in muddy water. I just can't see. . . . Now my parents show me such concern; but where was it when I needed it, when I was so desperate for their attention? It's too late, their caring, twenty-nine years too late; and probably it's all a charade anyway, and what they're really worried about is their grandchildren. I used to scream at Papa to notice me, to say something nice; but he would laugh and tell me, "Ruthie, stop the joking and get serious." And

then he criticized me for something, my hair or how I didn't give him enough respect. All I could do was stand there, hurting unbelievably, wanting to scratch his eyes out. But I did nothing; I ran into my room and sat on the bed, staring at wallpaper or tracing lines with my eyes. I couldn't do anything right as a kid; I even think my father hated me as a girl and later as a woman.

Ruth's struggles with her father appear persistently in her narrative. For example, a mental health worker reports, she felt she was going through a

"sexual identity crisis," explaining that her father always told her she was "more of a man—too thin, too bony, and my breasts were too small." She stated that when she first menstruated her mother "slapped my face" and also reported that her husband constantly tells her that she is not feminine in generally the [same terms] as her father. Pt. stated that she wants to get rid of "her *self,*" but "keep the person." For now, suicide, she says, is "on hold."

Ruth:

Papa threatened me if I misbehaved by yelling, "Ruthie, if you don't come here at once, I'll throw you in the pot and we'll cook you for dinner," a weird thing to say, actually grotesque, since both my parents had been in concentration camps during the war. Maybe my mother and father never saw me as a person; or what they experienced in the death camps depleted them of so much human feeling they came to believe the world, including their own family, was composed entirely of vicious animals who had to be trained to do right. It's not that they treated me this way all the time, but I often felt I wasn't part of them; we weren't a family but some kind of group trying to survive every moment of the day. What was important was not love but survival. And what mattered was not affection but the children excelling in whatever they did. I thought my purpose here in life was to prove, to demonstrate, my worthiness even to be alive, to be fortunate enough even to have parents. No doubt what happened in the camps scarred them for life, but it also has hurt me and my brother. Maybe their rage became part of me, or should I set an example as the daughter of survivors? You can't imagine how horrible it is to be a child of parents who made it through the camps. There are moments when I think of myself as living death, a monument to their suffering. Or am I already dead? And you're talking to my ashes?

The only time my parents noticed me was when I started screaming and carrying on. . . . My rage kindled theirs, and all of us were caught up in battles lasting for hours, if not days. We seemed trapped by it, like we were drowning in each other's hatred. Afterward, I gasped for air, trying to find the surface . . . no wonder anger leaves me feeling so helpless. If I wasn't escaping them with my anger, pushing them away, I made myself numb against their insults and indifference. I became a stone, hard and cold, protected from their insensitivity. Nothing they said touched me. I felt like a dead person, petrified but safe. At least a stone couldn't feel pain.

At school, in Hebrew school, everyone thought I was clever and admired me for expressing anger so directly. It amused the teachers: "Ruth has such a good sense of herself . . . Jahweh's right arm . . . When Ruth thunders you hear the voice of God!" Looking back on it, they laughed at me, but I believed them. I felt powerful, strong in my rage, like I spoke with God's will. I had God's wrath inside. What a blessing; my anger killed, and I better be careful how I used it! A girlfriend confided in me that if someone were to look inside and see my rage, they would see who I was. I sometimes acted like a monster; my anger had no boundaries. I yelled, ranted, until I got my way. I only stopped when another student stood up to me and told me to shut up; I took it so personally. When that happened I felt wounded, like the person hated me because she had insisted I be quiet. Of course, no one understood how terrible I felt inside after these outbursts, how I was hurting, what all that rage was doing to me. I never showed that side to anyone; and I've only shared those feelings since I've been here at Sheppard. I've always worn masks; and when the masks become too burdensome, I scurry around for pills like an alcoholic for his bottle.

Gradually, Ruth showed what lay behind her masks. For example, her dance therapist noted that she struggled "to accept the deep sadness and grieving and along with that, a great sense of need (of her doctor, of support from others, to be cared about) which, she acknowledges, is easier for her to handle through denial and rage." A nursing entry referred to Ruth's belief that the "Nazis are chasing her." Ruth claimed that there was "no basis" for this belief, but it became increasingly clear that her paranoia, her periodic rage directed toward staff, her hints at "something going on that no one knows about" indicated an internal or delusional world that she had yet to express directly. Her art therapist observed:

Feelings about herself are harshly critical and judgmental. Seems unwilling to listen to ideas which might lead to increased self-acceptance. . . . Aware of own feelings of wanting to defend and protect herself, seems to experience everything and everyone as potentially intrusive and destructive to her. Pictures especially reflect this theme; they showed her with eyes, ears, and mouth blocked and arms raised to defend her. Seems quite frightened but won't explain why.

A mental health worker wrote:

Ruth states that she has become confused about people and situations, but she is unsure whether staff here wants to help her or hurt her. Subsequently she is finding it difficult to communicate and was at times unresponsive during this conversation. She adds that when she feels confused, this "something comes to her and tells her what to do." When asked if this thing told her to hurt herself, she said that she wasn't sure yet. Also she says that she feels very compelled to comply with what this [thing] tells her to do.

By early winter Ruth's masks had eroded even further. At one moment she would perform like a model patient; at other times she would withdraw and break down into monologues on the horror of life. She expressed to one of the staff a need to "take a vacation from my mind." She complained about conditions inside the hospital being "unbearable" and wondered whether she would "make it through another day." She spoke about feeling "very alone" and how "everything seems meaningless." She reflected on her "self-hatred" and described how she had been "locked into the same pattern of depression since she was three years old." She wished she could "just disappear" and "become a speck" that would finally dissolve.

I've lost all hope. . . . And I despise people who try to get close to me. I don't deserve anyone's support, and the more people come to know me, the less they like me. I'm surprised you're not driven from this room by how horrible I smell . . . the stench must be awful . . . it's my rottenness, my limbs, flesh decaying . . . it makes me stink, dying meat. . . . What do you do with putrified meat? You throw it out, into the garbage pail.

At the end of February 1983, Ruth's psychiatrist observed:

This last month has been a difficult one for the patient for she has begun taking trips home to be with her children, her in-laws, and her family on an increasing basis. In addition, her closest friend, Pearl, also a woman facing divorce, left the hospital. These stresses have been upsetting to the patient but have allowed us to look more closely at her inner world. She was able to speak about her identification with her parents, their hopes and dreams for her as well as their memories of anger and despair from the Holocaust. The patient, in turn, spoke with great poignancy about her having failed her parents and her in-laws, also survivors of the Nazi Holocaust, by not being able to keep her marriage together. However, in addition she complained that she felt alone and that no one understood her needs. Ruth also grappled with the enormous tumultuous feelings within her children, their anger at her for not being away from the hospital and, of course, their great love and need for her. The discharge of Pearl, the patient described, as being a part of her; "we are one" or "I feel I've lost part of me." This precipitated a kind of mourning process, though the patient remains in touch with her [Pearl] and has taken several short sign-outs with her.

In early March Ruth again returned home for a visit. This time it was a terrifying, disillusioning experience. She felt absolutely no connection to her house or to the people living in it.

I felt like an observer from another planet, an outsider. And I didn't enjoy being with my parents or in-laws or my children. During most of the day, I had memories of how unhappy I was before any of this began. None of them seemed real; my parents acted like strangers, and my in-laws treated me as if I were some fragile piece of china they couldn't touch. It was so formal, so stiff and awkward. I wanted to die; it just didn't make any sense being there. It was like wandering around in a foreign country; who were these people? Why should I put up with this? Didn't they know I was sick, what a difficult time I'd been having just trying to stay alive? I thought to myself, it took twenty-nine years for this breakdown to finally come to the surface, and I'll always be broken. Nothing will help. Where are some pills? I had a panic attack and wanted to be out of there, to find a place I could lie down and disappear. I couldn't even play simple games with my children; I ignored them completely and wished they had been somewhere else.

Nursing entry:

At one point during the stay Pt. stated that she hit one of her children for not behaving. "It was the only time that I felt like myself, when I was hitting her." Children were apparently unruly; and [they] told patient to "go back to the hospital . . . we were happier without you." Pt. states she felt "empty" throughout most of her visit home. . . . When asked if she gained anything positive from the visit, she stated, "I can't think of anything."

Suicide became a topic again: "I'm thinking about all kinds of ways to kill myself. It's my major project; nothing else makes any difference. I have a right to die, and the hospital better not get in my way." The art therapist noted that she drew a picture of herself "being beaten by her father," and a week later her sketches dealt with "themes of World War II Holocaust. Ruth identified this but wasn't willing to discuss it further." She took a sign-out to a local motel with Pearl, and according to Ruth:

> All we did was talk about the conditions necessary for suicide. It was comforting; we stayed up all night and I knew someone was there who understood what I had been going through. But I told Pearl she shouldn't do it; she should live; she deserved to live. Me, I'm a piece of shit, and shit you flush down the toilet; you get rid of it. So I told Pearl to help me find the pills and to come and visit my grave every so often.

She told staff that if she "could be tortured, maybe she could get beyond the ever-present feeling of pain . . . being alive is such a burden." In her psychological testing she visualized "monsters, ogres, strange animals, ugly faces, and bleeding vultures zeroing in on victims . . . vicious fighting . . . [there is] a sense of doom and relative lack of control . . . a quality of Greek tragedy where these things need to be played out and there is nothing that can alter the sequence of things." In response to parables, questions, and pictures, she wrote: "Closer and closer there comes doom . . . if people only knew how much pain I was in . . . the best of mothers may forget that her children can hate her . . . a naked man walked into the gas chamber." Ruth was grappling with overwhelming forces. "The responses she gave in September," wrote the psychologist a few months later, "seemed troubled, but more tied to issues concerning her children, and about getting a divorce. She stated that she regretted having children, particularly by her present husband. However, there was not the sense of doom and despair to the extent that presently seems to exist."

By the middle of March, Ruth was complaining of "green bugs . . . in my plants"; they come out "at night and crawl down my back . . . I feel them going into my body." She threw her plants away; when asked why, she responded, "My green bugs have become bad bugs, naughty, they do perverse things to me." Staff thought Ruth might be "hallucinating, dissociating" at times. She had trouble describing her feelings: "I think I feel real, it's just that everyone else doesn't . . . things are going on in here you wouldn't even dream of." She was "edgy," "nervous"; she slept in the Hall's living room because "scary things in her bedroom . . . appear to take on different shapes in the dark."

Nursing entry:

Pt. also stated that she felt afraid and that she "should leave this place . . . something terrible is going to happen to everyone." She [keeps seeing] "ugly hostile bugs" and wants to "die." Pt. speaks of "feelings of doom" . . . observed to be trembling . . . she felt that she was "dead" . . . and she wondered out loud if she would feel any different if she actually took her life . . . refuses any contact with her children . . . she feels she's in a "different place . . . room and people here are unfamiliar to me" . . . talks about burning down her house and using her husband as the "wick" while he's asleep . . . feels that staff are not really staff but "someone else" and that the place [Sheppard-Pratt] is somewhere else.

During another visit home in late March she again tried to commit suicide. "The number of drugs she took was unclear. Her feelings of worthlessness and hopelessness were expressed. . . . [Ruth] requested that she be transferred to a state institution because 'I don't want to be a burden to anyone'" (from the psychiatric review). It was the beginning of the most terrifying period in Ruth's life.

5 /

The Destruction of Mind

In the midst of her regression, Ruth found no comfort; the world appeared as death, and her contact with external reality became extremely tenuous. Staff took on images that corresponded to the structures of a delusional identification. All experience held threat; all definition turned into a function of what internal images were dictating to her consciousness. Fear controlled Ruth's world. She lived in a Hobbesian terror.

> Papa never recognized my suffering; he said things like, "You can't suffer . . . you have no idea what suffering is." I thought that to suffer you had to be really special; and I could never be special enough. . . . I came home and said, "Papa, I hurt . . . I'm in pain," and his response? "That's nothing . . . how dare you call that suffering!" I was devastated, confused . . . I didn't know what to feel. . . . If you had to be so special to suffer, then I wasn't special at all. I worked hard at trying to be special, perfect; but for Papa, it was never enough. I wondered if I shouldn't hate God, since he hadn't made me special enough to suffer. It was unfair.
>
> How could I describe my father's experiences? How did they

come to me? It was a combination of his religious orthodoxy and what he endured in the camps. Sometimes I thought I lived only to confirm his religious beliefs and to atone for his pain. Papa took orthodox Judaism to an extreme. He believed we should rid ourselves of all physical impulses driving us toward pleasure. He saw pleasure as an evil, and we should do all we could to harden ourselves against any kind of temptation. Imagine listening to this as a child; to be righteous we had to earn the reputation for righteousness. The good Jew stood pure before God. Papa repeated this over and over: we should think nothing of our bodies and devote all our attention to the cultivation of our minds. That was how the Jew became righteous: if we performed well and looked good, God noticed. It reflected well on Him and on us. I thought if I received good grades and dressed nicely, God might tell my father to like me more. And if I was smart and clever and if I wore pressed clothes, I could stand before God and share in His blessings.

But Papa's philosophy made me unhappy, and as I got older, I came to hate God with a passion. It was too much effort to be righteous; it tired me out. If righteousness demanded all the sacrifices I was making, if acting righteous meant being unhappy, then I could never forgive God for *my* pain. But I felt so guilty! I couldn't please my father; I was unable to please God; whom could I please? Was I so worthless I couldn't please anyone? I could never be happy inside or outside the house, so I spent my entire childhood trying to be perfect. I could never be who I was: an unhappy, miserable, guilt-ridden kid. When my grades were good and when I looked nice, Papa noticed me. That was it. After each report card, he told me, "What a smart girl!" . . . the only compliment I ever received from him. What a sham! Inside I felt the opposite of what I showed to the world. I tried to be perfect, but the more effort I put into it, the more horrible I felt.

I never believed anyone perfect could like me. Truly perfect people have their own agenda, and I wasn't on it. The more perfect the person, the more worthless and desperate I felt being around them. I've always been attracted to people I thought were gods, who were unattainable. But if they showed an interest in me, there had to be something wrong with them. Like you, you're a fool for wanting to speak with me . . . you're probably as worthless as I am, since no one pays you to listen to these wanderings in my mind. Of course, on one level, obviously, you're not an idiot. But I have a real hard time imagining that anyone could find what I have to say *useful* or interesting. But people who show me respect or interest *must* have something wrong with them; why else waste your time on me? Look at it this way: if X likes me, X has to be an animal with no taste, a jerk who only sees the outside and doesn't have the insight to see beneath my surface. And if X could see what's really going on, he would be out of here as quickly as possible. Or maybe the reason X likes me is that he's as loathsome as I am; he sees a kindred animal. How could anyone find anything in such a disgusting creature as myself? There are moments when I feel like a thing, an object, a boulder lying in some desert. Do you find that so strange? My parents continually refused to acknowledge my deepest feelings; and what *I* felt was constantly being denied. Is it any wonder I see myself as worthless, so distant from everything human?

Papa was usually away for the week, working somewhere; but when he came home, the fighting and yelling began. Every weekend, each of them [mother and father] lived in some crisis. No one expressed any love or caring; we were admonished not to say anything to anybody, just to keep quiet. Papa held his anger inside, but you could see it. I felt it in the air, like a slingshot ready to explode . . . until he leaped out of his chair screaming he was "taking refuge in the Yeshiva" [seminary] and his children were trying to kill him, and why didn't his wife beat us . . . and all my mother was saying was, "Your father, he's just tired; give him a chance to calm down; it's been a hard week" . . . excuse after excuse. She cringed at the sight of him . . . I have almost no recollection of my mother through this. She didn't seem to be there, and why should she? Did her husband really love her? The only time mother touched me was when she paraded me before her friends at card parties and religious functions. She never touched me when we were alone; she never showed any tenderness; no hugs and kisses, just *tsouris,* you know, the Yiddish word for hassle, trouble. She was never excited or happy about her children or anything they did, their schoolwork, games, hobbies. Mother was a watcher, not a doer. . . . She also spent a great deal of time in her bedroom.

It was always grim, sad, in her bedroom. I go in there and find this pathetic old woman lying in bed, never noticing anything, staring at the ceiling. She looked so unhappy, so out of touch. She revived when she had to go out, to do her religious obligations. But around the house, if she wasn't doing chores, she lay in bed. As a child, I thought I might rescue her from her unhappiness. Then she would love me, and the whole family would live happily ever after. What a fantasy! Reality washed away these daydreams and wishes. . . . I never brought any feeling out of my mother; it was like trying to stir a corpse. Her indifference, her lack of emotion, pushed me into the most incredible rages. I stormed around her bedroom like a crazy person, screaming any insult that came into my head. She accused me of saying things to hurt her. I yelled back I hated her and wished she were dead. I cried for hours after these scenes; and I convinced myself my words had the power to kill. I put invisible daggers into her: "Ah, Mama, if you don't kill me first, I'll do it to you!"

Yet there were times when I saw her as a mighty princess who deserved servants, ladies-in-waiting. She could be so beautiful, so glowing, and my heart cried out for her. I wanted mother to love me more than I wanted anything else in the world. What a magnificent woman she could be! So austere, so perfect . . . so much a fantasy! I don't think I ever saw her as a mother, soft and affectionate. I never came that close; but she also shut me out. Either mother stood as this mighty princess, with her magnificent black hair piled high on her head, or a pathetic old woman refusing to get out of bed, looking as if she were about to die. I have trouble finding reality in my mother; it's as if she were never there.

Papa believed that everything we did, and this included my marriage, reflected on our faith and obedience before God. If we had to erase our emotions and feelings to justify our worth, he insisted we do it. His attitude toward my marriage and my responsibilities toward Aaron followed his religious beliefs, and he put tremendous pressure on me to keep an efficient, functioning household. He demanded that I cater to Aaron: "A man's wife," he said, "is a reflection of his value before God." The more children I produced for Aaron, the greater would be our family's righteousness. The *kinder* [children] became an investment in

God's goodwill. It was a terrible time for me because these messages also kept coming from my in-laws. My worth as a human being depended entirely on how well I served Aaron and how I fulfilled my duties as a childbearing Jewish wife. Papa kept reminding me I should take comfort in the tradition that the wife served a husband who dedicated himself to the greater glory of God. By taking care of Aaron, by tending my duties, I, too, could participate in God's works. When I tried to speak with a rabbi about problems in my marriage, the heavy burdens, he laughed at me and told me to go home, make dinner, and attend lectures on the "obligations" of the [Jewish] "orthodox" wife and mother. He even accused me of going "reform" [a more "liberal" tradition in Judaism] and that I should stop complaining and observe *Shabess* [Saturday, the Jewish day of rest] more faithfully.

I tried everything to please my family and in-laws: I volunteered for community work, spent time at the Jewish public service agency, collected for charity, took meals to the old folks' home. No one was more religious, righteous, or obedient to the law than I. . . . I could have written the book on how to be a good orthodox Jewish wife. Yet I'm not sure when it began, when I started to think of myself as a sacrificial animal. The harder I worked, the more I denied my own desires, I believed, the more God would favor me by demanding I sacrifice everything to Him. If I could die working, being good, I thought I could achieve some happiness because my sacrifice would be a glory, a blessing, a *mitzvah* [meritorious act] to the Jewish people.

I worked a twenty-four-hour day; I stayed up until 2:00 A.M. doing whatever I could, sometimes cleaning the bathrooms three or four times. I convinced myself sleep was a luxury and the truly righteous survived at most on an hour or two a night. I rose at 4:00 A.M. so I could do two hours of exercise and be beautiful for my husband. It was discipline! I became the Queen of Discipline; not a soul would be more perfect than me! I would be God's favorite; then everyone would love me. But it didn't turn out that way. I worked hard, but the numbness kept increasing. I filled up my life with activity, but all I could feel was emptiness. The more I did for my children, my community, my husband and my house, the more distant I felt from all of it. I was obsessed with being and acting perfect. All other feelings left me. I even had the thought of offering myself to a local hospital as a subject for special surgical experiments designed to improve on the human body, anything, surgery, whatever, to make me more perfect. I couldn't work hard enough. It's no wonder I had trouble feeling human. Would a human being do what I was doing?

I sensed that something was wrong, but couldn't define it. My belief system crumbled before my eyes. I started to see God as a tormentor; I hated my husband and children. I couldn't love. At least once a week I locked myself up in the bathroom; I ignored the kids pounding on the door, screaming, "Mama, what's wrong, what are you doing!" They must have thought I was dead. I curled up under the sink and tried to decide how many pills to take, which pills I should use, when would be the most effective time to take them. I stayed this way sometimes for five or six hours. Afterward, I unlocked the bathroom door and the kids rushed in, grabbed hold of me, screaming and sobbing. But I felt nothing and returned to the normal routine: keeping house, making beds, baking, dressing the kids, having breakfast ready, sleeping with my husband, although this was completely mechanical. No one understood. Outwardly, I became my old self, but inwardly I knew I was falling apart and I had been for years.

I felt responsible for everyone's suffering, for my neighbor's hepatitis, for the man down the street when he broke his arm. Not that I caused these things, but I took responsibility for them. All that burden lay on my back; their pain should be my suffering. I went to their houses, offered my help, told their families I would take care of them. When the Jewish social services agency called and said out-of-towners needed a place for the night, I said fine, send them over. Being charitable and neighborly, I might reflect well on my husband, our families, improve my standing with God, affirm my faith, and so on. When the service agency kept calling and sending people over, and with all the additional cooking and cleaning I had to do, my husband told me I should be proud because I brought glory to God. Besides, when people were around, we never fought, and it drained off tension between us. Judaism says if you put up strangers, it's a *mitzvah,* a sign of your good works and righteousness.

Aaron ignored all my efforts to please him, my need to be the perfect wife and lover. He said things like, "You look like shit," or when he wanted me sexually and I felt tired or sick, he accused me of shirking my obligations as a wife. "It's your duty as a wife. . . . I don't care what you feel . . . just lie there and let me do what I want. . . . It's my right!" He turned into a madman, and the sex was horrible. I thought this is what prostitutes feel like, numb screwing machines faking it completely, no connection whatever with their work. It was all I could do to keep from throwing up. Aaron heaped on the abuse . . . things like "the sight of you makes me sick . . . you sexless creature . . . they should have put you in the camps, burned you . . . used you as a field whore . . . you're the worst fuck in the world. . . ." It never let up; Aaron wouldn't, he couldn't, stop himself. At times it was so ugly. I ran out of the house and wandered around the neighborhood for hours. Or I'd lock myself up in the bedroom and stay there for days, just to avoid him. I wanted to die, disappear, become nothing and melt away.

I really felt nothing. . . . I go from numbness to rage; it's too painful. It's easier to feel nothing, to be nothing. . . . everything in my mind is tearing itself apart, coming loose, it's war in there. . . . I see no purpose in keeping myself alive. What a loathsome creature I am, a cockroach, one of Kafka's Blessed—a *meshuggeneh,* right?

Sometimes I hear a voice mocking me, saying I'm terrible, a voice outside my head commenting on my stupidity and foolishness. It tells me I'm a dead person, filled with pus and decay. The voice places tremendous weight on my limbs, and I feel like a massive granite slab that can't move. When I was a kid, I lay awake at night thinking about physically disfiguring things. Somebody broke my body into bits and fragments. Or they tied weights onto my severed limbs and threw them into the Ohio River. Or I was struck by a car, or a safe fell on my head while I played. These fantasies never really ended. I've used them for years to comfort me, to put me to sleep. When I have trouble sleeping, my mind wanders to scenes of torture and desecration, and I see myself put to death in the most vile ways. . . . You know what it is? Sleep is like dying, my need to escape the pressure. Part of me wants to live, so I fight with sleep, but a larger part of me wants to die. That's why I have this need to create fantasies. If in my imagination I put myself close to death, I might be able to lose consciousness.

Hope, beauty, love? None of it has any meaning. Look at the people on this Hall; read their hearts; run your fingers over the scars on their arms; study their twisted, ugly bodies. Do you see any hope, beauty, and love? We're the dregs, shells of human beings; we offer no beauty, grace, or charm. Our main topic of conversation is suicide and medication. We fight voices, demons, and devils. We struggle with realities other folks out there never see. Who would want to see it? It's better we're locked away so we don't contaminate society any more than we've done. Or is it the other way around; maybe we're the ones who have been contaminated? Our families want little to do with us; we embarrass them, drain their finances. What do we do here? We make suicide pacts and ferret out razor blades.

No one is ever really free of pain. It draws you into it; it kills feelings like hope, beauty, and love; it is particularly brutal with family. Are you surprised this is so? If you could scratch into my flesh the thousands of little cruelties that make me shy away from those words like the plague, I would be a crazy quilt of scars. I want to believe in love and family; everyone in here does. But it's going to take a long time. Truth is pain, and I'm too busy with it to see beauty and love. It's like Papa said: truth lies in the [concentration] camps, and we live on this earth to witness truth. You don't think I wake up in the middle of the night sweating *that* burden! All this terror and pain lie inside me like some octopus encircling every part of my being. Mama and Papa passed it on to me; and now I'm bequeathing it to my children; the hatred they must have for me! But it's not only me because I happen to have parents who lived through the camps. Look at Vera over there, whose parents never knew the camps. Vera grew up in a nice, genteel section of Atlanta, a sweet southern girl. Look into her eyes. Do you see anything except pain? Explain for me her torment; is it genetic? Is she a victim of a bad chemical in the brain? Does she scream herself to sleep at night or pick at her veins with a ballpoint pen because she has a biological dysfunction?

Papa told me his concentration camp guards had systematically robbed him of his humanity. He faced their brutality and lived like an animal. He slept on racks with fifteen other human beings who had been reduced to animals. . . . He woke up in the morning and found his rack piled with defecation, and all around him dead bodies and people dying. His teeth and hair fell out; he lost fifty pounds. . . . I don't want to go into it; it's too horrible. Am I repeating his nightmare? Is my father a "Kapo" in his own house? Why his cruelty to me, his own daughter? Is that how God metes out justice, having the father do to the daughter what the Nazis did to him?

He battered my soul and I hate him for it. . . . My whole life has been one unbearable holocaust of the mind. . . . I never felt safe or protected around Papa. He gave demands like his Nazi tormentors: perform this, do that, be obedient, stay invisible, don't get in my way. I never had that innocent feeling kids need, what I craved every minute of the day, knowing Daddy is there to take care of you, not having a worry in the world because Daddy's gigantic bear hug has the power to drive away pain and tears. I think Papa wanted his daughter to prove to the world the Nazis couldn't destroy the Jewish capacity to endure, to survive. But he went overboard with his severity and living in the past. I needed safety, protection and warmth, a father. And I didn't want to be a symbol for anything; I just wanted to live. My fantasies about "Papa Bear" and his care were torn down, destroyed by my real father; it was no good; how could I ever feel safe? How could anyone who saw themselves as worthless, as a stinking evil thing, a creature from another world, ever experience anything like innocence?

Sometimes I think I should be tortured like they tortured him in the camps. And I have this fantasy that the staff takes me outside, onto the lawn out there, and I'm publicly whipped and raped in front of the entire hospital population. Look at me; what do you see? No, don't answer! I already see it in your eyes. You see a monster, my crookedness, evil.

At this stage Ruth's psychotic suffering became increasingly pronounced. It was picked up in different ways by several members of the nursing staff.

March 13: Ruth asked to use the quiet room and sat on the floor, curled up, crying. She said she has murdered three people . . . they go away and she never sees them again. Therefore, she must have murdered them.

March 29: Ruth was observed sitting on a couch holding her arms tightly around herself. Pt. appeared depressed and anxious. Pt. told staff she had a dream about killing one of her children. Pt. also said she continues to obsess about the concentration camps and the events that went on there. Pt. said she feels that if she could be tortured, that maybe she could get beyond this. Then Pt. said that it probably would never be enough. Pt. states she must make herself talk with her therapist about the wards and the [concentration] camps [as being the same thing]. Pt stated that "being alive is such a burden . . . everything seems unreal . . . nothing matters."

April 9: Ruth has made several "emergency" phone calls stating that she has to get out of here immediately. The patient spoke angrily to this writer about the "physical trauma" she has suffered here. When confronted with the fact that any physical trauma has been self-inflicted, Ruth stated "that shows how ignorant you are." . . . Ruth is placed in seclusion after she refused to get off the phone; became abusive, started yelling, screaming . . . a profound display of agitation and anger.

April 14: Ruth talked nonstop about being afraid of her feelings and her anger and about the fighting scenes at home during her childhood. She spoke about being angry at her mother because she [Ruth] would lie on the floor saying she wanted to die. And Ruth was afraid she [mother] would leave Ruth alone. . . . Pt. told this writer she sees "this hospital as a concentration camp. . . ." Pt. explained that she wants everybody to know just how sick she really is.

April 20 [after a former patient committed suicide, and Ruth responded that she could "identify with the patient"]: Ruth was lying on mat [in quiet room] with covers pulled over her head at times, sobbing aloud on occasion. The patient came out of quiet room after one hour at staff's request but wanted to know "how soon" she should go back in. . . . [Ruth asked] why she cannot "spend the whole day" [in quiet room] . . . complains of this being her "worst day yet" at the Hospital, that she "feels good" it happened.

Ruth had taken on the reputation of being the most confounding patient on the Hall. She made extraordinary demands; she abused and shouted at staff. Some suggested that she be placed in another Hall; one nurse thought it would be better for everyone if Ruth were transferred to another hospital. Tension increased among members of the treatment team. Ruth was hallucinating green bugs with black spots and swastikas on their stomachs. She saw Nazis on the hospital grounds; she whispered that the basement contained sophisticated torture devices. She believed the CAT (computerized axial tomography) scan she received at a local hospital was a device designed to weaken blood vessels in her head, making her more susceptible to paralyzing strokes. She wondered if maybe it wouldn't be wise for her to kill her children before the Nazis could find them. "It's 1943; get me out of here!" she screamed at me. Time lacked all boundaries for her; we all, she said, live in the midst of 1943, and Auschwitz is our home. Objects, staff, patients, visitors, activities all tied into Ruth's belief that Sheppard-Pratt was Auschwitz. She experienced herself as a participant in a world where murder defines reality; she slept in a barracks; the staff were SS guards and Kapos; her therapist was Josef Mengele, waiting for the right moment to do experiments on her brain.

Ruth:

> Stay away from me.—Can't you see, all these people, these Nazis—the Holocaust—the Holocaust—it's ugly, the cold/hot water torture—boiling alive—they'll be doing it any minute now—filling up this room—leave quickly before you're caught in it—stripping flesh from my bones, throwing the raw meat to their dogs—snarling bastards.—Did you hear what happened to me? The CAT scan machine—they lied—told me it was for my own good—do you think I believed them?—It was an experiment—Mengele's henchmen sending rays into my brain, popping little blood vessels to see if I could have a stroke.—But then they took out needles, sticking them—everywhere—all over my body—deep—I'm in such pain! It's horrible! Make them stop, please! Do you see the guards over there, the beatings—Vera's teeth have been knocked out—the quiet room, operations—I hear it—the screams—I saw hooks in the ceiling—plans to string me up using electrodes and cattle prods to do God-knows-what—Papa told me they hung Jews up with wires in their cold-storage rooms—by their toes from meathooks and whipped them until their skin started peeling off and finally the flesh lay loose off the bone like a fresh piece of meat.—Speak about punishment! I deserve to be punished.—My evil, it smothers me—it won't go away. Please, kill me before they start with the tortures—I'm as bad as those Nazi pigs. Is it 1983, 1943? Does it make any difference?—Is anyone around here human?
>
> What will happen to my children? Should I kill them first? I don't want Mengele turning them into monsters. Remember

what the Nazis did to twins?—transplanting eyes, limbs—forcing them to have sex with each other—listening to their screams until they finally died. I know the SS—I know what it can do. They give operations without anesthesia—they cut into flesh, replace body parts, puncture organs. It's horrible—I'm sure these are the plans for me—they'll stop at nothing—ice water baths—heating devices—boiling—back and forth, first the cold water until you begin to freeze, then hot, the water quickly reaching boiling, searing you, peeling off your skin, then back again to the ice until your body collapses like a punctured balloon and your heart bursts from the strain. This battleground in my head, it hurts—it won't stop—rotting flesh, death camps, the fire, corpses stacked one on the other—smell it, that burning charred smell—those bodies melting in the heat. It's all out of control, helpless—they pick us up one by one and smash in our brains—why won't they let me commit suicide? I hear my children's screams and sit in that cold bath, getting colder and colder—numb—the sounds of skulls cracking open—the drilling, that sickening sound of bone being penetrated—I feel myself sinking in the water—I can't breathe—I'm drowning . . .

Shortly after that conversation, the following entry appeared in the nursing notes:

April 4: Examination revealed a bruise on patient's thigh within which were superficial scratches in the form of the Star of David. . . . the patient states that her attempts to injure herself were precipitated by a television show last evening depicting the torture of the Holocaust victims.

"I identified with those victims," Ruth said. "I shared their experience. . . . We're both in it together. . . . I felt their pain . . . I know what tortures they went through, what they witnessed. . . . That's why I marked myself; the Holocaust surrounds all of us. . . . It's inside me, in my flesh."

Ruth's religious identity as an orthodox Jew developed into a trap, a structure in her pervasive masochism. She believed that if she were rigidly orthodox, the Nazis would leave her alone. The more orthodox, devout, and obedient she was, the less pain she would experience. It was a delusional trap because the more orthodox she held herself out to be, the more the "Nazis," in their wanderings around the hospital and in her Hall, would notice her. Either way, running from her orthodox habits and practices or embracing them even more fervently, would land her firmly in the Nazis' grip. If Ruth tried to escape being a Jew, the Nazis would discover her and punish her for being too Jewish. She vacillated between an intense Jewish identification and actions like the one described in another nursing entry:

April 11: Ruth immediately started screaming that the contents of the tray [her evening meal] were all things she did not want. She went on to say she did not want a Kosher tray or anything else that sounded Jewish. Ruth then stated she wanted to forget "everything connected with Judaism."

Yet her masochistic superego prevented her from turning away from orthodoxy: "Every time I want to escape, to run from a God who lets his children be massacred, I hear my father's voice saying be perfect, be orthodox, be a good wife, a *mitzvah* before the Jewish people. But when I'm being orthodox, the Nazis find me out and start to hurt me."

If Ruth were to give up orthodoxy in her own mind, she would no longer be a good Jew; and in identifying with the Holocaust victims, she felt compelled to demonstrate how good a Jew she was. It was another way of obeying her father's conception of who she should be and how she should act. She struggled, therefore, in a no-exit situation. Her delusional world demanded punishment, but when she made fitful efforts to transcend her internal torment, the enormous guilt in the form of her father's voice and Nazi persecutors came crashing down. It was as if Ruth could not receive enough punishment. Further, through punishment she affirmed her identity, and during April 1983 all experience, real and imagined, funneled back to 1943.

Later in her treatment Ruth began to disentangle her own delusional conceptions of Judaism from religious beliefs she could tolerate. Her self-loathing, her masochistic assaults on her physical and psychological self, embodied powerful defenses that not only kept her riveted in delusion but prevented her from acknowledging the frightening pain of a lost and terrified two-year-old child. It was only when she could experience sadness and grief that her delusional world lost its hold on her consciousness. Ruth needed delusion for identity; in a

therapeutic sense, however, her identity possessed pathological qualities. And to move beyond pathology she had to frame or conceptualize
her identity in terms that allowed her to separate her own experience
from her parents' and to recognize the internal (not projected) source
(and causes) of her suffering.

As her therapist explained it:

Ruth at some point will be forced to "own" her rage and pain, to take it
back and place it inside herself where it belongs. She will be compelled to
acknowledge its internal source; and once she does this, her delusions will
diminish, if not disappear altogether. It will not be others tormenting her
[the Nazis or green bugs], but it will be Ruth, the small helpless child
creating a fantasy world filled with victims and victimizers. In accepting
her inner suffering as part of her, in seeing her rage as hurtful to others,
Ruth will be able to separate her delusional reading of reality from what
actually exists. When she sees she was as much a tormentor as her own
"inner Nazis," when she comes to understand that the delusional images
embodying her rage [Nazis seeking victims] are the other side of what
appears to be her unconscious identification with the master torturer himself, Hitler: at that point, she will be more capable of distinguishing reality
from delusion.

6 /

Return to the Human Text

In our final conversations, Ruth reconstructed what she found to be essential to her efforts at recovery or personhood: the acknowledgment of her own need to torture herself; the relationship between her narcissistic rage and the consequence of her actions as a form of torturing others; the interpenetration of her perceptions of consensual reality with delusional projections; and the gradual appearance of an intersubjective self that provided the foundation for her understanding of community.

Ruth:

> The last time I saw you, green bugs were rumbling around my room, monsters were attacking me. A *dybbuk** living in my throat kept telling me to go over to the corner, slit my wrists, take some pills, and find a noose to hang myself. Whenever it spoke, it

*A *dybbuk* in the folklore of Eastern European Jewry is a spirit presence or demon that takes over the soul and changes the personality. It occupies the self and induces profound transformation in action and consciousness (see, for examples, the stories of Isaac Bashevis Singer). In psychoanalytic terms, a *dybbuk* might be understood as a production of the unconscious, an unintegrated aspect of self that haunts consciousness in the form of delusions or hallucinations.

laughed hysterically. I thought the world was full of people who wanted me dead, and the *dybbuk* agreed. He said I should be dead; why should someone as worthless as me continue to live? I was a drain on the human race; I would be better off as meat on somebody else's plate.

I remember throwing things all over the [Hall's] living room and screaming at staff to stay away from me. While they didn't know it at the time, I convinced myself staff were SS involved in a plot to torment me. I wanted to hurt them, scald them with hot coffee. I felt trapped, enraged, *and* betrayed. The whole room seemed to be closing in on me, and I felt if I didn't act, I would be killed. It didn't work, though. Before I reached the coffee maker, staff had their hands on me, and the next thing I knew I was in LDS. Incidents like that kept happening; talking on the phone and refusing to get off; fighting with staff when they tried to take the phone away. It was a horrendous time for everyone.

Staff thought I was a maniac. I saw them as concentration camp guards, Kapos, SS lieutenants armed with rifles. I thought one of them gave me a ticket that said "Admit one to the gas chamber." Jay sneered at me; Ellie and Rick had traces of blood on their lips. My *dybbuk* threatened to scratch my eyes out if I didn't obey him. He choked me and clawed at my skin; he said I should be fed to the Nazis. I was terrified and screamed at staff to "open up the gas jets," to "get it over with quick," to throw me in the quicklime, "crush my bones," "take me to the euthanasia center." I felt death in my throat, and all my *dybbuk* could do was heap abuse on me. What a piece of dirt I am, why should garbage be allowed to live; stuff like that. . . .

I didn't want the hospital to keep me alive. I couldn't trust anyone. I believed Sheppard-Pratt was Auschwitz; it should end already, and why don't they put me to death? I hated being Jewish: all the suffering, too much pain. But the *dybbuk* screamed at me to obey the law or he would kill me if I questioned any of the religious practices or rituals. I know it sounds crazy, but the *dybbuk* insisted I dress orthodox, eat kosher. He wanted me to be more Jewish than Rabbi Hurvitz* so the Nazis would have even

*According to Ruth, her father had attached himself, as a young man in Eastern Europe, to one of the most fanatical schools of what was known as the *"musar* movement," a highly intense religious orthodoxy. The movement was characterized by "ethi-

more reason to torture me. It wouldn't leave me alone, taunting me, criticizing how I looked, how I behaved. I remember a dream where the *dybbuk* placed me on a roller coaster, and the cars fell off at the highest point and crashed down to the stands. Spectators cheered, pointing at me, yelling how delighted they were at seeing my body smashed into pulp. I even had dreams about being cremated and woke up disappointed it hadn't happened. I asked staff for matches, but they refused. It was rock bottom. I was in such terror I couldn't move.

I knew I had to escape. Sheppard wouldn't let me die, so I had to find a place that would. I devised a plan. I escape from Sheppard and find my way to Springfield [one of Maryland's state hospitals]. I locate their euthanasia center, which I convinced myself existed somewhere, and insist they put me to death. I imagined an elaborate facility with machines, devices of all kinds, special doctors trained in torture and death, solvents to dissolve the human body. And I thought it perfectly legitimate; why shouldn't the state support such a facility? What else would society do with all its undesirables, its refuse? What more logical plan than to simply make them disappear by removing all traces of the human body, melting human flesh, and then disposing of it or even selling it as lard? I became obsessed with thoughts about this place. And I had to reach it.

I was a voluntary patient; they couldn't keep me here against my will. I submitted a three-day notice; legally they had to discharge me within thirty-six hours. Nothing to it! Of course, what I hadn't figured into this was my doctor's reaction. He very calmly told me, when I informed him of my plan, that he would certify me if I went through with it. No going back and forth; he said he respected my beliefs and wishes but also felt he had to do what he thought best. And in his view of it, no such place as a euthanasia

---

cal perfection" and its "mode was rigorous self-discipline. A Musarnik constantly tweaked at his thoughts and behavior to seek out flaws in his character; he plumbed his good deeds to hunt out the tiniest ulterior motive lurking therein; he tried to subjugate undesirable tendencies. A Musarnik had to become more critical of himself than of others. . . . The Musarniks censored, reined in, muzzled every wayward trait to make it conform to a predetermined—perhaps impossible—ideal. . . . [The movement requires a] merciless curbing of all one's natural impulses" (from the introduction by Curt Leviant to Grade 1976: vii–viii).

center existed. It was a figment of my imagination, and he thought I should not try to kill myself. If certification was the only way to keep me alive, he would immediately initiate proceedings. He even called my parents and told them I needed to stay in the hospital and not to take me out of here. When I found out about that, I almost went through the roof. I called them and told them the doctor was lying; I was perfectly sane and they should come and take me home. They refused. The certification hearing was held, and the next thing I knew, my doctor informed me I had been certified. I felt disappointed. If I wanted to die, why wouldn't they let me? Was I so special they had to go to all these heroic efforts to keep garbage alive? I was angry; now I had to stay. *They* were the ones who were crazy!

Certification frightened me; it told me that everyone else thought I was insane, that other people questioned my interpretation of reality. How could I be mad? I believed in what I saw. It was the rest of them who were confused. How dare they question my beliefs! I had reached certainty: death was preferable to life; I was better off dead than alive. But the only way I could find death was by getting away from the hospital and checking into the euthanasia center. I know now, looking back on it, that if I had been released or if my doctor had given in to my wishes, or if I had convinced my parents to have me discharged, I would have found some way to commit suicide.

After the certification hearing and the hours I spent in the quiet room, I never felt so abandoned or so enraged. But it forced me to a choice. Either I destroy them [staff] and myself with my rage, or I try to hold on to what little goodness remained in me and climb back out of the pit. It was the loneliest week of my life; you can't imagine what it's like to know how absolutely shut off you are from the human race. No one can help you. . . . I had to decide whether to live or die. Each time I moved closer to life, the *dybbuk* would start pounding on my throat; the closer I moved to death, I saw images of my children crying out for their mother. Either I give myself up to the *dybbuk* and his Nazi henchmen, or I destroy him and come back into the world. Either I murder everyone around me and let myself be murdered, or I confront the pain I keep inside and see why it is I want to hurt people.

I began to put together what my therapist said about my need to identify with the torturer, with Hitler. Either way I turned I saw murder and suicide, horror and fear. I looked outside the quiet room, at the other patients, and all of them turned into trees and cows. Had they become raw material to be used to feed and house Nazis? I slid from life to death, from feeling dead to glimmers of hope. I thought about what Dr. —— told me about Hitler and my need to hurt others. The idea disgusted me, but a part of me knew it was true. It made me sick to realize this, but when I let myself think about leaving the hospital and trying to lead a normal life, I got terrified. Would I go into the grocery store and instead of seeing cabbages find skulls in the vegetable bins? Or would ketchup bottles fill up with human blood? Would the meat counter sell human flesh? I couldn't bear it. It was horrible.

Then suddenly—I'm not sure when, but I'm certain it was in the quiet room—I started choking, vomiting, retching. It didn't let up for hours. And with my guts being turned upside down came the pain, in waves rolling over me. It was, though, a different kind of pain. It drew me in on myself; it took me not to death but to sadness. And this might sound odd to you, but I wanted this particular pain. It hurt, oh, did it hurt, but it wasn't torture; it wasn't being administered by *dybbuks* or Nazis. It was like grief, since all I could do was cry. And the more I cried, the lighter I felt, like a lifting of burdens. But I was proud of it; it was my pain, my grief, not something caused by torturers. It draped itself over me, and I seemed to be moving through a mist.

It's impossible to pinpoint exactly when I decided to live, to come back into the human world. All I know is that I no longer had the sensation of something being in my throat; I stopped choking; air seemed to move freely through me. I couldn't imagine Sheppard being Auschwitz; I was amazed when Ellie and Rick told me I had accused them of being Nazi SS guards. I remembered my obsession with the euthanasia center and laughed at it. I thought it ridiculous when someone asked if I still believed it was 1943. No, I said, it's obviously 1983; and I'm here. I returned to humanity. People no longer were symbols for something else, just who they were, patients, staff trying to do the best they could. I saw beyond myself without facing Auschwitz barracks or watching my children murdered by Nazis. I thought about real things, like what I would have to do to be discharged, problems that might arise in the custody fight, what I would buy the kids for their birthdays, how they would respond to their mother leaving the hospital, what my friends would think. I thought it absurd to be rigidly orthodox, and I no longer heard voices telling me to be an obedient, compliant wife. Nazis and *dybbuks* became memories of a nightmare I would like to forget. I'm still depressed—that's obvious enough—but I don't think about dying every waking minute.

For the first time I appreciated staff's efforts through all of this. I asked Ellie about her kids and her divorce; I spoke with Rick about his girlfriend and if they planned to get married. I joked around with other patients and tried to be of some help to them. I discovered I could learn, from staff *and* patients. I also found out I could laugh and enjoy myself inside and outside the hospital. I had this need to talk to people, to anyone. I had a hunger for information; I checked books out of the hospital library, sent away for college catalogues, read newspapers. I contacted the social worker who would be following my case after discharge. I shopped in Towson, searched for an apartment, and began to speak seriously with my doctor about plans for leaving. But—and I want to emphasize this—I needed to be sick, very sick, before I could heal. I had to be in that pit, struggling. If all that horror hadn't come up, if I had simply tried to deny all my fear, I would have ended up where I started: feeling like a stone, only able to express myself through rage. By letting myself be sick, by traveling through all that terrible world, those awful delusions, I found my way through it. I needed help, lots of it, no doubt about that. But ultimately I alone had to be the one to discover the pathway out. I had to be inside whoever I was, whatever demented person I had become; I had to be the one at rock bottom.

For months Ruth had thought of herself as a citizen of another universe, a delusional world beyond this earth without any human qualities. She thought she had been permanently cut loose from the human race and was destined to live as a sacrificial animal chosen by God to be His offering to the devil. It felt good, she said, to see those beliefs crumble away. "And in spite of my past, I live like a human being. You have no idea what that means to me, to rejoin humanity and take pride in my *imperfection!*"

Ruth insisted that this was not a rebirth but a "coming together," a new understanding of the different components of who she was. It also brought an ability to be objective, to step back and examine her experience, to find meaning hidden in the contorted events of her past.[1] It was for her a beginning, filled with trepidation and uncertainty but still a vast distance from where she had been. In the words of her therapist:

After this [her certification] she seemed less angry, and gradually better able to see situations more clearly and began enjoying other people. Individual sessions were more intensively focused on father transference, mother transference, and the intense identifications with both her parents as well as her husband's close resemblance, in her mind, to her father. She was able to detach herself a bit from a former female patient [Pearl] who was very depressed and with whom she closely identified.

During this month [May], she struggled with her feelings regarding caring for her children, and by the end of the month began making very definite plans to live with them and care for them as their mother. Likewise, she said that she was much less depressed and suicidal but acknowledged that she had some "very bad feelings," which required further work.

The nursing staff saw deep and profound transformation:

May 18: Ruth also spoke about a new attitude to life based on the acknowledgment that every action taken involves some risk of pain and failure but that not to act ensures failure. [Ruth was referring to her decision to live.] Pt. also spoke about how she used to refuse to laugh or enjoy the little (and sometimes superficial) things in life, because she perceived such enjoyment as a way of avoiding, escaping the important and major problems in her life.

June 6: Pt. stated that she no longer thinks of her husband as especially intimidating or hateful, but as someone with serious problems of his own for whom she has little feeling left. Pt. stated that she used to see him as an oppressor and herself as a victim, but now she realizes that she fit herself into the role of victim and wonders how she stayed in the relationship for so long.

Occasionally Ruth hallucinated a disturbing image, but it lacked a compelling or lasting hold on her consciousness. These hallucinations were like afterthoughts, without the power to define reality, knowledge, or action.

I may be driving over train tracks and think they are headed for Auschwitz; or a German Shepherd dog runs across my path and I see an SS guard hiding behind the bushes, pointing his gun at me. I don't stay in these places. Images come and go quickly, and I know where I am: in the middle of Towson looking at the B & O railroad tracks, or on the street thinking the owner of that dog should keep him leashed up.

I'm proud of my accomplishments; I even like being alone and digesting my thoughts and feelings. I don't blow up at people; I control myself. Sure, I get angry, but it doesn't leave me feeling so alone, so empty. It's not easy moving closer to people, opening up; but I've worked hard to get this far, and I'm certainly not going to backtrack. It's difficult leaving the hospital; how would you feel if you had to go away from the only place where you ever felt like a human being? People hung in there; they stayed with me, stood up to my rage, refused to give up; and, of course, they kept me alive.

If it weren't for my time here, I doubt if I could have come to grips with the *dybbuk* or the Nazi delusions. I never felt safe enough with anyone to tell them about it; but it was different at Sheppard, like being held and knowing deep down, although I wasn't aware of it then, that there was some purpose or meaning in my craziness. I thought I could never endure grief and the sadness I now face every day. I felt more comfortable raging or screaming or just numbing myself out in terror at the delusions rushing through my head. All that is changed; I accomplish things and even with the hassle feel some enjoyment doing them. I've enrolled at Towson State; I have my own apartment; the children spend weekends with me. And I'm involved in this activity without wanting to kill myself. I go to bed at night; I don't think about torture or death or suffocating or drowning. I cry for a while; it's a good feeling—painful yes, but I'm alive. I don't think about slicing into my veins or slinking off to the all-night pharmacy for five bottles of Sominex. I wake up the morning without being in terror; and believe me, that's a real victory.

Empathy and the Rousseauian Position

When Ruth began articulating her unconscious fears, when she examined parts of herself that had previously been inaccessible, she initiated the very difficult process of transcending the radical character of her alienation from the human community. Ruth's sense of the political world, her "indwelling" in delusion, her identification with the Nazis (as both victim and persecutor) derived from the formative dynamics of an unconscious that was pathologically wrapping itself around perception and language. In her aloneness Ruth felt that nothing could reach her; compassion, in the form of the hospital's holding environment, finally broke the grip that delusion had exercised on her awareness.

Think of the circumstances of the self, in Ruth's narrative, as a history of intrapsychic and interpersonal disintegration (the decline of the "constitution" of the self). It is not fear or instrumentality that returned Ruth to a human identity—the argument of Thomas Hobbes (1950), for example. What brought Ruth back from 1943 was a concerted effort by all who were involved in her treatment to remain empathically connected with her tormented and delusional self. Figure 1 outlines the effects of empathy as a modulation of delusional terror.

For Rousseau (1950), community served, in Winnicott's terms, as a holding environment, a place encircling the self and breathing life into its action. To care for the community, to be attached to it, to participate within it are parts of the same emotional process. Empathy, or what Rousseau calls *pitié,* forms the bedrock of the community's sense of political relationship; *pitié* lies behind consent and deliberation. It enables the self to distinguish between individual will and the general will; it constitutes the psychological agent inducing a sense of the collective, what the citizens define as purpose. It is an emotional state that resonates not only in Rousseau's political recommendations, but in the work of such modern psychoanalysts as Kohut and Winnicott.

Winnicott (1965), for example, addresses himself to holding environments, the importance of containing and caring, transitional objects, the movement from inner (or nature) to outer (the interpersonal world). It is his view that the self's natural movement is toward sociality and away from isolation. It is a movement impossible to undertake unless the infantile self internalizes an empathic regard (trust in

FIGURE 1. Ruth's movement away from delusion

Delusional Phase	*Postdelusional Phase*
—Anger overwhelming	—Anger more modulated
—Self as object of anger	—Anger more accurately placed outside of self
—Everything seen in black and white, "all or nothing"	—Appreciation of ambivalence; tolerance; capable of understanding different sides
—Lack of trust; incapable of intimacy	—Willingness to trust; more open and communicative about her depression
—Relations to her children abusive: "Once I threw syrup over them"	—More restraint with her children; acknowledges their anger toward her as legitimate
—Feels hopeless about future	—Acts on the future; believes in it
—Induces anger toward herself from staff and patients	—Staff find her the "hope of the unit"; becomes favorite patient; other patients look up to her
—Belief system defined by *dybbuk* in throat and Nazi tormenters	—Belief system defined by consensual values and attitudes
—Reality defined by 1943	—Reality defined by the present
—Incapable of organizing or responding to stress in her personal life	—Capable of organizing her life: relations with children, divorce, custody, school, apartment
—Hypersensitive to others' feelings; taking those feelings into herself as her own	—Sensitive to others' feelings but capable of maintaining a boundary between self and others

the caring Other) and establishes transitions in the form of specific objects such as teddy bears or pieces of blanket. This regard and attachment to the transitional object (I have more to say on this concept in Chapter 7) modulates between the isolation of the self's psychological nature and rudimentary association represented in the growing independence from the mother and the infant's increasing awareness of autonomous others outside the self. Empathy induces humanity and integrity; it is critical in collaboration; it forms the core of interdependent being; it draws human beings from isolation into contact. Politically, it binds the community; it is vital in the creation of value. Cooperation, tolerance, understanding, equality: all these *political* values rest on empathy.

Ruth's capacity for empathy—her internalization of a sense of purpose and acknowledgment of the importance of community—was not blind obedience or simple acquiescence to hospital authority but an active effort to engage both herself and her treatment in a collective movement toward healing. Ruth substituted an interdependent and "moral existence for the physical and independent existence nature has conferred on us all" (Rousseau 1950: 38). It was moral in the sense that she came to understand living, acting, and participating with others as involving acceptance of consensual or public values shared by an identifiable community. Ruth's movement, then, from distrust to trust; from a private, closely held being to a public and participatory one; from anger, rage, and isolation to sharing and cooperation effectively overcame her withdrawal to a nonhuman world and opened up the possibility of return to a citizenship equally shared with others. Yet that return (as I show in Chapter 8) had not been fully completed.

Fragmentation and Disintegration: Failure in the Empathic Position

An important modern psychoanalytic argument may be usefully situated within a political tradition of commentary emphasizing community and relatedness. Aspects of the thought of Heinz Kohut, particularly as his concepts illuminate the Rousseauian position, can add to an understanding of Ruth's inner world and the forces provoking it. Even though his theoretical concerns are strictly focused on narcissistic personality disorders, his observations refract Ruth's language against an interpretive background that emphasizes the lifesaving properties of empathy and intersubjectivity.

Kohut addresses his theory to the "enfeebled and fragmentation-prone self . . . [a self that] has not been securely established" (1977: 74). The signs or symptoms of the "fragmented" self, the self without cohesiveness or intactness (Ruth's psychological position throughout her life) are "low self-esteem and depression—a deep sense of uncared-for worthlessness and rejection, an incessant hunger for response, a yearning for reassurance . . . a feeling of inner deadness and depression. As children, these patients had felt emotionally unresponded to and had tried to overcome their loneliness and depression through erotic and grandiose fantasies" (1977: 5). It is the presence or absence of empathy, a *relation*, which determines the course of development: "The child that is to survive psychologically is born into an empathic-responsive human milieu (of self-objects) just as he is born into an atmosphere that contains an optimal amount of oxygen if he is to survive physically" (1977: 85).

Within the infant's perceptual field a "self-object" develops; the infant identifies with its primary object or objects; the self-object (the consequence of this identification) becomes both the world and the embodiment of the infant's will and power. Under normal circumstances, grandiosity in its infantile form (fusion or merger with the omnipotent object) is given up; the parent or object comes to be seen in realistic and limited terms; reality-based perceptions replace both the sense of grandiosity and the idealization of the object. The self facing and overcoming frustration is optimally left with a healthy sense of its own capacities ("ego syntonic goals and purposes . . . realistic self esteem"; Kohut 1971: 107) and a core set of ideals consistent with dignity, self-respect, and tolerance of others.

If, however, "the optimal development and integration of the grandiose self [the core of the narcissistic personality] is interfered with . . . this psychic structure may become split off from the reality ego and/or may become separated from it by repression" 1971: 108). It was precisely this split-off self that haunted Ruth for most of her life. If such separations or splits develop, the grandiose self, rather than disappearing, remains as an archaic structure in the personality. It is not modified by reality; it is not subject to external forces; yet it exercises a powerful influence over how the self experiences need and desire. And it may come back to haunt consciousness, as it did Ruth, in the form of fantasy or delusion. Its retention as a split-off structure in the self has a corollary effect in inhibiting both the necessary de-idealization of the parental *imagos* and the construction of realistically based assumptions and values about self and Other.

"Self-objects" have been defined as "figures who inhabit the external world but are not perceived by the infant as separate individuals" (Ehrlich 1985: 388). Empathy-absent environments result in serious disturbances to the child's psychological balance, particularly the relation to self-objects. Self-objects, then, are images or reflections of the parental figures understood as the self's own being. Self-objects and the relationships established with them are essential for the infant's (and self's) development and maturation. It is impossible to escape the power of the self-object in the *internal* frame. Kohut defines empathy as "'vicarious introspection' . . . the capacity to think and feel oneself into the inner life of another person . . . our life-long ability to experience what another person experiences" (1984: 82). Failure or lack or emptiness within the self-object reverberates through the infant's experiential world. "Defects in the self occur mainly as the result of empathy failures from the side of the self-objects—due to narcissistic disturbances of the self-object" (1977: 87). Or, to put it another way, psychopathology in the parental objects may be internalized by the infant: for example, the "merger of the nascent self with the self-object's depressive and/or manic responses" (1977: 89).

Kohut consistently returns to the idea that the nonempathic world and its effects in producing "disintegration anxiety" threaten the cohesiveness of self and its capacity for community. "What leads to the human self's destruction . . . is its exposure to coldness, the indifference of the nonhuman, the nonempathically responding world. . . . It is not physical extinction that is feared, however, but the ascendancy of a nonhuman environment . . . in which our humanness would permanently come to an end" (1984: 18).

Empathic absence, "by depriving the child of maturation-promoting responses" (1977: 188) may bring with it secondary reactions, particularly in the form of rage and anger. And in a passage that echoes sentiments in Rousseau's *Discourse on the Origin and Foundation of Inequality among Men*(1950), Kohut observes: "Man's destructiveness as a psychological phenomenon is secondary . . . it arises originally as the result of the failure of the self-object environment [the environment of the mother/father] to meet the child's need for optimal—not maximal, it should be stressed—empathic responses" (1977: 116). Kohut criticizes in its broad outlines the Hobbesian view that aggression is innate to the self (insatiable drives, impulsions to power, the will to dominate). Aggression (the Hobbesian egoistic self) "as a psychological phenomenon, is not elemental"; and "destructive rage, in particular, is always motivated by an injury to the self" (1977: 116), an *effect* (not cause) of the disturbances to self/self-object relations. Further, the presence of "destructive rage" becomes a social event in the sense that the relation between the infant and its mirroring others constitutes a social field that the self internalizes and identifies as its own (the self/self-object relation): "The primary psychological configuration (of which the drive is only a constituent) is the experience of the *relation between the self and the empathic self-object*" (1977: 122; my italics).

Kohut frequently criticizes psychoanalytic drive theory because of its lack of a concept of the self and what he regards as its narrow focus on the drives as the primary cause of conflict and feelings of hostility. He rejects the view of a "primal infantile viciousness" (the psychoanalytic restatement of the Hobbesian position) as "part of the primary psychological equipment of man" (1977: 124). In this respect Kohut moves quite a distance from the rather grim Hobbesian view of the self represented in the theory of Melanie Klein (1948).[2] Nor does he see the "isolated striving to search for an outlet for rage and destructiveness" as a "primary given—an 'original sin' requiring expiation, a bestial drive that has to be 'tamed'" (1977: 124)—again, the Hobbesian and, in Kohut's view, Kleinian argument. Rage "is a specific regressive phenomenon" induced by faulty relations in the *existent* social world (the Rousseauian interpretation). Rage, therefore, appears as the "dehumanized and corrupted" product of a self "isolated by the breakup of a more comprehensive psychological configuration" (1977: 124). This "loss of control of the self over the self-object . . . leads to the fragmentation of joyful assertiveness [certainly a constituent of individuality] and in further development to the ascendancy and entrenchment of chronic narcissistic rage [an impediment to individuality]" (1977: 130). What the psychoanalyst sees (in the transference relation) as a conflicted, impulsive ego are the products of a "seriously damaged or destroyed" self where "the drives have become powerful constellations in their own right." Such drive "constellations" inevitably influence the self's sense of its own individuality, its being in the world. Ruth's anger became a clue to the nature and origin of the products of a self that had been seriously damaged throughout critical developmental moments.

Therapeutic intervention addresses itself not to the structure of the drives as primary factors but to "the threat to the organization of the self . . . the experience of the *absence* of the life-sustaining matrix of the empathic responsiveness of the self-object" (1977: 123), precisely Ruth's inner dilemma. The language of the transference enhances the relational capacities essential to the self's being-in-community.

Empathy-filled experiences (the Rousseauian world) define individuality as a function of shared, reciprocal purposes; empathy-absent experiences (the Hobbesian world) construct individuality according to the demands of egoism, separation, and isolation. Empathy as a political value enhances the ties of the public; it diminishes hostility by leading to a willingness to listen. It encourages face-to-face relations where conflict might be transformed into concrete tasks and actions; and it facilitates the pragmatic approach to specific issues. (Kohut's psychological theories would certainly be consistent with the pragmatic liberalism of John Dewey.) Notice how Kohut describes empathy as a political relation *in the context of a psychoanalytic view of the self*: "The social reformer influenced by the imagery of the fragmented self . . . will focus not on an aggressive destructive drive but on the poor cohesion of the self of slum dwelling youths; and he will attempt to institute remedial action by enhancing self esteem and by supplying idealizable self-objects" (1977: 130). Kohut aims his political recommendations at principles consistent with the foundations of self psychology: (1) the firming of the self, and (2) a "diminution of the diffuse rage that had formerly arisen from a matrix of fragmentation" (1977: 131).

Tragedy and Self: The Loss of a Sense of Place

Kafkaesque figures such as Gregor Samsa in *The Metamorphosis* (1976) and Joseph K in *The Trial* (1969), metaphors for a dissociative alienation, the "loss of contact with reality," represent for Kohut the tragic consequences of the empathy-absent world. Gregor Samsa, cut off from his family and treated as an object, a thing that ends up worthless in the family matrix, and Joseph K, driven to states of unbearable distraction and contemptuously regarded by unfeeling and sadistic bureaucrats, find themselves encased in states of being that are striking precisely because of the profound absence of empathy and community and the impact of this absence on what each experiences as a disintegrating and fragmenting world.

For Ruth, the idea or concept of a shared reality, a communal world, had no significance; she possessed no sense of common purpose, no affective alignment with the consensual world, no empathic connection with others.[3] Her situation resembled the desperate aloneness of a Gregor Samsa; she was closed off, locked into herself, experiencing a vast silence between herself and other persons. She refused to accept the interconnectedness of human desire; she rejected mutual dependencies (particularly the idea of community). She saw herself as an outcast in a world she found threatening and without meaning. It was as if life had somehow missed Ruth and passed her by.

Unable to feel empathy from her surrounding world, sensing a deprivation that intensified as she grew older, desperately attempting to escape despair through suicide attempts, Ruth found herself oscillating between periodic narcissistic rages (a radical frustration in being) and overwhelming sensations of being bad, dirty, and corrupt. Who she was as a person, her identity, revealed massive cracks in her being. Ruth's values, then, her attitudes toward persons and experience, the metaphors she chose to define her identity, her selfhood (her individuality) all reflected this shattered internal sense of being.

To survive effectively as a human being requires trust in an external world and a sense that others can accept, confirm, and echo (the Kohutian notion of mirroring) the self's needs. For Ruth, however, until the very end of her stay at the hospital, trust had no *affective* significance. She felt compelled to construct psychological barriers against the "painful feeling of self-fragmentation"; she resisted anyone's standing in for the "gleam in the mother's eye"; she refused to believe that people "echoing, approving, and confirming" her (Kohut 1971: 119, 116, 117)—that is, the Hall staff, the social worker, other patients— actually did so because of any genuine regard. Rather, she believed that any show of affection degenerated into sham and mockery.

In tenaciously defending her isolation and exclusion, Ruth unconsciously testified to a despair over the loss of self, to a massive disappointment and cynicism over trust. If Ruth's tenuous relation with trust were to be described as a function of her concept of truth or reliable knowledge, its frame of reference would derive *completely* from the secrets or fantasies she had held inside. It would be totally dependent on her solipsistic universe, which (from the outside looking in) appeared to be thoroughly nihilistic: no value or meaning resided in consensual reality.

Emotionally sealed off from others, Ruth had lived most of her life in a primitive world of archaic self-objects; locked up inside herself, bitter and frustrated with life, she was convinced that the deadness of the world would swallow her up and transform her into an empty, inert shell. It had been a universe where, in the words of an ancient Gnostic text: the body is "the dark prison, the living death, the sense-endowed corpse, the grave thou bearest about with thee, the grave which thou carriest around with thee, the thievish companion who hateth thee in loving thee, and envieth thee in hating thee" (quoted in Bultmann 1956).

7 /

The Wish for Nonbeing

The Oedipus whom Sophocles (1960) describes at Colonus demonstrates the terror and despair of living on the borders, of being kept outside the city, experiencing the public or associational self as an outcast that is lost to time, to honor, to the acknowledgment and esteem of the political world. Oedipus falls from power; he wanders with only his daughter to lead and comfort him. He suffers the knowledge of exile, the loss of home and name, the terrible shame of having his life and his being shattered by the unexpected. "For kindness' sake, do not open / My old wound, and my shame" (2.515–16). He relinquishes his civic identity, his practical usefulness to the polity; he endures exile in his own body. "That stranger is I / As they say of the blind. / Sounds are the things I see" (1.138–39). But Oedipus survives in darkness and anguish, fighting bouts of intense rage and overwhelming defeat; it is in this sense that his *desire* becomes connected to the wish for death. I return to this understanding later in the chapter; for now, Oedipus's plight at Colonus illuminates or frames the intensity of the borderline self's despair.

The Wandering of Consciousness

Oedipus's emotional isolation, his experience of that isolation, is an event that replays itself in the borderline's relation to culture and to the values of human association. The borderline self, with its fragmented internality and often striking intelligence, enacts the fate of Oedipus at Colonus, *not* Oedipus the King. Consciousness suffers from an affliction that it neither understands nor accepts; it rages at an existential universe it sees as inhospitable and cold. I am not arguing that Oedipus is "borderline" in any formal psychiatric or diagnostic sense; rather, his fate, his sense of being a wanderer, an exile in a hostile and malevolent universe, contains properties that the modern borderline experiences in very real forms. The borderline self knows itself to be an exile, to be condemned to a terrible fate because of its horrible badness, its worthlessness even to live. The self understands, like Kafka's Joseph K, that it is guilty and that suffering, pain, and shame constitute the defining properties of life.

This fate, however, is not immortalized in drama; it lacks the illumination and high tragedy of an Oedipus. It is not transcendence in defeat and at the end the recovery of dignity, amidst lamentation, as it had been for Oedipus. It is rather an endlessly repeating history of humiliation and failure; it is the self as Oedipus appeared, for a moment, before Theseus: defeated, bitter, resigned, and enraged. "I come to give you something," Oedipus says to Theseus, "and the gift is my own beaten self: no feast for the eyes" (3.576–77). It is the self speaking of itself as denied, forgotten, unrecognized, rejected, an unwanted, unwelcome thing amid the society of persons. "Time disquiets / Earth wastes away; the body wastes away / Faith dies; distrust is born . . . I am oppressed by fear" (3.609–11, 654).

I recall a young Israeli, a former mental patient whom I met on a kibbutz, telling me that he felt as if he were a stone lying in the middle of a vast, dusty road going nowhere. And when I asked him what happened to that stone when a traveler came walking down the road, he replied that no one would ever walk down that road; but anyone who did would simply kick the stone away. To this young man the hardness and impermeability of the stone defined his existence; the coldness of a nonliving substance turned into the defining element of his life. In his kibbutz he lived like an exile, never fully in or entirely out of the organized daily routine. He clearly occupied a special status within this tightly knit and self-conscious group structure. Or as Julia, on whose narrative this chapter focuses, put it, "I wander alone in these cold interstellar regions."

Aristotle's *Politics* (1978) speaks of "justice for equals" and of moral excellence, but the borderline feels no equality, no sense of justice, no moral worth.[1] The world is a radical injustice filled with inequalities, with various patterns of domination and violence. Not only does hope for equality (equality of happiness and of function) disappear, but there is even less hope for justice, since the self feels its own inner world to be in a state of disruptive chaotic injustice. It is beyond the capacity of the borderline, suffering from the threat of imminent fragmentation, to consider even the possibility of political justice, since what the self experiences every moment is horror and futility. Consciousness is constantly on the brink of flying apart; pain and death preoccupy the self—hardly a state of mind receptive to justice in association.

The Aristotelian citizen/self exists in relationships extending through time and history, through community and networks of association, participation, and administration. Such relationships contribute to the self's sense of esteem and respect. The borderline, because of its peculiar psychological position, is precluded from drawing on these sources of self-esteem. Yet in the tragedy of Oedipus at Colonus and in the misery and destruction of Kafka's protagonists, as well as the reflections of borderline patients, human and social connections take on a certain ominous cast. They appear fragile; the world of relationship and community seems radically unsatisfactory; and human conduct finds itself victimized by chance, unprotected by the stabilizing networks of civil and political association.

It is all too easy to lose the Aristotelian position, the commitment to association, friendship, and community. In the fragmented and contingent existence of late twentieth-century society, it is indeed possible to lose one's identity (or way), to find oneself falling through the cracks of civil society, to be forgotten or dishonored, to wake up and discover—like Kafka's Gregor Samsa—that one's being has no meaning or recognizable human identity. The borderline's internal tragedy is played out on a very private level, invisible to the rest of the culture, hidden behind psychological walls, yet is as stark in its own way as the images of an Oedipus at Colonus, alone and blind, furious at the injustice and violence of the universe. What appears in this language is the battleground of the self, the annihilation of an Aristotelian citizenship, and the power of despair in defining human purpose. Existence turns into a tortuous enterprise, an activity without value, an effort riddled with failure, uncontrollable anger, and frustration over the cruelty of even being. Justice, humanity, goodness, and virtue mean nothing in the isolation of this border. In Julia's words:

> Dear Anybody:
>   If anyone is out there please hear me. I fear I am in the grip of some terrible nightmare. First of all, I have to tell you I am very sick. I feel like an animal on a leash but no one tells me what to say. . . . And I am sick, so very, very sick.

Julia: The Fascination with Annihilation

Julia sought both a spiritual annihilation and a penance expressed through physical mutilation. She lived as if in a prison, locked up inside herself; she tortured her physical being by periodic laceration and binge eating. By the time she reached her twenties Julia's sense of threat, her inner insecurity, had been written in her body as massive weight gains and losses and incessant cutting. She described her insecurity as an infection, a sickness that took on increasingly virulent properties: "I want to smash at this thing in my body that is making me so unsettled." And smash it she did: through the use of razor blades as instruments of self-mutilation and the ingestion, at fairly regular intervals, of such enormous quantities of food that she might put on as much as sixty pounds in a three-month period.

It was her way, as she put it, of "getting used to a world that hated me." And that hate she carved into her flesh, a self-hatred understood through the flow of blood and the scars on her body and stored up through the symbolic medium of an obesity that she carried as a sign of her essential poisonousness. Julia could also shed her weight, but even that victory had a terrible emotional cost: she bought thinness at the price of an extraordinary anxiety that had the effect of tormenting people close to her and throwing her own self-perception into a despairing tailspin that could become, very quickly, suicidal. To be thin was to come closer to the human community, and for Julia that prospect had always in her life brought terrifying consequences. In Winnicott's terms (1965: 47) Julia possessed no "continuity of being. . . . The alternative to being is reacting, and reacting interrupts being and annihilates; being and annihilation are two alternatives." Before coming to Sheppard-Pratt, Julia had chosen annihilation.

Julia never made it easy for people to know her. She made it clear to me that research meant work and that I had better be prepared to endure whatever she "dished out" if I wanted to speak with her. She warned me to expect torment in my research relation with her. Torture and self-torture for Julia had been a way of life. People lived to torment each other, she believed; torment defined human relationship; torment enclosed the self. She was obsessed with Jean-Paul Sartre's play *No Exit* (1949); it was difficult, then, for her to imagine any kind of relationship other than torture. And her self-hatred led her to see the world as filled with disgust and distrust.

> There is a deep vein of self-hatred that runs so far it scares me. I hate myself enough to want to destroy this body that I've worked so hard for. I get bloated and swollen with food, my belly distended, because I have no self-image to center on. I start at the top, not the bottom, trying to nurture a healthy loving view of myself, forgetting that I have none at all. . . . I want to eat until I am so fat and ugly that there will never be hope for me again. I must be the worst person in the world.

Yet Julia's existence-in-torture suggests broader, political implications. Torture places the self on the borders of the culture; torture transcends the elemental boundaries of humanity. Torture is a profound act of negation and renders consciousness impotent in its own internal forms of self-governance, a position that Frantz Fanon eloquently argued in the final chapter of *The Wretched of the Earth* (1968). To be tortured or to feel compelled to torture the Other, in whatever form, is to be out of balance in the Aristotelian sense.[2] It is to fall victim to a sadistic superego heaping endless abuse on the self. This incessant torture had placed Julia on the borders of her own family. It had completely alienated her from community.

Other modes of being were unfathomable to her: she had no inner image of innocence or playfulness, no inner sense of security; to hold herself meant literally to torture herself. Or to put it another way: to feel herself close to nonexistence, to wrap herself in fantasies of imminent death and the infliction of pain, meant paradoxically that she could exist. Pain, then, affirmed existence and being; how could she live if she weren't in pain? But people close to her, particularly her parents and sisters, had in fact not acknowledged her pain. Shortly before coming to Sheppard-Pratt, in an act of desperation to get her busy mother's attention, Julia had carved in her thigh the words "Dear Mom, I love you all." She had used a kitchen knife—even so, it had taken her mother several minutes to notice her daughter's bleeding. What the borderline suffers is not an act of imaginary pain; there is a strong reality-based component to the self's sense of its estrangement from a common humanity.

Like Kafka's Joseph K waiting for, even willing, his execution, Julia found herself convinced that death was the only route out of her sense of entrapment in a world of endless pain. She survived only as a victim of her own uncertain and contingent knowledge, a casualty of emotional forces that, while taking her to uncharted territory, left her adrift without compass, emotionally blinded, without a language to decipher or interrogate the horrors she faced. A terrible emptiness assaulted her consciousness and drained her will to live. She despaired of ever making sense out of the chaos, the darkness that surrounded her. Like one of Epicurus's atoms, she drifted haphazardly in the universe; in Derrida's terms (1984: 8), she understood herself as a "twisted entanglement . . . mass, swarm, turbulence, downpour, troop," tossed about by "the play of necessity and chance."

> I was very agitated when I first came to the hospital. I felt like I would die, like I was going to die, and that was the most horrible thing of all, knowing that you are about to die and not knowing how to deal with that knowledge. I was convinced nothing out there could save me, no God, no truth, no mother or father. I was totally alone, without any sense other than pure unrelieved fear. That was the most horrible feeling of all, knowing you are going to die and being unable to deal with it or keep it from happening. I had stopped believing in everything, and now that I think back, I wonder if I ever believed in anything at all.

It was enormously troubling for Julia to do what normal people do, what normal persons take for granted: to make friends, to pursue intimate relationships, to perform common tasks. Such actions were "like climbing Mount Everest." She felt like "one of the many who do not feel that they exist in their own right as whole human beings" (Winnicott 1971: 29). It was as if she were saying that the Aristotelian concept of friendship lay beyond her capacity, that the intricate balancing of self-regard and the regard of others could not be realized. Aristotle (1978) writes: "Community depends on friendship; and when there is enmity instead of friendship, men will not even share the same path" (4.1295b7). For Julia the universe spawned enmity, malevolence, and evil; in her view people brought with them torture and misunderstanding, not friendship and community. Julia, then, acted in the only way she could: to others she became cold, brutal, cruel, and manipulative. She was incapable of what Winnicott (1971: 56) described as coming "together" and existing "as a unit, not as a defense against anxiety but as an expression of I AM, I am alive, I am myself."

She often spoke of her body as in pieces, disintegrating, fragmenting, disappearing. For example, shortly before readmitting herself to the hospital (after a six-month period of living and working in the local community), she told of having attended a local rock concert; thousands of people surrounded her, but she had little sense of them or of the music. All she saw was her body dissolving, changing into a "million molecules . . . even my blood seemed to float away"; she felt herself as "beyond pain. . . . I had dissolved into something else. I was not recognizable. . . . I saw pieces of myself." She returned home that evening to a night filled with hallucinations. She lost any physical sense of the integrity of the body or its boundaries; she thought she had literally been disembodied and described it as being in the crash of a plane that "exploded in the sky and fell fifteen thousand feet to the ground below." It was as if her "self" had disintegrated and been left "scattered around and . . . lying about" (Winnicott 1971: 67).

Self as Poisonous: The Destruction of Being

To be poisonous meant to be not an admired being but a denied and unwanted presence, an aberration in the community, a "nothingness" whose will was manifested in obsessions with death and dying. Early in her hospitalization Julia wrote:

> I feel condemned to some shadowy border-life, always hurting underneath, nothing wonderful. . . . I forever fight to make it from one day to the next. . . . I wonder if anyone could ever love me like this: depressed, fat, ugly, dreary, boring. . . . Why don't I get it over with now [suicide]. I don't care; no one sees me, no one hears me. . . . Someone, please make this better. I feel so alone; no one's caring.

This sense of existing in a "shadowy border-life" had plagued Julia as far back as she could remember. As a child she had believed that the expectations of others defined who she was or should be as a person; therefore, she could be only what her parents wished her to be. "Compliance," writes Winnicott (1971: 65), "carries with it a sense of futility for the individual and is associated with the idea that nothing matters and that life is not worth living." And if her parents' wish was to see her dead, Julia believed that *her* project in life was to achieve this wish: that is, to please her parents by becoming nonexistent.[3] She retreated inward; she turned to maneuvers to protect her threatened internality; she lived in fantasy productions that had no audience. Consciousness desperately tried to retain some place in the world, even though that place was invisible to the Other. By her teens Julia had successfully constructed an elaborate false self-system that acted as a buffer between the world and her desperately frightened inner self. "One has to allow for the possibility that there cannot be a complete destruction of a human individual's capacity for creative living and that, even in the most extreme case of compliance and the establishment of a false personality, hidden away somewhere there exists a secret life that is satisfactory because of its being creative or original to that human being. Its unsatisfactoriness must be measured in terms of its being hidden, its lack of enrichment through living experience" (Winnicott 1971: 68).

If no one loved Julia for the hurt, wounded child she felt herself to be, she reasoned *unconsciously,* then there must be something poisonous about her, something so terrible, so unmentionable, that to reveal her internal feelings would bring disaster. She therefore developed a view of the external world as unreasonable and brutal, a place full of deceit and unhappiness. Living became a strenuous effort at trying to satisfy others, at protecting the fragile boundaries of an inner self that she kept locked away, out of sight. Julia's identity *to the world* never anchored in a firm separation of self from others; it became an empty space to be filled and molded by whatever expectations happened to be surrounding her at the moment. But that deeply hidden self remained as a split-off source of incessant despair and pain.

Badness had no existence inside Julia's highly successful and talented family. It had to be kept secluded, out of sight, invisible. The family, in effect, said that what mattered most to *her* had no public existence, no significance. It was simply not important. What mattered was what people saw; nothing else. Eventually Julia came to hate that external compliant self, the self that was visible, the physical embodiment of what the world saw. Her hidden self registered itself on the physical boundaries of body: to be real was to scratch the flesh with razor blades, to draw blood. To confirm being was to ingest soft, sweet foods, which, rather than bringing comfort, became a desperate action to preserve a threatened being, a hated reminder of the pain she felt inside.

As a bloated fat person, Julia could be *seen* as ugly; to be thin, however, was to suffer with the knowledge of her disability, her pain. To be fat meant to run from the pain, to be the person who could live on the margins of society in that "shadowy border-world," who could fill up her emptiness, dull her sensibility, and receive the attention of her mother. Eating, like cutting, became a form of control over the terrible fragmentation she felt in her internal world. The heavier she became, the more separate she felt from the world. The more she allowed the expression of that illness to take place in her feelings and in her interactions with others, however, particularly in her therapeutic transference, the less insistent was the urge to binge and the more manageable the compulsion to eat. Binging resumed at those moments when inner pain became intolerable, when she felt she was "getting somewhere in therapy." She had little faith in the possibility that she, the ugly poisonous being, could lead a productive life, much less attain some kind of happiness or fulfillment.

If Julia could poison herself with food, she might not poison others with her being. If the poisonousness could be registered on her body, as the palpable sign of her essential and abiding badness, it might not infect and thereby contaminate others; to keep poisonousness from others, it had to be held inside. *She,* her body and self, had to be the object of the poison's consequences. If, therefore, she could not control her external experience, she could certainly control the fate of her physical being. She had that much efficacy in the world.

> When I would visit home from college, or even on sign-outs from the hospital, I had this fear my parents would kill me; I don't know why; nor did I know how they would do it, what kind of tools for killing they would use. All I knew is that they wanted me dead, out of the way; and I would stay in my room for hours because I actually believed that if I left the room, they would hack me up into pieces. So I would eat; the eating kept the fear under control. I stuffed donuts, cookies, candy, anything, into my mouth. And as I was chewing, as I felt the food going down, the fear lessened, and I felt much less panicked, not nearly as anxious. Well, it was more than anxiety . . . more like dread. And as I ate, I would think to myself: I wish I could be another person; I wish I could have more courage, more stamina, more strength, more beauty. That thought would make me happy; and I would eat even more. Then I would begin to feel leaden, heavy, like a great weight lay on my back; or my arms would feel like wooden sticks, and I couldn't move them. I asked myself, what good was it to do anything.

Life indeed had been a grim, joyless business.

I want to emphasize this theme of wandering, exclusion, experiencing oneself as an exile, and the fascination with death. Lacan (1978b: 1032) writes about Oedipus at Colonus that his life "is made of death, that sort of death which is exactly there, beneath life's surface." This movement toward death evolves into a matrix of interweaving contexts forcing the self away from Aristotelian association and toward the delusional world of an unbounded nature, Epicurus's endlessly colliding and "swarming" atoms. Everything that happens to Oedipus at Colonus revolves around death and the embodiment (and mythologizing) of death in language. "You will have to read Oedipus at Colonus," Lacan observes (1978b: 1028). "You will see that the last word of man's relation to this discourse which he does not know—is death."

Again, I am not arguing that Julia is Oedipus or that she occupies a similar literary space. Rather, what Lacan discovers in Oedipus at Colonus, as a mythic *presence* in the Freudian drama, appears in Julia's ruminations on death and exile.[4] Julia's desire *is* the wish for and the project of death, and her self becomes a commentary in language *and* action on what death and its power mean as a way of life—as it had been a way of life for Oedipus at Colonus, in Lacan's view (1978b: 1032): "What Freud teaches us through the notion of primordial masochism is that the last word of life, when life has been dispossessed of speech, can only be this ultimate curse which finds expression at the end of *Oedipus at Colonus*. Life does not want to heal." Nor for Julia did life "want to heal"; she lived with the terms of an inner language, the discourse of death and masochism that served to isolate her from others and give her a picture of experience filled with bleak, despairing and hopeless images. In Lacan's terms, this grim speech constituted her self; she became, acted out, the language with which she identified being. For her as for Oedipus, the driving force was the desire of death.

In his analysis of *Beyond the Pleasure Principle,* Lacan (1978b: 1032) writes: "The key to *this mystery* [negative therapeutic reaction], it is said, is in the agency of a primordial masochism, that is, in a pure manifestation of that death instinct whose *enigma* Freud propounded for us at the climax of his experience"[5] Yet negativity had become an enigma for Julia. Masochism had been inescapable; it filled out the context of her being; it structured her language, her sense of self-description. It impelled her use of razor blades as a statement about life and "healing." That compulsion to cut—a repetition-compulsion in the classic Freudian sense—constituted a mystery and terror until its therapeutic demystification. Julia discovered new symbols to replace a deadly history, to remove from her linguistic self a storytelling of death and self-annihilation. The therapist as *other* became the mirror for this process of discovery and renewal. Shoshana Felman (1983: 1045) writes: "The psychoanalytic myth, in other words, derives its *theoretical effectiveness* [and its practice as a form of therapy] not from its truth-value, but from its truth-encounter from the other, from its capacity for *passing through the Other;* from its openness, that is, to an *expropriating passage* of one insight through another, of one story through another."

Julia's resymbolization of her experience, her discovery and recognition in the otherness of her therapist, enabled her eventually to move beyond the compulsive terror of her own project to die into a linguistic reconstruction, narrative as insight. To put it another way: the inter-mingling of Julia's narrative and her therapist's refraction—her otherness—created a stage, a dramatic text for unraveling the mythic or unconscious terms of her exile and alienation, her sense of seclusion and isolation, and most important, her preoccupation with death.

The Physical Body as Text: "Nature" as a Form of Torture

Aristotle calls the ends of the self *eudaimonia,* a term that Ernest Barker defines as a state of being "which means something higher than the mere happiness of pleasure (*hēdonē*) and involves an 'energy of the spirit' impossible to slaves and animals" (Aristotle 1978: 118n). *Eu-daimonia,* then, in its classical Greek sense, entails the "energy and practice of goodness," an effort to attain through association what Aristotle calls a "good quality of life" (certainly a phenomenon alien to the borderline, who hovers precariously on the brink of psychosis and total exclusion from the polity and its language): "But the end of the state is not mere life; it is, rather, a good quality of life" (3.1280a6). To be *eudaimonic,* to be attuned to integrative and social principles of happiness, entails an acknowledgment of the body as central to the being of the self; it requires a moderation and respect for the very physical bases of life and its political context: "a system of good laws well obeyed (*eunomia*)" (3.1280b8). To hate one's body, then, would be to deny goodness. Further, it is difficult to imagine an Aristotelian conception of goodness in which the body is experienced as alien to the self. Nor would hatred of the body facilitate goodness or friendship. To denigrate the body is to violate both the ends of the community (the polity) and to repudiate the essential goodness defining the ethical aims of the self and "the pursuit of a common social life" (3.1280b13).

To pursue goodness in the Aristotelian view is to accept association as something more than sheer existence: if mere life were the end, "there might be a state of slaves, or even a state of animals" (3.1280a6). It is to regard the body as more than an impediment or as a text for registering the pain of the self. But the borderline does experience the body as a place on which to register preoccupations with death, suicide, and emotional mutilation. Physical being becomes a site for specific messages, for symbolic statements about self. In Aristotle's terms, that sense of existence signifies a self trapped in a form of enslavement, and consciousness finds itself so preoccupied with death that it is incapable of living within the sphere of civil association. In addition, to attack the body as an enemy of the self would, in Aristotelian terms, constitute a violation of the central principle of the self's moral ends: the pursuit of *eudaimonia*. A striking example of this kind of repudiation is the physical self-mutilation so characteristic of borderline patients. The denial of felicity and goodness are literally written, as if they were texts, into the flesh of the body, in its mutilations and distortions.

By cutting, Julia knew herself to be alive, and the knowledge that she bled relieved tension. Anger (and disillusionment) revealed itself in the etched surfaces of the body-as-text, as a series of marks that stood out as signs, stigmata of the self's utter alienation. For her, well-being and completeness depended on the power to control her own life by literally regulating the flow of her own blood. Even in the hospital it was discovered that "the patient had been scratching herself with her fingernails and tops of the soda cans" (nursing notes). She could, through the depth, extent, and severity of the incisions, determine the rate at which the blood flowed from her body. Julia believed she had ultimate control not only over her life but over *the rate (or pace) at which she might allow herself to die.* Contemplating that possibility gave her life meaning, as she put it. That knowledge became a source of pleasure. It also provided a future, since it was an action she could undertake by herself at her own will.

Cutting, then, had given Julia the illusion of control; razors functioned both as instruments of self-mutilation and as assertions of will. Not only did she have the power to control the pace of her dying through the release of blood and mutilation of tissue; she also possessed control over the sense of well-being accompanying the knowledge that she had the power to harm herself. She thought, "Why should I hurt myself? I want to feel good; I want this feeling."

The razor came to take on a symbolic meaning, assuming a significance that transcended its importance as an instrument of self-torture. At some point in her treatment it became significant as a symbolic presence that reminded Julia of her will-to-be. If she could store the razor and *not* use it, she could prolong the feeling of well-being that accompanied her conviction that she had control over her life. She could do this because in fact she had the power to end her life, to exercise her will not to be. It was as if she had discovered in the sheer presence of the razor—designated as the one to do the job—a linkage to life, a symbolic advance over her earlier *instrumental* view of the razor as a tool with which to mutilate the body. It may seem strange to use Winnicott's term (1971: 6) transitional object for a razor blade, but there was a meaning attached to its presence that brought Julia from a deadly preoccupation with annihilation and disfigurement into a relation with the external world, with life.[6]

As her preoccupation with death diminished, the *presence* of the razor functioned as a link to the embodied world of association and facilitated Julia's efforts to find within herself the will to be, to exist, to discover the "continuity of being." In this regard, Volkan (1981: 366–67) writes: "There are thus clear similarities between the transitional object of infancy (a bridge between "not me" and "mother-me") and the reactivated transitional object (substitute object) of the borderline and psychotic, for whom the object is a defensive buffer between what can be admitted and what must be kept outside." For Julia to keep the razor blade meant, paradoxically, that she was more capable of relating to the outside *in the context of a project to live*. To have it and not use it relieved her of the fear of death and annihilation and drew her closer to forms of social relatedness. To possess or contemplate the razor yet not act was to commit the self to living; she felt good *as long as the razor was around*. She felt secure with the existence of the razor not as a tool for killing or cutting but as *a symbol that had the power to enhance the feeling of well-being*. The razor contained her feelings; it brought her comfort and safety; she could use it as an object to enhance her relatedness with the outer world. The razor had indeed become a "transitional phenomenon," a teddy bear invested with transitional properties, which provided her with a connection to the world outside, at the same time assuring her that life could go on and she could feel safe.

As I understand it, Winnicott's term "transitional object" refers to the link established by the infant "between inner objects and external objects, between primary creativity and perception" (1971: 6). The object stands in for the mother or part of what the mother is (whether the good mother or the bad mother). In its form as teddy bear or blanket, for example, the object allows the self to move from inside (from being fused with) the mother, to outside; it "describes the infant's journey from the purely subjective to objectivity . . . [a] journey of progress towards experiencing." It allows the self to feel safe in the presence of the mother's *absence*. It is a primary socializing dynamic, the beginning of the creation and development of an autonomous self fully appreciative of the interpersonal world. The transitional object signifies the infant's entrance into the world of symbolic understanding and human association. The term also possesses a broader philosophic meaning for Winnicott, one that is useful for understanding the significance of these objects as transitions from states of nonbeing to being, from solipsistic inwardness to participation with others, as an "intermediate area of *experiencing,* to which inner reality and external life both contribute."

Likewise, the transitional object for the adult becomes a "resting place for the individual engaged in the perpetual human task of keeping inner and outer reality separate yet interrelated." It is neither real nor unreal; it is rather the "substance of *illusion,* that which is allowed to the infant, and which in adult life is inherent in art and religion." Illusory experience is the first step on the "journey" to accepting real or embodied experience, the facticity of the self/Other relation. Illusion is a bridge between the demands of the internal world (the intrapsychic) and the necessity to establish social relations and consensual foundations. However, illusion "becomes the hallmark of madness when an adult puts too powerful a claim on the credulity of others, forcing them to acknowledge a sharing of illusion that is not their own." It is not the object itself that interests Winnicott (the particular shape or form of the transitional phenomenon) but what the object represents, the "first possession . . . the intermediate area between the subject and that which is objectively perceived" (for example, in the adult the creative or artistic production). Further, Winnicott argues, illusory experience is essential for the larger social processes of cohesion and continuity. "We can share a respect for *illusory experience,* and if we wish we may collect together and form a group on the basis of the similarity of our illusory experiences. This is a natural root of grouping among human beings" (Winnicott 1971: 2–3).

It was in the sense of a kind of "first possession" of life, a statement about her inner world and the external reality she confronted, that

Julia's razor blade became transformed into a transitional object. Taking on the properties of a teddy bear, it allowed her to move from the trapped subjectivity of her inner life, with its total desperateness and isolation (manifested in persistent cutting), into a relation with external experience that ultimately left behind even the need to possess or store up the razor. Like the child's discarded teddy bear, it was a shed aspect of the self's commitment (and adaptation) to social reality, to being.

To summarize: as teddy bear, the razor's function lay in comforting Julia, in bringing relief, in sustaining her desire to live and her need to find connection in outer reality. Storing the razor, then, not only brought relief from the horror of the outer world (and her subsequent withdrawal inward) but was vital in initiating a process that over the next several months would slowly lift Julia from the hopelessness of her despair. Subsequently, she never returned to cutting as a form of self-expression. Her unconscious identification of the razor as teddy bear prevented her from using it (or anything else, for that matter) as an instrument of death or mutilation. Having control over the possibility of her own annihilation led Julia to disavow annihilation altogether. It should be stressed, however, that even the idea of a razor as a comforting, containing object indicated the deep roots of Julia's illness and the extent of her alienation. Nevertheless, her decision to store up the razor suggests in retrospect that she had altered, fundamentally, her project to die, and she ceased being enslaved to the internal compulsions whose effects had been registered on her body as scars and cuts.

Fear as the Condition of Being

Fear defined Julia's life. It lay at the center of her intersubjective world; it motivated her nihilism, her self-mutilation; it intensified her feelings of extrusion and homelessness; it led to her fascination with razor blades.

That kind of existence, however—finding the burdens of association intolerable—is not, as Hobbes (1950) would have it, proof of the antisocial character of the self, of its essentially destructive and anomic impulses. It is, rather, a statement about what happens to selves that suffer extreme emotional injury and for whom the world, throughout their psychological development, appears to be an uninviting and hostile place to live.

Julia's efforts to kill herself, to mutilate her body, to use razors as teddy bears all reveal a self in extreme desperation. Existence could take no other form; her inner world understood only fear, and her experience of alienation and nothingness convinced her of an utter and absolute isolation. Not to be *seen*, to live in the distortions of false self-systems, gave rise to an internal regime of terror and uncertainty. The unacknowledged self was a self driven to distraction; it lived in perpetual pain. Julia's preoccupation with violence—to her self, to her body— was not due to some innate characterological flaw, a kind of Hobbesian psychology manifesting itself in unrestrained drives. Rather, her self-destructive acts were derivative of what Winnicott (1970: 71) called the "environmental provision," the consequence of surviving in what Kohut would see as a world without empathy, a universe without attachment and safety. For Julia, to feel anything meant to be afraid: she perceived coldness, alienation, isolation as the facts of an existence defined by disillusionment, silence, and pain. She lived like the Hobbesian natural man, with "anxiety over future time" and "fear of imminent death" facing her constantly.

Persons who cut themselves, who find themselves obsessed with suicide, torture, razor blades, who experience themselves as less than human, as possessing animal-like features, can hardly be expected to be good citizens, to "practice" the ethics of mutuality and participation. But exclusion by virtue of psychological alienation does not mean that persons like Julia are condemned by their histories to antisocial positions and inevitable self-destruction. Rather, their illness, their psychic injury, suggests a complex set of interpersonal and intrapsychic processes that radically separate the self from the existing premises of communal and social life. In other words, persons who inhabit society's psychological borders are there for a reason.

It is Julia who has told us why it was impossible for her to be fully within the *polis*, why it was that psychically the mean lay beyond her capacities, why she found moderation and balance so difficult and painful, why what the normal world considers consensual were for her tortuous exercises in adaptation. But she never argued that she harbored within herself an abiding hostility to what might be termed the civil passions (cooperation, mutuality, tolerance, and empathy). In fact, she fantasized about these passions and often expressed in her diaries a despair of ever attaining them. Nor did she glorify her status on the borders of civil society; it was not an ideal or a revelatory place to be but, rather, like living in hell, and to live in hell brings torment.

Julia's struggle during her treatment was nothing less than an effort to move from the borders of the community and its alienated interstices into what the community regards as an intersubjective life. It was an effort to exist as a productive and creative person, a self whose existence in the world possessed meaning for others, whose inner reality demonstrated possibility and potentiality rather than poisonousness and death. Although at this stage Julia's battle was to build the basic structures of becoming a person (establishing trust and relationship), it was nonetheless a psychological movement to transform the percept "razor as teddy bear" into the much more Aristotelian view that acknowledges the self as a moral and reflective being.

The borderline self, then, reflects on a microcosmic level a political culture. It is the political culture of alienation, fragmentation, all-or-nothing demands, the skidding from extreme dependency to intolerable rage, living in the extreme—the very state of being that Aristotle feared and believed constituted an impediment to a participatory citizenship.[7] It is not that the borderline self, which experiences the world as danger and fragmentation, necessarily represents a threat to social order—although this certainly has been the case with cults and political leaders whose commitment to participatory citizenship is tenuous if not nonexistent. But I am not speaking here of borderline types who manage to harness groups to attain political ends at the fringe of society, although such types can exercise a significant effect on the society. I am speaking rather of the *victim:* Kohut's notion (1977: 7) of the fragmented self and its "chronic enfeeblement"; the Kafkaesque conception of consciousness fighting its inner sense of shame and badness; Kierkegaard's (1954) theory of "shut-up-ness"; the self that feels cut off from all acknowledgment.

In speaking of the borderline personality as a political category, I have addressed that side of being borderline which appears as alienation and separation: the self as victimized, fragmented, excluded from community, isolated from the social order, obsessed with suicide, consumed by despair, futility, and the belief that torture defines human relationship. I have not looked at other politically defined borderline types: for example, the political actor (or movement) who, because of the fascination with power and domination, seeks to subvert and overturn the historical and communal roots of the political culture and its patterns of participatory representation. It is important to distinguish such types and their pathologies from the disconnected and terrorized worlds of borderline patients and victims like Julia.

Finally, Winnicott's theory of the transitional object points to the importance of illusion in assuring the movement of the self from its isolation (the solipsism of infancy) into intersubjective and communal modes of being and relating. Such objects, invested with powerful psychological properties, become agents that bind the society, forming psychological underpinnings for social cohesiveness. Illusion is, from a political perspective, a bridge between inner and outer which takes increasingly intricate forms as the developmental process proceeds. It may be that complex forms of illusion (political belief systems, major religious orientations) are manifestations of this early phenomenon in the socialization of the self; see, for example, Freud's argument in *The Future of an Illusion* (1927) that religious belief constitutes a mass projection of a collective neurosis. Winnicott is insistent on the illusory quality of the transitional object, on its "intermediate" status as a symbolic tie between inner reality and outer frames of reference. If such transitional objects are constants in the movement from inner to outer, is it not plausible to suppose that this constant repeats itself continually over time, that it is the realm of belief which provides social cohesion, binds societies together, and prevents massive regression to anomic states of nature?

In this respect I see Winnicott as Rousseauian; he argues, like Rousseau, that it is not aggression (with its accompanying reaction formations) that coalesces the social order (the Hobbesian position). Rather, he suggests that empathy, intimacy, and the wish for community (represented in the infant's need to attach to the transitional object as a bridge to attaching to more complicated social entities) lie behind the illusions that the self builds to defend against contingent experience and the fear of being left adrift in a boundless universe. It was, in fact, the use of the razor blade as a transitional object that brought Julia from her tormented isolation, her Hobbesian withdrawal, into a relation with experience that provided some belief or trust in the illusions of community and association.

Political theorists persistently face the question of how individuals consent to be in society; it is a theme that preoccupies, for example, social contract theory, particularly the thought of Hobbes and Rousseau. If we think of the transitional object as a form of consenting to be in a social world (the object moves the self from isolation to relationship), then the function of these objects, their illusory quality and character, may indeed provide some clues to the psychological foundations of political culture. Persons who feel alienated from the culture, excluded from its premises, may have lost that capacity for transitional relatedness. Locked into internal worlds that completely remove them from the consensual processes of civil society (the reality of consensually validated *illusions*), the self has no opportunity for shared forms of relatedness.

One of the interesting differences between illusions and delusions lies in the fact that social illusions have shared histories. Illusions are not as frenetic as delusions, not as isolating and destructive. Rather, the *shared* illusion (for example, religious belief and symbolism) possesses a history, a common language, a common set of values, which have been the subject of historical evolution. Delusion, on the other hand, is ahistorical; it is the product of the movement away from history, a massive regression, whether collective or personal; it is the epitome of the denial of history.

Illusions have consensual structures validated over time, and such historical illusions are real and binding for the societies that share and believe in them. They provide continuity, a voice through time; delusions disrupt that continuity and create strident, unrecognizable voices. The illusory belief structures provide a certain element of cohesion and security; they become agents of social empathy. Delusions lack any empathic capacity; their function lies in fragmenting, isolating, destroying, and dominating. If Winnicott emphasizes anything in his analysis of the communal functions of transitional relatedness, it is the fact that the transitional object becomes the first step in a movement toward shared realities, trust, and eventually what he calls play.[8] Delusion, however, destroys the function of trust and play and therefore represents an attack on the historical structure of the community.

PART II

EFFORTS AT RESOLUTION

8 /

"Mama, Make Me Dead":
The Power of Depression

In the spirit of Lacan's notion (1978b) of narrative as an action of uncovering, witnessing, and progressing into deeper reaches of the self, I return to Ruth's narrative (see Chapters 4–6). The different levels of her understanding illustrate both the tensions and possibilities in the sense of being an exile (that part of the self which figuratively reenacts Oedipus at Colonus),[1] and the importance of language as the agent of the self's dramatic resymbolization.

Delusional Phases: The Language of Place

First, however, I suggest a typology of delusion, conceiving of it as a volatile psychological environment with four distinguishable phases (see Figure 2). Each phase erodes relationship and community with different degrees of intensity; each contributes to the regression of the self and the disintegration of ego structure; each annihilates the Aristotelian concept of the mean.

Phase 1 delusion takes the self back to an almost hermetic isolation, a pre–transitional object state, in which the self lacks any psychological connection to historical or social frames of reference. All experience is

125

FIGURE 2. Phases in delusion's impact on reality

Phase 1
Delusion as world defining, an alternative epistemology

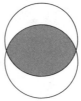

Phase 2
Delusion fixing reality in specific frames

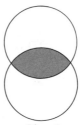

Phase 3
Delusion as an occasional structure of perception

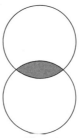

Phase 4
Delusion as one method among many for organizing consciousness

Shaded areas signify the extent to which delusion encircles reality; light
areas signify extent to which reality is defined by consensual factors

126

assimilated into a delusional epistemology that totally absorbs consciousness. Phase 2 keeps the self just beyond the border. Delusion fixes reality in specific images that have the power, when present, to locate time and experience in a definable delusional frame. In Phase 3, a less severe state of alienation and exclusion, the intensity and duration of such specific frames diminish, and the self may experience both periodic contact with consensual reality and occasional descents into a delusional symbology possessing some specificity (but not as clearly delineated as in Phase 2). In Phase 4, delusion appears as perceptions that, while intrusive, remain secondary to epistemologies grounded in social contexts; the self no longer feels the need to rely on delusional symbols but still knows that something is not right with the external world and its structures of meaning. Consciousness remains unstable and fluid. Chuck, whom I talk about below, may be thought of as occupying Phase 1; Ruth (in her first hospitalization) and David (in a manic episode), Phase 2; and Ruth and Julia, at different times, Phases 3 and 4.

Phase 3 delusions situate consciousness in a psychological no-man's-land. Neither fully delusional nor integrated in community, the self moves back and forth; it feels lost, out of control, ineffectual, and terribly confused. Lacking the certainty of any firm belief structures but not so psychotic that consciousness has been completely absorbed by delusion, the self searches for moorings and familiarity. Delusion fails to provide any comprehensive or detailed epistemological direction. While inwardly the self experiences despair and hopelessness, its outward appearance may seem organized or together. It is a state of mind and being characteristic of borderline psychological states.

A Phase 3 delusion might contain, for example, detailed reference to a set of events or happenings; the delusion figures in the self's knowledge world, although it may not be all of it. Delusional thoughts may even for periods of time eclipse reality altogether and completely transform relations between inner and outer. Phase 4 delusions, however, compete with consensual reality; often they exist simultaneously with the self's rational perceptions. It is a matter of degree and intensity; consciousness may still function effectively in the external world and be capable of reflecting on the day-to-day problems of living. What is important here is the resilience of the self's connection to consensual reality: Phase 4 delusions fail to dislodge completely the self's capacity to maintain firm links with what is out there. But they are a good indicator of the extent of the self's affective or emotional disorganization.

As an example of Phase 1 delusion, a schizophrenic state of mind where delusion constitutes the governing epistemology, consider Chuck's explanation of the meaning of death. Chuck argued that death occurs on three levels: the first is "shaking, a kind of preparation where the body moves to the wrestler's crouch. I lie on my back looking up to see when it's coming." The second level appears as torture: "Someone breaks my spine and I can't feel anything." The final level is dismemberment: "'I'm ready for the final blow; the cutting of my jugular vein, a cyanide tablet thrown down my throat for insurance. That's how I'll die; that's what death is all about." Chuck believed he had "died three or four times in twenty years; the doctors here made me dead; I'm a dead man. I'm already dead."

In describing the voices he heard, Chuck said:

> The nukes and voices are put together in a kind of kit; when the nukes explode, the voices explode.

Certain physiological systems, strategically placed, control the voices:

> I have fat pads in my brain to deflect the voices. Scar tissue from psychotherapy forms around my ears; it lives on the inside of my skull; but you know scar tissue keeps the voices out. I've been dead for a hundred million years and I just woke up. Actually, I'm feeling pretty good, kind of dead, though.

Chuck described a special voodoo that performed voice-blocking functions while simultaneously repairing damage done to his body by the ever present violence.

> My voodoo protects me; I ate my special chicken yesterday but when my head was chopped off, it grew back. The chicken contained a potion, real magic, making my head come back.

While voodoo possesses a creative, regenerative quality, it also has the power to harm.

When I was an infant, someone did voodoo to me; they put it into me, made me crazy, or maybe my mother fed me bad voodoo food; something like that; a hex. Ed [his voice] did it to me, threw bad voodoo over the radio waves [Chuck believes Ed transmits voices and voodoo from a radio station located in Honduras].

Delusion defined reality for Chuck; he believed he has two jobs at the hospital:

To listen to the voices and to flush toilets; that's what my mother taught me to do, flush toilets, shit flushers go a long way back in my family; there's big money in it.

Pain and violence fill these symbologies:

Staff cut you up into pieces or they take dead pieces from the people and then stuff a brain into it; you can do all kinds of things with body parts; I live for pain. Last night in my sleep, staff cut off my head with a chain saw, a small one because my neck is not so big. It went zip and my head fell off, just like that. It didn't bleed too much but dropped right off and then grew back.

Phase 2 delusions may be as complex as those of Phase 1, but the self is not as irrevocably trapped or tied down to rigid and inflexible conceptions of reality. For example, Chuck remained completely enveloped and surrounded by his delusional world; he had no way out of it, whereas Ruth (whose first hospitalization centered on Phase 2 delusions) even during her most regressed moments could occasionally step outside her delusional environment. It would be as if she had moved from one reality to the next, although her capacity to sustain consensual connections would be quite brief. In this regard, she suffered moments of psychotic disorganization.

Ruth could doubt her own delusional experience when that experience periodically lifted from her consciousness. For example, in the morning she might look through the window and see visitors to the hospital as SS agents sent from Berlin to plan her torture, then in the afternoon wonder who the visitors were and why they had come to the hospital. She could think that her Hall's quiet room secretly contained electrocution devices and demand that she not be put there, then a few hours later request to use the quiet room because she "needed a place to think, to feel some calm." It should be emphasized that Ruth's Phase 2 delusions were not minor hallucinations or vague premonitions but concrete knowledge systems forming the underpinnings of a distinct view of the world, a factor that distinguishes her experience from Julia's.

During most of her first hospitalization, Ruth lived within a Phase 2 delusional environment. Her beliefs defined the way she looked at the world, what she saw around her, how she assimilated experience. Occasionally she put on the mask of sanity:

> I needed a sign-out, so I let staff think I was okay. Of course, I didn't tell them I thought that behind their "kind" exterior hid the fact that they were SS agents planning my execution. Or there were times when I sympathetically spoke with patients; I let them feel I was sincerely interested in their problems; I wanted to be their friend. But underneath, in my world, I knew them to be spies for Hitler's medical experiments team.

Ruth could use her "sanity mask" without revealing her profound delusional core. In a Phase 1 schizophrenic delusion the self remains trapped by the delusional introject on all cognitive levels. But Ruth could speak in a normal, conversational style even while her convictions remained delusional. Patients had become spies; staff who spoke to her were enemies; such people might be friendly, but they intended to kill her. She felt forced to "bide her time," to "try to survive the fires of Hell." Not until the last few months of her hospitalization did Ruth begin to substitute more consensual references for delusional ones. She finally came to see that staff were not SS guards, that patients could be distinguished from spies sent by Berlin, and that Sheppard-Pratt was not planning her execution.

In Phase 3 delusion the self maintains a distinction, at least consciously, between what it recognizes as delusion (usually after the fact) and what it regards as appropriate or normal. Delusions may appear only at night, with spirits coming into the room and speaking. Ghosts may pop out of doorways; strange beliefs may suddenly materialize during a meal; Ruth, on a sign-out, might mistake a policeman for a Nazi guard searching for her. Yet these images, while distinct and often complex, remain outside the self's epistemological system. Psychically, the balance lies on the side of consensual reality; and these delusional moments, unlike Chuck's delusional *epistemology,* appear to be regressions, with the self mounting a desperate effort to move in the other direction. Delusions may be recollected as dreams, funny thoughts, hallucinations, or bizarre visions. The critical element is the distance the self places between its imaginative projections and its rootedness in consensual reality. The self in Phase 3 delusion develops a greater facility for observation. Delusion ceases to be a living, ongoing present. Nor do delusions for any period of time disrupt conventional conceptions of cause and effect. Julia's relation to razor blades and cutting, for example, did not interfere with her acknowledgment of social frames of reference. Will and volition directed toward consensual objects take on increased meaning and significance, and movement away from the delusional symbology is seen by the self as desirable and even necessary.

An observation of David's suggests something of the impact of Phase 3 delusional thinking, in which imagery appears as an isolated phenomenon explaining a limited series of events. The delusion is not part of a complex system of meaning or even of naming, as it is in Phase 1 and to a lesser extent in Phase 2 (like David's, for example, during his manic phases). Delusion, here, lacks an epistemological frame; it is distinguished by the immediacy of its impact. It constitutes not a world view but a sense of things expressed at a specific time. Such delusions affect consciousness as a single overpowering event; delusion appears, then disappears.

> No one understood why I refused to shower. It was like having my skin washed off. It wasn't a normal thing, not like your day-to-day shower. Clothes became my skin and when staff took them off, I felt my skin being pulled apart. Taking a shower terrified me; it stripped me of my dignity or what remained of it. The dirt showed me I was alive; it extended my flesh, my skin. Being in the shower, then, was like finding myself in an acid bath, my skin burning off, taking bits and pieces of me down the drain. I be-

lieved the longer I stayed in the stall, the more of my identity would dissolve down the drain. And by the end, when I became clean, there would be no David left, just a memory, the scum on the bottom of the stall.

David's belief that his skin was peeling away, however, lasted only during the duration of the shower. Afterward he felt normal, healthy; he remembered his reaction in the shower, but the memory ceased to influence what he did or how he perceived himself. It was as if David, no longer bound by the *philosophic* frame of delusion, moved away from these images as soon as the experience giving rise to them dissipated. Similarly, during her Phase 3 period Ruth's delusional images functioned not as knowledge systems riveting her to an alternative world but as fragments of experience passing in and out of mind. When the experience faded, so did the delusion. Even though David had been consumed by the "acid bath," the delusion possessed *affective* impact only in the context of the moment when, in the midst of a shower, water splattered like acid over the surface of his skin. Precisely at that moment David understood his body, his skin, and his flesh to be dissolving; it was torture. Phase 3 delusions, then, are real, imminent or present; they frame perception; they contain discrete elements that orient consciousness toward the present. But they are permeable: almost as soon as they happen, they find themselves rejected by consciousness, only to reappear as bad memories, despairing liabilities, or horrible nightmares.

Ruth's Depression as an Example of Phase 4 Delusion

Phase 4 delusions create a sense of dread or foreboding without severing the self's connection to social reality. They are a powerful threat to the belief structures of community. What Ruth saw in her depression and what she held inside on her return to the hospital offered a fascinating insight into the function and operation of these vague and confounding thoughts. Her consciousness or mind encircled reality with a number of different assumptions or what I call perceptual methods and values. And her delusional world intruded when she felt it necessary to call it to consciousness. When delusion filled up what Ruth saw, it functioned as the dynamic organizing her experience; it also drew her away from her associational ties. It was as real as any other method for organizing percepts but, unlike her earlier delusional phases, was only one among many for approaching reality. It never threatened to tear her perception from its foundation in the social world. Though Ruth sometimes hallucinated perplexing and disturbing visions, she never found herself separated in any basic or fundamental way from the consensual environment.

It was five months after her discharge that Ruth readmitted herself to Sheppard-Pratt in a state of acute, psychotic depression. Delusion no longer involved Nazi guard dogs, SS commandants, or *dybbuks* poking iron rods into her side. She complained of difficulties in moving; her body "sagged"; she felt like a "heavy mass," without "will." She had no "desire to do anything" and just wanted to "sit and let everyone do for" her. She needed to "sink into the floor and disappear"; she saw herself as a "piece of dirt in the flower pot." In sharp contrast with her earlier terror—centering on staff as SS, the human-flesh butcher shop in the hospital basement, the fear of execution by firing squad, and the belief that she and her children were destined for "death experiments"—she now experienced a diffuse but intensifying depression.

Ruth's return to the hospital was literally the action of a refugee. She came asking for asylum; she presented herself as a person without place, a wanderer in a world having no boundaries, no frontier. She felt that the world "out there" (civil society) would petrify her, would turn her into stone. It struck her as a hostile environment filled with unpredictable danger. She thought she might kill herself.

Ruth remained at Sheppard-Pratt for an additional three months. An entry in the nursing notes suggests something of her state of mind during the first week of this second hospitalization:

Ruth ate a tray on the Hall, spent time watching TV with peers and time lying down in her room. Minimal interaction with peers . . . spoke quietly and briefly with staff . . . states she is "extremely depressed," feeling helpless and hopeless, doesn't know what will help her to feel better, and lacks energy to do anything. Pt. started being so depressed that she didn't think she would be able to make it through this stage . . . having tightness in stomach and not having enough energy to take a shower . . . spent the greater part of the evening lying down in her room. . . . As patient stated: "I feel so bad and am in so much pain emotionally that it is too difficult to be on the Hall" . . . attended Hall meeting . . . sat with body slumped forward, head in hands, eyes closed, much of the time. . . . Ruth continues to be very slow in motor activities and speech, stating that she has "no energy."

Ruth's psychological and perceptual relation to experience was determined not by a delusional epistemology (like Chuck's) or periodic psychotic regressions (like David's) but, primarily, by undefined feelings, sensations, and thoughts involving a belief that she should kill herself, which accompanied her wherever she went.

During my interviews with her, Ruth spoke of despair, fear of freedom, her desire to have decisions made for her, to become the slave of a rich and powerful person who would dominate and take all responsibility out of her hands, an omnipotent authority who would be alternately sadistic and protective. Depression showed in her face and the movements of her body; it defined her interactions and self-perceptions; it lay around her like a dense cloud. She spoke of the depression as an "it": "it" was there; "it" could take her away; "it" had the power to destroy her and me; "it" cut her off from people. She expressed fear at having to look at invisible ghosts who had turned her into this "empty person," a "shapeless mass" with no idea how to complete herself. She spoke of being unfamiliar with the flesh inhabiting her body, of being detached, of lacking an identity, of feelings shattering inside her.

> I do everything by rote, nothing lives inside me, and what there is keeps repeating itself, like a machine doing the same thing over and over. That's about it, endless repetition, without end. I feel like I've been released from the death camp and I'm standing outside the gates wondering what's going to happen next, how many of my family died, why I escaped. It all seems to useless, so without meaning; and if no meaning exists, why do anything? Why not just go back inside those gates and lie down?

The Wish to Be Mortified: Masochism as a Dynamic of Depression

Ruth persistently returned to the theme of an inner voice that dragged her down. At one point she described the following dialogue with an Other who spoke in an indistinguishable mumble.

> R: Are you there?
>
> H [for "He"]: —— (mumble)
>
> R: Yeah, I guess you're there, I can hear you.
>
> H: —— mumble
>
> R: What did you say?
>
> H: —— (mumble)
>
> R: That you hate me?
>
> H: —— (mumble)
>
> R: You said yes?
>
> H: —— (mumble)
>
> R: I guess you said yes; what do you want me to do?
>
> H: —— (mumble)
>
> R: You said you want me to kill myself?
>
> H: —— (mumble)
>
> R: Yes! kill myself; that's what you want me to do! I filled in the blanks, and hoped what I said would please him.

Ruth granted agency to a presence she could never make comprehensible; however, the real agency lay in her wish to die; *she* "filled in the blanks," the demands she thought she heard. The delusion possessed reality or force only when she represented what she thought was this speaker's wish. She replaced vicious Nazis, guard dogs, *dybbuks* with a sadistic voice, but all her delusional phases sent the same message: to be loved or acknowledged or defined by an Other inevitably involved abuse (the Other as sadist). It was a law of the universe; it appeared in her earlier delusions as complex symbologies of domination and victimization, and later as an unintelligible voice inside her head demanding that she die.

For Ruth, to be abused was to be loved, but her feeling of having to be abused depended in large measure on her guilt at not having suffered enough, or at least *not having suffered as much as her father*. By taking into herself the wish to die, Ruth attempted to atone for her own insufficiency in suffering and to relive in her fantasy her father's anguish by offering herself as a sacrifice to his pain. The "he" or "it" of her Phase 4 delusional world served as an embodiment of this fantasized wish, the wish to die as a form of sacrifice, as atonement for her father's suffering in the camps. In placing the abuse inside her in the form of voices, she became both victim and victimizer. She could now author her own destruction, yet she lacked control over internal psychological functions that might dissipate the commands of a voice, which in the classic *political* sense possessed power.

It had been drummed into Ruth-the-child that she could never suffer as much as her father; further, his suffering became the yardstick against which to measure both the family's collective pain and its collective sense of guilt at having survived the camps. Ruth became the living extension of both guilt and pain; because of this, she felt that her existence could not be justified. It had no meaning when compared to the magnitude of her parents' grief. How could she live when so many others had suffered and died? That fantasy served as the driving dynamic for Ruth's later delusional identifications. Not only did she deserve to die, but the manner of her death had to be as painful and agonizing as her father's suffering had been. It had to match the intensity of the horror experienced by those who had perished in the Holocaust. This burden evolved into Ruth's delusional core; it became her identity. It was what she felt she had to be.

Ruth saw herself as an instrument of atonement or sacrifice. Since embodying or acting out her fantasy in reality was impossible, the stage for actions of sacrifice shifted to the imagination and, later, to complex delusional systems. Prevented, because of the family's collusive network, from expressing her own pain, the part of Ruth's self which carried the suffering and rage had to be split off from her conscious awareness. She could never be with her own pain; it hurt too much; it was too explosive. And when, in her twenties, she repeatedly tried to kill herself, or when she unconsciously encouraged abusive relationships, or when she heard voices, it was as if she were desperately trying to establish contact with the split-off, denied part of herself that contained all her pain, her suffering and rage.

As a little girl she could not realistically make her father feel better, but in her imagination she created scenes that, according to her fantasies of sacrifice, might alleviate *his* horrifying burden. The real *affective* side of her life, then, developed around these delusional wishes. But it was a part of Ruth that lay outside her will; she had no control over the feelings generated by these wishes and fantasies, even though they stood at the center of her emotional being. Nor could she permit herself to suffer, or even admit the suffering to herself, because of her crippling sense of guilt. It was as if her guilt said: "How can you measure your pain against the infinitely more powerful pain of your father? What a bad, horrible person you must be even to try to construct this comparison!"

> For years I protected my father from my rage; I never dared express pain in front of him or my mother. I became a terrific actress, to the point where I eventually came to believe my role. I had the mask so tightly fitted; I identified with what everyone thought I was: pretty, talented, witty, intelligent, even brilliant. That other side of me, full of pain, had been buried; and nothing could make me suffer. Underneath I knew myself as a stone, hard, unyielding, like a rock. Who could hurt me? No amount of hurt could ever equal Papa's hurt. I forged a thick iron shell around what later became the real Ruth, the "me" you saw when I was crazy with fear and hate. That "me" never had a stage; it never appeared when I was a child. It was locked up in a cave no one could find. And when finally I found that cave, when I lived in it in the seclusion room at Sheppard-Pratt or in the privacy of my own mind, it was like unlocking a Pandora's box of demons, bats, rats, pestilence, all sorts of underworld creatures whose only purpose lay in persecuting me.

When Ruth first left the hospital, she had no job; her acquaintances and friends provided little comfort. Their actions, she felt, mocked and misunderstood her despair. The company she treasured, desired, was the man inside her, the garbled, disembodied voice she translated in her Phase 4 delusion. She wondered during this period whether this bizarre voice came to her as a phantom of her husband, her father, or God. She believed she would never lead a normal life; she took excessive sleep medication; she made frequent and unscheduled visits to her therapist's office. She felt physically sick and psychically ill. The voice, however, had the effect of inducing in her a growing preoccupation with the reasons motivating her despair, her feelings of hopelessness.

Yet the voice never pushed Ruth back toward more systemic delusional constructs. For example, she no longer felt, as she had on signouts during her first hospitalization, that her neighbors might be in league with the Nazis or that policemen were the SS in disguise, or that German Shepherds were guard dogs assigned to burial squads in and around Towson (Phase 2 and 3 delusions). Nor did she find in the vegetable bins of grocery stores cabbages turning into skulls or tomatoes engorged with blood or carrots looking like pieces of bone and flesh. She found herself beset primarily by vague images and sensations whose effect induced a depressing hopelessness and a conviction that she needed to die. However, she was conscious that these images were in part her creations. She believed not that "a voice speaks to me" but that "I hear a voice, I can't make it out, I'll guess what it says." This was an important difference: her *own* voice had to define language and command.

Unlike Chuck, Ruth went far in demystifying the hold of delusion on consciousness and eventually came to think of the voice as an unwanted aspect of a self she perceived as sick. Chuck had no such hold on his delusional system. The belief that a neutron bomb inside his stomach lay ready to explode any minute demonstrated for him a fact of nature, a true phenomenon having nothing to do with "inner feelings." Neutron bombs existed "out there," facts to be perceived, realities to be confronted. For Chuck, nothing imaginary existed in the world. Neutron bombs, heads being chopped off, brains growing back, teeth as adhesive for chopped off heads: all these possessed an undisputed reality. In Chuck's world delusional happenings came from outside; he refused to believe that he had anything to do with either their creation or their action. Each event possessed an autonomous and therefore independent quality. Voices whispering in his ears, a computer sending "beeps" from Honduras, radio waves "zinging" his head, gases traveling through the hospital's air vents to suffocate his bronchial tubes were all coming from sources outside his mind or self.

For Ruth, however, all delusional experience emanated from inside herself. She acknowledged the difference between inner and outer; she saw that her voice was not part of common ordinary experience but an event inside her that she desperately needed to untangle. She had, unlike Chuck, the capacity for reflexive distance. Ruth's voice never transmitted intricate theories of knowledge, nor did "he" reconstruct the physical laws of the universe. Her delusion centered not on the organization of matter but on feelings that interfered with her actions in the consensual world: "I stood guard over the man inside me; I protected him; I turned from the outside to him. He took all my time."

Ruth's final efforts at dismantling her inner voice began with what appeared to be a minor incident. At a Hall meeting, about a month after her return, Ruth requested a sign-out; other patients and some nurses were opposed on the grounds that it was not safe for her to be out of the hospital. Much in her therapist's reaction to this decision depended on what the nurses conveyed to him, both about Ruth's behavior and about what other patients had observed. Ruth objected to the nurses' interpretation; she thought they were exaggerating her potential for self-destructive action. But even more important, she was outraged at her therapist's apparent agreement with the nurses' views; she felt that he was questioning her truthfulness. Further, the fact that her therapist believed what the nurses told him became for Ruth a sign of his betrayal, an attack on her capacity to be truthful. She saw him as doing to her what her father had done countless times years before: denying her experience by refusing to accept her view of it.

To understand Ruth's process of resolution, one must examine how the power of her therapeutic transference broke down the power of her depression. A person she idealized—her therapist—had, like her father, rejected her words as incorrect and wrong. That recognition threw her into a panic; she felt she had become a little girl all over again. She transformed Dr. K. into a tormentor, a cruel and vicious tyrant who wanted to abuse her, denigrate who she was; his explanations were "malicious"; he harbored a "secret desire" to inflict pain. Dr. K. evolved into the living images of her father, a distant, spiteful, and sadistic man who had little or no feeling for either Ruth or her views. It never occurred to her that Dr. K. might be interested in what she had to say, since the unconscious fantasy had been that what she had to say, as a little girl, was in fact worthless. This belief was so binding on her consciousness that the process of validation never entered her mind; she refused to ask Dr. K. to check the facts and see whether either she or the nurses might have made a mistake. As she put it: "I wanted him to hurt me; I needed to believe he lied to me, wished me harm, enjoyed watching me suffer. I was convinced Dr. K. wanted to hurt me." That conviction became the central issue in her language of historical reenactment.

Ruth's feeling of betrayal bore no relation to reality on the unit. She felt broken and incapacitated by what was in fact a relatively minor rebuke that could have been worked out with little difficulty. She found herself so enmeshed in rage that she could not step back and examine the refusal of her sign-out request and her therapist's relationship to that refusal. She was too involved emotionally with the incident; it stirred up too much from her past; and she could not empathically read the event either through her therapist's or the nurses' eyes. It had been this way with her father as well; she never saw "Papa" through his eyes: "I had no ability to be inside his skin, to be in his mind, to be tolerant of his feelings."

It was difficult, if not impossible, for Ruth to conceive of his reactions as those of a person emotionally and physically devastated by his experience in Auschwitz. As a child, she said, how could she be expected to understand what Auschwitz meant, what it was? Could a little girl just beginning grade school see that her father's preoccupations and psychological debilitation might have made it extremely difficult for him to behave in accordance with what her wishes expected of him? "Maybe he could love me but not listen to me; maybe his capacity to show love had been all twisted up by the Nazis; I see that now, but then? When I was a kid?" The only time her father appeared to demonstrate any feeling or tenderness, according to Ruth, was when he listened to Mozart, and he did that only by himself; he refused to let anyone in the family sit with him. "I used to watch him weep, but he never saw me; in his mind he had gone far away." Ruth never experienced love, affection, or care from a father who both fascinated and terrified her. Instead, then, of taking in a father's love, which would certainly have contributed to a stable self-representation, she internalized her father's anger as rejection. She came to understand herself as *deserving of that rejection*. It was this self-blame that formed the core of her later masochism. "It was the only part of Papa I could identify with, and in my mind, I became angry like him." Yet she split off the anger, stored it up, and became psychically what she thought everyone expected of her: a dutiful, polite, sweet child, an elaborate but false self-system that met the compliance demands of the outside world.

Initially, following the sign-out incident, she had reacted to Dr. K. as she had to her father. Ruth accused him of hating her, of wanting to cause her pain, of doing to her what her father and husband had done for years. In the therapeutic transference, parts of Dr. K's *imago* stood not only for Ruth's historical father and historical husband but for the fantasies attached to these figures: the imaginary father and imaginary husband, the linguistic projections of her unconscious. She felt guilty and mortified: why did Dr. K. work with such a "worthless person . . . such garbage, dung in a manure heap"? She told Dr. K. he should "murder" her and "be rid of a horrible pestilence. I had been corrupted, polluted. Could he not see this cesspool in front of him?" She screamed that he had betrayed her, conspired with the nurses; the entire Hall wanted her dead; friends were enemies; she demanded another therapist. She thought of all sorts of ways to hurt Dr. K. by poisoning the day-to-day affairs of his life; she would break up his marriage, turn his children against him; tell his patients about his lies and deceits.

Yet at the same time she *could* ask, why would *she* want to hurt *him*? Why had she felt like a little girl in his presence, invisible in relation to him? Why had she carried around this sense of poisonousness? Why had she confused intimacy and torture? Why had being close felt so painful, and why had she used anger to defend herself from being too close? All these questions initiated a process that brought speech into a direct confrontation with the pull of her unconscious fantasy. She saw enormous flaws in the world she had believed to be true, her symbolic world of tormenting fathers and victimized daughters. She began to see her parents as victims of a historical drama with inevitable human and family consequences, and herself as authoring imaginary plots and subplots that fed into a corrosive masochism and unbearable inner hurt. It was, then, not a matter of *fault*.

Her therapist's office, as she put it, "turned into a stage, a thousand-act play with scenes interposed, juxtaposed, confused." She refused to run from the memories and their action.

> Images of my mother and father, the fights in the living room, broken dishes, yelling, Papa's indifference toward me, all this broke in and out of my consciousness. And in the privacy of my room, and my mind, I screamed at Dr. K. for opening up these wounds, for exposing me to such pain. I thought the anger, the sadness would never stop; I hated Dr. K.; I wanted staff and other patients to come over and hug me until the fury died down. Images of Dr. K.'s face, my father's voice, my husband's rampages, all flowed out. The dam had finally burst.

In a delicate interplay between symbolic and historical truth, the language of Ruth's unconscious spilled out into the conscious field of her therapeutic relation: the jumbled-up feelings, the doubts, the injustices of her distortions, the insensitivity of her father (and an appreciation of his pain), the fantasy that Dr. K. was brutalizing her, her desperate need to atone for a father's pain that she had taken inside herself as a little girl. All these images found a context in speech. And as this historical unraveling and interpretation gained strength, the inner voice began to recede. She heard less and less of its garbled mumbling; she listened more closely to her own thoughts, which seemed to arise with increasing frequency. And her depression started to lift. With the demystification of her masochistic fantasy, Ruth looked forward to the project of *life*, the will to be climbing out of her delusional obsessions and reentering the patterns of historical existence.[2]

> It wasn't that suddenly I had been cured or made happy; nothing that miraculous. But the immobility, the depression, lifted for short periods. The man inside me rarely made an appearance, his voice disappeared for great stretches of time; and I felt like a huge burden had been taken from me. I found myself responding differently to people. I became more interested in what they did, their sense of the world. I think I was healing. I felt a need to be outside with my children, to teach them things. That urgency to be told what to do and how to be, the desire to have a person

control and dominate my life, seemed less important. I thought about being on my own without feeling petrified or incapacitated by anxiety.

It was a painful process because Ruth glimpsed aspects of her father's world—a world twisted by Auschwitz—and her own unconscious distortions, the little-girl-Ruth retreating into a nonempathic internality and suffering from intense environmental deprivation. Her therapeutic field, however, brought her own history into sharper focus. For example, she understood that she had made her father's words into the acts of a willful tormentor; she also acknowledged another possibility: his memories and pain had been so overwhelming that his coldness and disdain had nothing to do with her, or even with his deep feelings for her, but with a historical fact—the Holocaust—that she had been powerless to control or change. "How was I to know that his words were signs of the frustration and limitations of a man incapable of listening to his children? He was so caught up in his own pain that his kids became an intrusion into a private Hell." It became clear to her that her yelling at Dr. K. was Ruth-the-little-girl making an appearance. It was a dreaded memory of the past intruding in the consciousness of the adult, yet the more that little girl appeared in language, in speech, the less insistent was Ruth's need to torment herself and distort her object relations. The more the child intruded into her conscious symbolizations, thereby subjecting them to observation and analysis, the less demanding was the sadistic tormentor inside her and her underlying conviction she was worthless and bad. "I saw something of the difference between what actually happened to me and what I did to myself."

Demystification of Fantasy: The Language of Intersubjectivity

Finally, in the space of her therapeutic field Ruth unraveled and demystified the central structure of a fantasy she had carried as a concrete belief system. It went something like this: She believed, as a child, that her father literally wanted her dead; he could then live without having "this disgusting little girl" as a liability. Not only was her existence the source of intolerable pain to her father, but her badness was worse than the pain unleashed by his Nazi tormentors. "I was the child who made her father suffer" was how she defined her being-in-the-world. To defend herself against that frightening source of pain and knowledge, Ruth constructed a counterfantasy involving her death and annihilation, an event that her father, she thought, would welcome. She saw him rejoicing at her funeral; she convinced herself that her life's purpose was to deliver herself into the hands of the fantasy, to discover that form of slow death which might satisfy what she perceived as her father's wishes for a tortured and messy annihilation. The fantasy, then, solved two problems: Ruth could find a way of pleasing her father, and she could remain alive. Torture was less final than suicide. To torture herself continuously meant that she would be condemned to life *and* pain, as her father had been in and out of Auschwitz. A swift painless execution or suicide would be too easy; it would not do justice to her existence as a living reminder of the world's essential badness, nor would it demonstrate the stigmata of her sacrifice, her need *to suffer*.

This distinction had become less and less tenable in the three years preceding her hospitalization, as the frequency and potential lethality of her suicide attempts increased. The fantasy, however, had contained an additional component. Ruth not only wished she might torture herself to please her father; she also fervently wished that "Mama" might make her dead. Not only would her mother's murderousness, which Ruth saw as the other side of her indifference, bring joy to Papa by realizing his wish to see his daughter dead, but the act of murder would bring mother and father closer together. To guarantee their happiness, Ruth would be the sacrifice. It was a fantasy played over in her mind countless times, a compulsive, recurring thought that plagued her childhood in infinite permutations. Later, as a young woman in her twenties, she transformed the fantasy into concrete activities that brought pain: her marriage to a sadistic, unfeeling, and narcissistic man; her rage at her children, which came back to her as *their* hatred and denial of her; her efforts, leading to exhaustion, to please various authority figures in her orthodox community; her hatred of her body and feeling numb, stony, nonsexual, thinglike (a systemic *anhedonia*); her repeated attempts to harm herself physically through the ingestion of pills. The Imaginary had indeed become the

Real, or at least it encircled the Real with powerful perceptual and behavioral force.

The fantasy of her own annihilation and sacrifice functioned for Ruth-the-child as a source of knowledge, an epistemology that informed her interpretation of self and experience. By dying in her imagination, she constructed scenarios of slow death; she atoned for the crimes and anguish she inflicted on Papa; her death would bring him out of his despair and depression. And if Mama made her dead, her family had that much better opportunity to prosper and survive. (I am reminded here of the end of Kafka's *Metamorphosis* when the Samsa family seemed to grow more robust and hearty, with prospects looking up particularly for their daughter, after the final disposal of their son-as-cockroach.) Further, Ruth believed that her death would be a sacrifice for all the Jews destroyed in the Holocaust; maybe, she thought, if she died a painful death, her suffering might even bring them back to life. This fantasy of her death as signaling the resurrection of her family and the victims of the Holocaust provided the only link she had to any sense of self-worth; it was the *imagining* of her sacrifice in its various scenarios that kept her going.

This play, the permutations of the Imaginary stoked by the unconscious fantasy of sacrifice, became her real world—not school, not the knowledge in her textbooks or her relations with friends. All of that was ephemeral and meant nothing to her; it was part of the disguise, the false self-system that she enacted to keep the real play going inside her. What mattered as *knowledge* were the symbologies of sacrifice and self-effacement represented in an inner dramaturgy, without audience, that Ruth authored and directed. The fantasy "sustained me in my periods of deepest despair; it was the only tie I had to my parents' love." What greater gift could she give to her father than to be his personal and historical sacrifice? If she were dead, Papa would live as a free and happy man. If she were to die, the millions of dead Jews might return to the world. If this "worthless" child's dying were to bring back all those millions, particularly the children, would that not justify her tortured, agonizing death and show her parents what a good little girl she could be?

That inner drama (the Imaginary as a form of atonement), which for the child had been the central pivot of her existence, became for the adult psychological patterns defining how life should be lived. Ruth-the-adult would live her life as a perpetual, living sacrifice; her every act contributed to that end. Even though the fantasy had become unconscious (that is, Ruth believed that the concrete actions of her life, no matter how self-destructive, were freely chosen), she would perpetually atone for her father's anguish by herself becoming the object of anguish. She would literally give herself up to pain by either exacting abuse from others or so abusing others as to encourage a kind of infinite sado-masochistic cycle. By constructing an elaborate sado-masochistic dialectic, by turning the elemental facts of pain and abuse into the governing forces of her existence, she would transform her very being into a lesson in sacrifice.

In sum, Ruth harbored an unconscious fantasy, one that was never directly in her consciousness but still controlled much of her behavior and, more important, her sense of self and self-worth. She felt herself to be a sacrifice for her father's will, and she expressed her worthlessness in persistent acts of self-torture and mutilation. This suggests highly charged *affect* lying inside a terribly wounded self, feelings Ruth could never formulate in language; she represented or embodied this side of who she was in suicidal action and delusional projection. She could never visualize, either in concept or language, this dimension of her being, even though it informed everything she said or did. It was as if an invisible curtain separated Ruth as a hurt, injured, rejected, worthless child from the little girl her parents wanted her to be: a performer, a charmer, a well-dressed, intelligent, shining example of the family.

The demystification of Ruth's unconscious fantasies, then, owed a great deal to what she brought to the present in language, image, and recollection. Her linguistic constructions were reenactments of critical moments in her past; and the closer she moved toward these reenactments, the less dependent she became on delusion. Language served as the primary instrument allowing her to heal the split inside herself; empathy and mirroring transferences became the primary therapeutic approaches. Language made it possible for her to take back or reintegrate the rage, horror, and anger that had been such prominent factors in her unconscious identifications. That Ruth did recover, leaving behind *all* delusional phases, is attributable to a treatment that contained and held a horrifying inner self with considerable potential for self-destruction and suicide. In this respect the hospital provided a safe environment that allowed for the full play and *representation* of these suicidal themes. It is not likely that Ruth would have survived without such containment, yet most important, within such containment it was Ruth's own resilience and courage that ultimately enabled her to overcome her childhood wish, "Mama, make me dead."

9 /

Spring Lake Ranch and the Rousseauian Bases of Community

For the person who moves in and out of delusional frames of reference and being, whose attachment lies primarily with the internal world, integration into a community is a compelling issue. That such integration is impossible to sustain completely or practice fully in a mental hospital is understandable: the hospital tends to represent dominant social interests; it is not a polity but an institution within the surrounding society. As an agent of socialization, even the most progressive mental hospital still falls short of replicating the conditions and structures of a participatory community, with the exception of informal communities that appear from time to time in the daily life of the Hall. By its very nature and bureaucratic organization, the hospital with rare exceptions tends to enforce a hierarchical conception of goal or purpose and control. It is therefore an institution governed not by the sovereignty of its inhabitants (although in isolated instances it may practice such sovereignty) but by an administrative necessity that covers a broad range of professional interests persistently competing over power.

Spring Lake Ranch, however, a residential therapeutic community

148

located on some five hundred acres in the mountains of Vermont south of Rutland, has about it elements of a polity, a *res publica:* it offers its residents a public life. Its organization departs radically from the split bureaucratic and professional interests of the hospital. It is more than a residential farm. Spring Lake draws participants into a community persistently representing itself in public forums and collaborative action. It offers an alternative perspective on the demands of technological rationality and the relation of self to labor and work. It provides the experience of citizenship; it confronts the private delusional world with a natural environment requiring human intervention and action. The ranch thus creates a collaborative public, a collective response to a natural setting requiring a considerable expenditure of energy to make it productive. It is a way of life which, rather than beginning from the premise of sickness, accepts the proposition that collaborative activity possesses the capacity to both absorb and transcend sickness. It is a refuge, a place where the self may struggle to regain its visibility in society and its humanity among others. This chapter focuses on what Spring Lake Ranch reveals about a theory of community whose primary objective lies in creating a sense of public selfhood.

As a counterexample to instrumental and technological rationality and its administration, Spring Lake Ranch defines its identity through the implementation and extension of the concept of intersubjectivity as a form of community. It is based on a social contract in the Rousseauian sense: its residents make explicit agreements regarding the place of a public life (comprising both work and decision-making) and self-governance. In many respects, residents leave the isolation of their inner nature (delusion, hallucination) and the hopelessness of their social world (withdrawal, hospitalization) for what Rousseau in *The Social Contract* (1950: 15) sees as the "interdependent" qualities of human association: *"Each of us puts his person and all his power in common under the supreme direction of the general will, and, in our corporate capacity, we receive each member as an indivisible part of the whole.* At once, in place of the individual personality of each contracting party, this act of association creates a moral and collective body, composed of as many members as the assembly contains voters [at the ranch, both residents and staff] and receiving from this act its unity, its common identity, its life and its will."

The operating assumptions of Spring Lake Ranch, I argue, follow the broad outlines of Rousseau's conception. And in moving from patienthood and isolation to citizenship and community, the resident undergoes a painful struggle that occurs along three lines: integration into a group that refuses to acknowledge sickness as a way of life; the attempt to forge distance between delusional reality and the demands of consensual reality; and the extraordinary effort to participate in an environment where the interest of the community remains primary to the divisive effect of what Rousseau calls individual wills, where the politics of exclusion is *not* practiced.

For those who leave the ranch, the experience of community may provide a foundation or perspective for life within the surrounding society. In my view, however, the measure of success or viability is not so much what happens after the resident leaves as it is the effort Spring Lake makes to construct an environment that respects and recognizes the importance of the self's public being as a matter of therapeutic and political significance. It is therapeutic in the sense that the ranch acknowledges that no human being survives without trust in the self's essential productivity, that self-esteem and laboring with one's hands are intimately related. It is political in the sense that the ranch's emphasis on community, decision-making in common, and participatory action suggests that consciousness is more than a passive receiver of others' actions, that collaborative activity, decision, and association lie at the center of the human project. Spring Lake residents learn that what is communal depends on their own creation; that productive activity requires action, transformation, and an effort to mold the natural environment; that being active affirms a sense of well-being and faith in one's own capacities in relation to the production of others.

Rousseauian perspectives abound in the life of the ranch: the insistence on equality; the commitment to the concept of a common and general will; the deemphasis of private interests and an effort to focus attention on what is common; the dedication to a concept of *civitas* and citizenship as the uniting vision of the community; the firmness regarding a civil religion (in Rousseau's terms) centered on work. I look at these perspectives through an examination of the ranch's daily activity, its residents' observations, and case analyses that demonstrate both limitations and possibilities in the Spring Lake Ranch environment.

Spring Lake Ranch: Setting and Context

The ranch is considered under the licensing requirements of the state of Vermont to be a residential therapeutic community, not a hospital, and residents may not remain for more than two years at a time. However, they may in practice leave the ranch and then return; the two-year requirement applies only to the duration of a single stay, and those who were in residence prior to the establishment of the licensing codes are exempt even from this limitation. The population varies; when I visited there in October 1984, twenty-two former mental patients were in residence, although the capacity is forty to forty-five. Most are referred to the ranch by mental health professionals for a variety of psychological and emotional problems. (See Figure 3 for a description of the population during 1983–84.)

The facilities consist of a large main house (dining room, kitchen, living and common areas, reading room, offices) and smaller buildings scattered within walking distance of one another. There are a barn, a machine shop, and several smaller sheds or pens for livestock. Residents live in simple but comfortable cottages, usually two to a room; each cottage or house is responsible for its own cleaning and maintenance. At least one staff counselor lives in each house.

Life at the ranch, since it is basically a farming community, is quite simple; residents and staff eat and socialize in work clothes; there is a pervasive informality that defines relations between staff and resident. Everyone calls others by first names; doors to the offices in the main house are left unlocked. The only room with a doorlock in the entire building (except for bathrooms) is the small nurses' office where medications are stored. Food grown on the ranch is consumed there, and meals are hearty and fresh, usually with several different vegetarian and nonvegetarian dishes placed on a large buffet table. In nutrition, taste, and abundance, food at the ranch gives one the feeling of dining in a solid and authentic country restaurant. There is a hired professional cook, but residents help with various chores in the kitchen.

Chores are paid work assignments for which wages are determined by assessing how much time it would take an average worker to complete a task and the average per-hour wage paid for such work. Five hours per day (with weekends off) of noncompensated work, however, is considered part of the resident's responsibility to the community.

FIGURE 3. Resident composition, 1983–1984

Resident population as of 9/1/83	31	(11 women, 20 men)
Admissions during 1983–84	44	(15 women, 29 men)
Resident population as of 9/1/84	22	(6 women, 16 men)
Total residents during 1983–84	69	(24 women, 45 men)
Left during the year	47	(18 women, 29 men)

Two of the forty-four admissions were people who came, left, returned, and left again in the same year; nine others had been here during a previous year.

The following statistics refer only to the 47 residents who left.

	1983–84		Previous five years	
	Actual no.	%	Average no.	Average %
Age				
Teens	4	9	5	10
20s	33	70	32	68
30s	6	13	8	17
40s	3	6	1	3
50s+	1	2	1	2
Average age	25.9		26.0	
Length of Stay				
Under 1 month	5	10	8.6	18
1–3 months	12	26	9.4	20
3–6 months	13	28	9.4	20
6–12 months	9	19	10.8	23
Over one year	8	17	8.8	19
Average length of stay	6.8 months		7.1 months	

1985 Status of residents who left in 1983–84

2 residing at the ranch again
6 living in halfway houses
2 in hospital
3 living in their own apartments
2 living in their own apartments, working or volunteering, and part of the SLR aftercare program
1 living in her own apartment and volunteering
2 living at home and working
9 living in their own apartments and working
3 away at school
1 living in a halfway house and going to school
10 living at home
1 deceased
5 unknown

Source: Spring Lake Ranch annual report.

152

Physically, Spring Lake Ranch is surprising to anyone who has spent time working or doing research in a mental hospital, particularly one with the modern facilities of Sheppard-Pratt. The isolation is striking: to reach the ranch requires a two-mile drive up a rather steep dirt road; it is at least an hour's walk to the nearest village, Cuttingsville, and it is possible to wander for hours in the woods without coming into contact with civilization. Everything about the ranch is self-sufficient: water supply, sewage system, food production, governance. There are none of the trappings of hospitalization: no intercoms, heavy metal doors, keys and locks, nursing stations, shifts—or hopelessness. Nor is the professionalization characteristic of mental hospitals present in relations between staff. There is a marked absence of hierarchy, members being distinguished only in terms of how much time they have spent at the ranch: some people have been there for at least ten years, others less than two.

Staff divisions are nonbureaucratic. Senior staff, by virtue of sheer longevity, have developed a certain expertise in farming, organizing, and administering scarce resources; they assume responsibility as necessity dictates. The director and admissions counselor deal with admissions and handle correspondence with the outside world (with professionals referring residents to the ranch, prospective residents, families, therapists, and so on). The other senior staff organize and plan the farming regimen and tend to its physical survival and maintenance. Leadership is collective; no single person, not even the director, makes decisions unilaterally or claims anything like a bureaucratic prerogative. Senior staff are not gurus, spiritual leaders, or anything of that sort; if anything, there is a noticeable effort to be as nonimposing as possible.

Junior staff are generally former college students who for the most part come to the ranch because of dedication to what it represents. Primarily in their early twenties, they reflect an idealism and commitment to participatory action *and* democracy; they enjoy working outdoors and see their relation to the residents as that of counselor, friend, and listener. Occasionally, students from local colleges will spend a month or two or an entire summer as staff interns. Since salaries for junior staff range from $75 to $100 per week (plus room and board), their connection with the ranch clearly has nothing to do with material incentive.

With the exception of one nurse, no health professionals (therapists, psychiatrists, social workers) live at Spring Lake or involve themselves in its daily activity. The ranch does hire a consulting psychiatrist, but his major responsibility is monitoring medication levels; he administers no psychotherapy. Occasionally the ranch recommends that a resident see a local psychologist in Rutland, but no formal, ongoing psychotherapy is part of the Spring Lake regimen. Though it is not often stated, the fact clearly emerges that neither senior nor junior staff see the therapeutic purposes of Spring Lake Ranch through the lens of professional caretakers. Authority—or, in Rousseau's terms, sovereignty—is shared, and lacking bureaucratic structuralization, the ranch's administrative functions appear to be fluid and adaptive. The split between administrative and clinical staff so characteristic of hospitals, the competition among professional departments, simply does not exist. Therefore, a huge source of potential political conflict disappears. The disagreements that do arise center primarily on issues of implementation: which area of the farm needs tending, the nature of fund raising, the assessment of residents' progress, the distribution of work. Power as a matter of defending an entrenched interest (at the expense of another perceived threat within the same institution) possesses no function or arena at Spring Lake Ranch. The sovereignty is, in Rousseau's terms, indivisible; it is not split into spheres of private advantage.

Because of the close relations between those who administer and those who work (with one or two exceptions, the same people do both), there is no separate bureaucratic *interest*. If anything, the ranch is organized as a natural bureaucracy where tasks are accomplished because they have to be done, not because a prescribed function or role is assigned to any particular person. Certain individuals are responsible for various sectors of the ranch's operation: livestock, garden, farm maintenance, the admission of residents and provision for their living arrangements. Yet no one appears to order anyone to do anything; each staff person knows the extent and scope of his or her responsibilities; each sets up work crews and responds to specific seasonal needs. Decisions as to what to do on a given day, where to devote effort and time, derive from collaboration and discussion among both residents and staff. To administer the ranch is to live and work on it, not to be separate from the day-to-day activities but to be involved in all aspects of the total life environment. Administration, then, is not a matter of enforcing will or imposing dominion; it is an effort to mobilize action on behalf of what the community projects as its general and common purposes.

Both junior and senior staff and their families eat with the residents; the children obviously enjoy themselves, and each has a favorite group of residents. Furthermore, the extent to which staff's and residents' lives intermingle and intrude on one another is remarkable. While this occasionally causes some friction and frustration, it also suggests a nonjudgmental acceptance of the residents' internal reality which would be difficult to find elsewhere. Integration as a community occurs at several different levels: living arrangements, common meals, shared decision-making processes, the public quality of participation, the social relations that govern production and work, the intergencrational fluidity of shared experience. It is hard to imagine a therapeutic environment more at odds with the assumptions that govern life in the traditional mental hospital.

The distinguishing structural feature of Spring Lake Ranch is the work crew. It represents the ranch's governing assumptions and in the view of staff constitutes Spring Lake's distinctive contribution to the idea of rehabilitation and therapy. Further, staff argue that without the resident's participation in work crews, the ranch's per diem cost ($60) would be considerably higher. While chores produce an opportunity to make a little extra spending money or to help defray per diem costs, it is clear that the chore bears no relation to the kinds of social assumptions that govern participation in work crews. To be on a work crew at the ranch is not only to labor; it is to gain an experience of working in common, of sharing productive labor that returns benefits to the entire community.

Not only does work narrow the operational scope of delusional knowledge and frames of reference; it also enhances the self's potential in consensual reality. It encourages the *res publica* and builds the associational roots of being. Work at Spring Lake is not performed for the purpose of receiving a wage; it is not compensation that is sought after but cooperation. The structure of work, then, depends not on the enticement of wages but on a collective awareness that work lies at the center of both the enhancement of being and the survival of the community. No resident therefore understands work as "working for a boss" (even though residents frequently complain that work crew leaders act too much like bosses). Rather, the prevailing ideology encourages the view that each person works for the benefit of the community, that each worker should see his or her task as contributory to the welfare of the whole, the group.

This outlook was often stated to me in the following terms: in the factory you work for the bosses and wages; the purpose of work is to leave work (eventually) and get as far away from the workplace as possible. But work at Spring Lake Ranch is not a dehumanized process to gain wages. It is rather a commitment to improve the quality of life in the place where you live, the place that contains and houses the self's inner and outer being. It is as if the workplace becomes home, and you never really leave it. It encloses all aspects of life so that there is no distinction between the world where your hands produce and the world where you live.

Let me try to put it another way: working at the ranch, it is argued, extends beyond the activity of the labor itself. It is more than, say, just dumping a crateful of apples into the cider vat, or tending to their fermentation and soaking, or repairing a chicken coop. It is as if in every action taken, every work crew engaged, the resident participates in and affirms the connection with the people who have been through Spring Lake Ranch or may eventually find their way there. The following paraphrase summarizes various expressions of this feeling, this sense of a continuity with the past and an obligation to the future:

> I feel like my work extends through time; that it connects me to a history I am active in creating and producing. So when I work, I not only labor, I construct, through the very activity of my labor, my identity. What I expend out of myself, I put back in. It is not stupid labor, make-work; I am not oppressed or patronized. It is just the opposite: by working I expand the shared reality of this place and I contribute to its future well-being.

Work at the ranch, then, is both an act of production and an activity of recovery, a rebuilding of the humanness inside the self and an ongoing transformation in identity. For the resident who has struggled with delusion, for example, to acquire serious doubts about his "animal nature" and to wonder if in fact he might be a human being would in any context be an overwhelming transformation in identity (and self-knowledge). But to have that question and possibility (of being human) arrived at through the action *and* speech of a social relation involving productivity becomes, in the environment of Spring Lake Ranch, a therapeutic event.

Staff members are sensitive to the charge of exploitation. When I suggested that labor at the ranch appeared to have a non-alienated quality, to embody what Marx (1964) called "species" imperatives (work as a collective expression of the community's need), one staff person raised the question of remuneration and wondered whether in fact there was an exploitative dimension to the system of unpaid work crews. Yet work crews are not treated like capital; their labor is not stored up as part of a complex scheme for the enrichment of the few, nor is the welfare of the individual ignored or neglected. Most important, the worker is not regarded or treated as a thing, as a calculation designed to increase the profit of those who own or possess. What that worker produces as surplus finds its way back to the welfare of the ranch; it is wealth used to benefit the community. One could, then, justifiably argue that labor on the work crews possesses a true non-alienated quality. It is not the kind of work or accumulation that Rousseau saw as increasing privatization and separation, the work of egoism and self-interest, the appropriation and disregard of the other.

Further, from the perspective of many residents, it would be extremely difficult to see in their labor any exploitative dimension. As Annie puts it: "What I get back in terms of self-respect is worth at least fifty dollars an hour." For Liz, it is "the first time in my life I have known work to be part of who I am. To see that and to finally understand what that connection means suggests to me that I'm not being exploited by the ranch. The ranch's life fills *my* life; and the work crews open you up and allow you some glimpse outside your shell, your misery."

Let me approach what labor means at the ranch from a somewhat more theoretical perspective. Hannah Arendt (1958: 125) writes: "Labor, to be sure, also produces for the end of consumption, but since this end, the thing to be consumed, lacks the worldly permanence of a piece of work, the end of the process is not determined by the end product, but rather by the exhaustion of labor power, while the products themselves, on the other hand, immediately become means again, means of subsistence and reproduction of labor power." She speaks of "the compulsory repetition inherent in laboring, where one must eat in order to labor and must labor in order to eat." Yet at Spring Lake, what motivates labor (at least in principle) is not its power to create consumption, to exhaust itself, but what it signifies about the integrity of the ranch itself. Labor is not a "means of subsistence and reproduction of labor power" but an activity that more closely resembles what Arendt implies about action in a public space. The motivation is not the end so much as the activity of *doing*, the being together, in both speech *and* deed. At the ranch that "action in public" revolves around the work crews, plus meetings scattered throughout the day.

It is important to understand what labor means in this context. It is not laboring for wages or laboring for a specific end in a cycle of consumption—although consumption is part of it, since goods are produced and consumed. It is rather more like what Arendt (1958: 142) implies about an existence in public. For example, she speaks of a "togetherness" that is lost to the worker "while actively engaged in production"; she distinguishes "laboring" from the older tradition of craftsmanship, particularly the isolation of the craftsman producing an end, a product, a durability: "Only when he stops working and his product is finished, can he abandon his isolation." Clearly, what goes on at Spring Lake is not work in Arendt's sense of *homo faber;* it is not craftsmanship, with fine pieces being carved or nature transformed into durable and lasting things. Nor is it the activity of production, that endlessly repeating modern cycle of consumption, annihilation, and activity that leads nowhere, that depends so much on machines. It is, then, more like what Arendt calls "the specifically political forms of being together with others, acting in concert and speaking with each other." It is that sense of relationship and action that describes labor at the ranch. Laboring is not for the purpose of establishing an "exchange market," the "last meeting place which is at least connected with the activity of *homo faber*," the marketplace. Nor does Spring Lake resemble the *agora,* since the residents do not produce only to sell—although, again, selling what is produced is part of the activity. But the production of what is to be sold is not for the *end* of selling or exchanging; rather, the residents produce and act to affirm a much broader principle: labor frames the ranch's *public space* and its *public life*. What the ranch represents is less a laboring community than what might be called a *political* community, one whose primary method involves an organization of labor which lacks the traditional attributes historically connected with laboring for wages, laboring for consumption.

Work and Psychotherapy: The Divisiveness of the "Private"

Psychotherapy—that is, regular visits with a professional psychotherapist—has no place at Spring Lake Ranch; the consulting psychiatrist prescribes medications, nothing else. It would be wrong, however, to assume that discussion of emotional conflict is discouraged. Quite the contrary: staff continually encourage residents to talk about their feelings. The bias against psychotherapy comes not from a refusal to deal with the inner world but from the belief that psychotherapy reinforces the self's preoccupation with the private and therefore diminishes interest in what is public, common, and general *to the community*. I present the ranch's position not because I entirely agree with it (in many ways it is too limited and too hostile to psychotherapy) but because it represents, in the context of what staff members see as divisive tendencies in the therapeutic relation, the same criticism of the private or the private will that Rousseau constructs in *The Social Contract*. What creates certain parallels in the two arguments is the belief that the realm of privacy turns attention away from the *res publica*, from the sovereignty of the public self, from activity that represents the general will. Both Rousseau and Spring Lake believe that intrusions into the community's pattern of sovereignty not only threaten the collective's internal coherence but also bring to bear entropic dynamics that endanger "public enlightenment." Those at the ranch feel that the professional listener draws attention away from the shared reality of work crews and other efforts to establish a sense of communal identity.

While it is understood that residents will express their feelings, staff believe their function or response as listeners develops within the context of the ranch's shared reality. Listening to the resident involves a refusal to separate the function of listening from the activity of doing. It provides a context that allows the private expression of pain to develop within mutually supportive and public environments. That is a kind of listening or hearing considerably different from the relation established within a therapeutic transference. In the one-to-one transference (where the therapist receives and mirrors feelings—projections—that derive from critical persons in the self's past), a single human being occupies the self's primal attention and becomes the central pivot in untangling confusion and despair. At Spring Lake Ranch the emotion or passion invested in the therapeutic transference is projected into and onto the community. The will of the community replaces the gaze of the therapeutic Other. It is almost as if the community becomes the mirror through which the self begins to see pathways into *and* out of its unhappiness and incapacity.

Feelings therefore find themselves refracted not in the gaze of a single, solitary other, in the privacy of a hidden relation, but against the backdrop of a public consciousness, a community that replaces the *functions* of the therapeutic transference. This replacement or displacement makes a difference in the way language is understood and how staff conceptualize their place in the residents' internal preoccupations. To the criticism that the self's internal object relations may have a great deal to do with how it perceives and acts with others, Spring Lake staff might respond somewhat as follows:

Even though the inner world is important and affects perception and feeling, it is also possible to restore a sense of dignity and self-worth through a listening that focuses on shared experience. For most of the residents who come to the ranch, what has been left out of their experience is the belief that they can find it in themselves to assert their humanity through efforts that involve other human beings. That's what we teach here; that actions need not be a continuing series of failures, that human life survives in a social world, that work lies at the core of recovering self-esteem and a belief in one's own efficacy, that there's a limitation to the idea that one can be treated with any "technique" into a sense of health. To restore wholeness to the human being whose life has been plagued by misunderstanding, whose awareness periodically reflects the terrifying consequences of fragmentation and regression, requires a sensitivity to the self's public needs.

The emphasis on the *res publica* as an experience that attempts to break through a resident's self-conception as a patient, or as hopeless or ineffective (feeling passive or dead) guides the ranch's philosophy. Further, several residents observed that secrets shared in the past only with their therapists would spontaneously come up among members of a work crew, or in review meetings, or at late-night sessions with the house counselor or other residents, or during a walk through the woods with a friend. At times, there appeared in resident observations to be a kind of continuum between the public and private; private feelings would often find their way to the surface as a consequence of some sort of work in common. The very lack of formalism, including techniques of behavior modification, facilitated residents' openness, making it easier for them to discuss what was on their minds. *Not* to receive a chip or a cigarette or some other token for doing something—common practice in mental hospitals—residents found to be a welcome relief; to do was not a matter of reward or sanction but an extension of the resident's sense of obligation and responsibility to the whole, the community.

Spring Lake's critique of psychotherapy is not premised on its lack of usefulness or importance. Rather, in the context of an attempt to offer a therapy that focuses on the public self, on citizenship, on the integration of work with a sense of being human, psychotherapy constitutes a competing and counterproductive force. The following reconstruction from extended dialogue with staff sets forth what I found to be Spring Lake's point of view.

In psychotherapy so many patients take on the role of patienthood; they become their sickness and tend to identify with it. And in identifying with it, they become part of the system that sustains it. It is comforting to be a patient, to be acted upon, to be treated and nurtured by a number of different individuals. It is comforting because patients no longer have to think about broader responsibilities that eventually may hit them head on and because passivity responds to a deeply felt need to be held. It may even be necessary for them to be passive to keep themselves from exploding in rage; their silence may be part of massive defenses built against intolerable and guilt-ridden rage. It's difficult to know. What is clear, however, is the presence of patienthood and an identification with sickness rather than health. For whatever reason, the patient becomes victim-prisoner, an implicit inferior, and projects onto professionals qualities of superiority, intelligence, wisdom, and benevolence and the power to banish pain.

But in reality it does not work that way; and on a deep level the patient knows that patienthood is a role that, if not shed by the time he or she leaves the hospital, will bring all sorts of pain in the outside world. Passivity is not the way to survive in modern society. It leads to exploitation and domination. Yet passivity is subtly enforced even in the best of mental hospitals. Nor is it in anybody's interest that the role of passivity and patienthood be shed. Staff need the role to confirm their own reality. Patients need it to validate their self-conception as sick, debilitated, and tainted. What is even more important, when patients take on that role, they lose their capacity to attach to a more human conception of who they are. Being evil, debilitated, inferior, sick, diseased, tainted, it is easier for them to maintain links to their own inner worlds of delusion or identification with animals or belief in supernatural beings.

In the psychiatric hospital the primary energy lies for the most part with the psychotherapist. Therapy is the space where desire, feeling, and need are cultivated and explored. It stands to reason that this space constitutes for the patient the most passionate relationship established during hospitalization; it has the most emotion, negative and positive, attached to it. Connection to the psychotherapist, then, means a commitment to and an attachment with the privacy of psychotherapy and the exclusivity of that relationship. While at times such exclusiveness may be necessary, there are certain costs or trade-offs. For example, in the hospital the therapeutic relationship is jealously guarded; at Spring Lake Ranch, however, the communal relationship is the central one. The consequences of this shift in focus are significant. First, the passion that the patient directed toward the therapist is at Spring Lake Ranch projected outward toward the community; the individual's relation, therefore, with the group, the "whole," is going to be considerably different in an environment where psychotherapy is absent. Priorities obviously will shift; passion and feeling will have as their objects representations in the community, not in the privacy of the therapist's office.

The consequences of shifting passion from the exclusivity of the therapeutic relation to the commonality of general purposes is fundamental and basic. Instead of trust directed at a single person, trust is placed in a series of actions: shearing sheep, hauling wood, picking apples, keeping the vegetable garden weeded, collecting maple syrup, tending the chickens, and so on. This kind of activity takes the self out of its isolation and psychological hibernation: it gives the entire range of human feeling and desire a context and place.

The privacy of the psychotherapeutic relation shifts the focus away from interpersonal relations organized around the basic human need for association. There is something unreal and abstract about psychotherapy cut off from any integration into a larger community. It is too enclosed and closed off, too exclusive to be adapted to the self's need for a public life.

We are not arguing that psychotherapy is useless or irrelevant or trivial; quite the contrary. But for individuals as disturbed as those who come to Spring Lake Ranch, psychotherapy works against their interests as persons. It becomes a hindrance to directing passion, energy, and trust toward the collaborative externalities of community.

After patients leave hospitals, after residents leave here, they will have to find their way to a productive environment if they are to survive as active, sentient members of a community. But if they have no experience of that integration, or if what experience they have remains shattered by their own emotional immobilization, then life will be disastrous. Learning and adaptation often happen through concrete actions; we discover ways of taking measure of our self-esteem and translating that measure into productivity. A good art therapist for instance, draws out the patient, takes the figures and representations, and turns them into insight. It is a beneficial and useful process; it often clarifies and leads to deeper understanding. But it is not the same as receiving payment for painting a house or for slapping rustproofing onto a half-track to keep it from corroding. Both forms of activity involve paint and the action of painting, but the relation of the action to the self is radically different. In one case painting leads to understanding in a very private discourse, but in the other it leads to self-respect in a public environment where action requires collaboration with others. Both are necessary; unfortunately, both are too often neglected by society.

In the outside world, individuals will be asked to work; they will be judged—praised or condemned—according to the nature of their work. And if their essential and innate productivity (we believe all individuals to be innately productive, even the most disabled amongst us) is not cultivated, their spirits, selves, whatever you call them, will wither and die. We offer a kind of asylum at Spring Lake Ranch, the time and freedom to come to be aware of oneself not only as a citizen but as a human being containing an innate potential for production. If that recognition does not hold, whether it is learned here or anywhere else, it is unlikely that the self will have much success or gratification in the outside world.

As long as patient and therapist relate through the common bond of sickness, it is sickness that defines the relation; the patient often uses a model of sickness to define health. At every opportunity we question that model; we try to demonstrate to residents that work, productivity, and self-esteem are intimately tied together; that work requires the expenditure of energy; that it is often frustrating but that much in being human involves internalizing collaborative experience as one's own. As a patient you may have to make your own bed, but you certainly don't have to clean your own toilets or milk the cows that contribute to your breakfast. It's not just that we farm here; rather, the collective effort involved in farming possesses its own therapeutic consequences.

The mental hospital comes from a specific social environment and value system. It is organized like political systems in the surrounding society and reflects what that society represents: hierarchy, jealousy, program competition, struggle over power, jurisdiction, dominion. At Spring Lake Ranch, however, organization has little in common with the economic and political drives of the larger institutions. In the hospital, sickness ties the institution's power system together, gives it identity and definition. Here, not sickness but the persistent assumption of an innate health, *borne out of concrete acts,* gives us a sense of pride and fulfillment, direction and substance. [I read this as a Rousseauian position.] We try hard not to be put in the role of therapist or surrogate doctor or nurse; we constantly impress on younger staff the need not only to resist such definitions but to consciously shy away from the tendency to act as powerful and knowledgeable figures in relation to impotent and powerless residents. Doing so is difficult, because residents often want us to act like mental health professionals. In many instances they need the security of that relation; it reinforces their essential core belief of sickness that allows them to avoid the prospect of interdependence (and all its fears). We often find ourselves, consciously or unconsciously, put in the place of being powerful by the residents or by our own needs. It is something we're always looking at, and we keep it open as a dialogue. We try to avoid the closed circle of definition that sickness imposes. And by maintaining the community's openness, we also keep fluid the relation between staff and resident.

It may seem that life in a mental hospital possesses extraordinarily public qualities, but this may not always be the case. The appearance in some institutions is certainly one of publicness: the expression of feelings to therapists and nurses; the emphasis on activities and therapies. However, the effect may be to reinforce privacy. There is little collaborative effort beyond mutual encouragement to express whatever happens to be on one's mind. Now that obviously has beneficial aspects, and we are not saying that the therapeutic interest of the individual in the hospital is being ignored. What is being neglected is the interest of the self's productive relations, the creation of any sense of public context that both holds and metabolizes disturbing feeling. What individuals express in the various hospital milieus (ward meetings, group and activities therapies) is generally put to work in the service of the *individual* ego. After all, the paradigm of treatment focuses on the individual; mental wards often have the appearance of being aggregations of isolated individuals gathered together because of necessity, tolerating each other because they must.

The hospital, then, is not an environment in which shared experience takes precedence over the tendency to withdraw inward, even though that may be the objective of milieu or treatment programs; and patients have very little interest in working with one another. More often than not, the Other is used as a medium or instrument to clarify the self's inner experience. It may even be that the net effect of therapies in mental hospitals is to reinforce separation and isolation, since there is so little opportunity for individuals to create and produce collectively, to combat loneliness and despair through common action. The patient often perceives "being" as a series of fragmented experiences dominated by a range of professionals who administer treatment (everyone from the nurse to the psychotherapist to the vocational therapist to the dance therapist, and so on).

Further, each therapy or interest has prerogatives to maintain and advance; each consistently moves around other competing centers of power and jealousy—all of which is bound to affect the patient and treatment. Even though such therapies and therapists may be empathic, nurturing, and sensitive to patient needs, the administering of therapy is not sufficient to overcome the political context and relations that surround it. Within the hospital the upshot is to keep the patient in the role of subject and not citizen. But how can any person fully assume the responsibilities of human association without effectively participating in a citizenship that engages the public dimensions of external reality? If the place where treatment is happening is not regarded by those who work there as a community, it is not likely that an education in self-governance will be even a desired outcome.

It is true that an institution—particularly a mental hospital, which is preoccupied with the struggle for power, with gaining advantage and furthering private or specialized interests—is not likely to represent itself (to use Rousseau's term) as a sovereignty. Nor are its purposes likely to be perceived in terms of a general will. The hospital is an agent of society; its membership shares similar values; and no matter how benign the institution, there remains a Hobbesian component within the hierarchical structure. Still, certain units or wards, mini-communities within the larger institutional aggregation (for example, at Sheppard-Pratt), do make efforts to embody and emphasize community interest over private, isolated wills. Occasionally an individual patient such as Julia or David will focus the unit's efforts, or provoke special concerns that put interdepartmental competition in the background (or on the back burner). And of course, many patients *do* benefit from treatment. In this respect, I think Spring Lake's critique of therapy is somewhat harsh and perhaps overly ideological. In addition, the ranch does borrow from technological psychiatry in its reliance on a psychiatrist to monitor medication levels and to adapt and change prescriptions. But the issue here is not the extent to which institutional considerations enter into treatment but the atmosphere, the environment, in which the self has the opportunity to explore not only its private world but its world-in-common, its being with others.

10 /

Boundaries of a Public Selfhood: Labor and Work

At Spring Lake Ranch I spent a day on the work crews. As a member of the morning crew, which mulched the asparagus field and weeded a blueberry patch, I worked with two residents and the staff person who coordinated the activity. In the afternoon a rather large work crew was assembled to search for apples; a number of staff and residents went on a long trek through the hillsides looking for unpicked apple trees.

Both residents on the morning crew had spent several years in and out of mental hospitals, and both at one time or another had been diagnosed as schizophrenic. During the work period and later, over lunch, I spoke with residents about the ranch, their views on it, what it had given them, what bothered them about the experience. While at times they complained about the work and its routine, they persistently returned to the themes of fellowship, a shared sense of accomplishment, and an improvement over the enforced isolation, separation, and inactivity of the mental hospital.

Louis, for example, who had been at the ranch for only a few months, spoke about his delusions: the CIA had been after him; he heard voices telling him to kill himself; he saw spaceships coming down to kidnap him and take him eighteen galaxies away from earth. At Spring Lake these delusions had gradually receded; their presence had become less imminent, less threatening.

167

I'm able to concentrate on working without hearing voices; for me that's a victory; and the work crews take the edge off my sense of pain. I'm not as frightened or terrified when I'm hauling hay or cutting wood pile. Before, I could hardly make it through a day without thinking I was going to be killed or massacred or torn apart by space rays. I hated to go outside because I thought spaceships hovered over the hospital waiting for me. Sometimes, late at night, I might hear voices, but if I'm frightened, I'll go downstairs and talk awhile with Bev [the house counselor].

The majority of residents had been at the ranch for relatively short periods of time. One exception was Annie, a forty-five-year-old woman from a wealthy West Coast family, whose own history read like something out of a Kerouac novel. Her connection with the ranch spanned fifteen years; as a result she had a fascinating perspective on what it created and gave through its work programs and on residents' attitudes toward the experience. I focus on Annie's observations not only because of the expansiveness of her analysis but because her own past and history seem to bear out Spring Lake's capacity to hold and contain entropic aspects of the self's inner life.

Annie: The Desire for Place

For Annie, Spring Lake Ranch had become a refuge, a haven from her self-destructiveness and her need to flee her own home and seek environments where she experienced herself as an absolute stranger, disconnected from daily life (for example, she lived by herself for a year in a small village in central Africa). Annie had no fixed, constant sense of reality, no grasp of a place where she should be; throughout her life, her voices would tell her what to do. The ranch however, gave her a sense of meaning in a social context; its very physical activity provided her with measures of her capacity and effectiveness; it also framed and defined her will to live and diminished her persistent confusion over who she was and how she should conceive her purposes in life. From what she told me, it appeared that when she was not at the ranch, from her early thirties on, she embarked on a number of projects distinguished by a need to annihilate herself.

I spent several hours speaking with Annie; I found her a woman of considerable insight, intelligence, and expressiveness who, I believe, managed to capture the feeling of Spring Lake Ranch as an asylum from the terrors of the world.

Annie divides Spring Lake Ranch residents into two types: those who see the ranch as giving something to them, who are willing to participate and take from the ranch through participation; and those who hate the ranch, who resist the work program and do everything they can to run from the ranch's imperatives. In Annie's view, selfishness ought to work in the interest of community; and by selfishness, she means engagement with the work program and the willingness to take from the community not as an act of greediness but as action essential to a common survival. Taking from the community means life, the willingness to live. From this perspective, selfishness, literally forcing oneself to take from what the ranch offers, constitutes not an action of separation but a striving toward unity, an effort at joining together and expanding the self's potential. The imperative to take, she argues, accompanies the action of giving (work, labor, participation in council meetings, and so on); the more one wishes to take, the more one ends up giving. But taking is not running away or isolating oneself; it is more like sharing. To take from others is to fill the self up; it is to feel replenished in public acts that bind individuals together.

Annie, then, understands selfishness as an activity of filling up with or taking and giving out or expending energy; the entire process involves conflict, struggle, and sometimes unhappiness and frustration. But she sees these feelings as essential to the ranch's identity as a community. The resident who refuses to take from the community ends up withdrawing from it, seeing in it a barrier to the cultivation of private interest. Such persons require the community to be endlessly supplying them; therefore, their taking is passive and represents a radical disruption in the ranch's system of reciprocity. The passive recipient of what the community offers inevitably feels alienated from it, because he or she has refused to participate in the taking and giving process. Such persons prefer the privacy of the internal world to the shared confusion of the ranch's various public spaces. Further, these persons only subsist at Spring Lake, and for Annie, merely to subsist suggests not only a passive relation to experience but ultimately a refusal of life itself. It is this refusal that provokes her hostility and disdain of residents who expect the ranch, in Annie's words, to "do for them."

The act of taking becomes not appropriation or greed but participation in a common sense of fulfillment and accomplishment.

> When the side of that barn is repaired or you have finished picking fifty pounds of apples, or the garden has been seeded, you have taken something inside yourself. It's obviously not tangible, but it's real. That experience, completing an action and knowing you have completed it, is yours; it is no one else's. You have therefore transformed a part of yourself, and you have brought what this place represents into you.

Taking creates community; it is not an act of destruction. It is the self's giving to the sovereignty.

Annie, in my conversations with her, repeatedly came back to the issue of work and participation. It was almost as if she were saying that residents who refuse work should be banished, even punished.

> There are people who come here who are always "slouching towards Bethlehem," lazy types waiting for salvation or rescue or a God to lift them from their misery. Their eyes lie "towards Bethlehem," but it's a mirage, a fantasy. If they blink they might see emptiness. These people sit at the end of the table; they don't join conversations. They are off by themselves, twiddling their thumbs, staring into space. It reminds me of what it was like in the mental hospital, with everyone sitting in corners, or on the edges of their bed, muttering or lost, a million miles away, not getting any better, and for a few of them, not even moving any distance from their rooms or the ward. It was frightening, and I sometimes see those stares here and it scares me, like ghosts stalking around. Slouching towards Bethlehem leads to nowhere; it takes you deeper into hell; it strangles, maybe even kills you after a while. Eventually I guess you become so marginal that you end up being like a fly spinning off the flywheel. You have control over nothing; everything that touches you hurts you. There really is no hope for individuals like that; they use the ranch as a way station in their passage to Hell.

To survive here, to really learn from the place, you have to open yourself up, or at least make the effort. It has to become a part of you, part of your being, your soul, your sense of self. Without that, you're bound to feel imposed upon, constrained, even violated. Look, if you join a church and decide not to obey its religion, it's a bit absurd, right? Why join? So, why do people come here who hate to work or who feel that it's beneath their dignity to stoop and clean up the cowshit or tend the septic tank? It's like they stumbled into the wrong place, signed the wrong papers, went to the wrong house. And you have to tell them, firmly, they've got the wrong address, and why don't they go down the block and take a left and keep on going. But maybe I see this place differently than most residents. For me, the ranch is home; it's inside me wherever I go.

Look, you're talking to somebody the professional community regarded as hopelessly incurable, with the exception of my therapist in Switzerland who at least held out some hope. I seem to have confounded psychiatrists, driven nurses on three continents to distraction, made mincemeat out of social workers. I have been certified, been dumped in back wards, languished in expensive sanitaria. I've seen it; I've been there in the pits with the most pathetic human beings you can imagine. I know what it's like, the end of the road, to have a mother who literally disowns you, who won't let you soil the carpets in her house. But it's the ranch that kept me alive, that reminds me over and over again that I'm a human being and I have a will. It settles me, gives me a sense of place.

You know what I really like about the ranch are the kids. Look at them—could you ever imagine the staff in a mental hospital allowing their kids to eat with patients? That should be a clue to our being human, since many of us here sometimes wonder. If kids eat with us and enjoy us, does that speak to our humanity? Would staff let their kids play and eat with dirty, disgusting, dangerous animals? It's probably very difficult for you to understand this, to know what it means to feel so outside the human community that your only friends are the animals, and you see your own reflection as a creature with no human features. But with kids around, we have proof that we're not lepers, animals, or creatures. Eating dinner next to a kid is something that normal human beings do all the time, but for us it's a revelation, a joy!

This view of community, however, does not go uncriticized. For example, one resident who had been at the ranch for about six months complained that it duplicates the mother-infant relation, keeping residents in a state of permanent symbiosis with a community that replaces mother and therefore diminishing and even absorbing their autonomy and independence. It was significant that Ed voiced these complaints on the day he was leaving. I asked him whether he had expressed these feelings to other residents or to staff; he said no, it was just an idea in his head, and he thought I might be interested. I related this conversation to Aaron (another resident), and his reaction was as follows:

> Ed misunderstood what the ranch was doing; he wanted to be tied into the group, but something about it frightened him, so he withdrew. Whatever the reason, Ed would not let the group help him; he refused to see his life in relation to others around here, and he kept to himself. I suspect the fear of becoming too close was Ed's problem and not anything specific in his day-to-day routine. Besides, Ed never fully understood what the ranch was all about.
>
> Look at Billy. You were with us this afternoon; you saw what he accomplished, how he picked those apples and kept up with us. Sure, he wandered off every once in a while or sat looking at the trees and talking to himself. But for Billy, just to do what he did would have been impossible in a mental hospital. Look, you can go to a state hospital, like the one I was in, or any VA hospital, and see hundreds of Billies in the back wards, drooling, sitting around doing nothing, pumped full of medication every four hours, slobbering over their food. Where is Billy better off, in the mountains of Vermont or in some stinking locked ward? In my view, that question shouldn't even have to be asked; but critics like Ed don't want to see; they have a fantasy about independence, so they back away from what they might give to the ranch. They run from it and then accuse everyone of being an infant. That's ridiculous; just the opposite happens. We learn how to be independent and interdependent at the same time. I would much rather have Billy driving around in the back of that pickup truck, with his hands dirty, than see him prostrate on a couch in some hellhole of a hospital.

It was difficult for me to disagree with Aaron's position. During the brief afternoon I spent with him, I was struck by how useful Billy made himself, how a person so obviously schizophrenic could adapt and work with others. Billy was without question better off on work crews in the isolation of Vermont than in a hospital back ward.

But the peculiar Rousseauian quality of Spring Lake Ranch also allowed Billy a measure of liberty, an interdependence not only containing his madness but demonstrating to him a glimmer of hope. Billy was twenty years old, a young man who had been in and out of several mental hospitals; his diagnosis was "schizophrenic, chronic, undifferentiated." Yet though he had been at the ranch for less than two weeks, he managed to adhere to the regimen, including regular participation in work crews. And though he never engaged anyone in direct, one-to-one conversation, he made his presence known: at every chance he could maneuver, he sat at the piano in the main commons area and played until he was told it was time to go. His playing was often chaotic and dissonant, but the piano constituted for Billy a kind of language, a connection with others. If speech was too threatening, perhaps the sounds made by his hands and emerging through an impersonal thing composed of wood and wires seemed safer and therefore tolerable *as a language*.

In the mental hospital, patients like Billy wander about (psychically and physically) in a kind of Rousseauian "natural independence," a state of mind and action radically cut off from others. The isolation manifests itself as a tremendous fear of intimacy or closeness, a dread of any collaborative activity, persistent delusional interpretations of reality, and a feeling of being cut off from identification with any historically embodied community. It is an existence that revolves around the lostness of an internal state of nature; the self, trapped by its own introjects, refuses the demands of human interaction. There is a peculiar and unsettling independence in schizophrenic patients. Voices, demons, hallucinations, delusions all keep consciousness preoccupied and busy. There is no real need to be *inter*dependent.

Further, like Rousseau's natural man, during the most autistic phase of the state of nature the schizophrenic appears to need no one and demonstrates an indifference to human association (like natural man, for example, wandering *by himself* haphazardly in the woods). It was preferable for Billy to exchange this kind of independence for the liberty and interdependence of a social contract that recognized and cultivated his human qualities, his potential for action with others. While he might not be as free to wander in his own internal nature, what he received was grounding in a reality committed to association. The social compact Billy established with Spring Lake Ranch brought him closer, or probably as close as he had ever been, to being an integral participant in an ongoing community.

Billy was never in any danger on work crews. Staff and residents kept an eye on him but never constrained or patronized him; if he wandered too far off, someone would simply go after him. It was gratifying, even moving, to see such an obviously tormented and fragmented human being laughing and running around in the woods, picking up apples, eating a few, filling up his bag, working with other men and women, and generally having a good time. There is a vast distance between the despair and resignation haunting the hospitalized schizophrenic and the images I witnessed on a Vermont hillside.

Persistently, in my conversations with her, Annie kept referring to the "silent pain" that she believed plagued all former mental patients and radically distinguished their pain and its intensity from what she understood as normal pain. Normal pain comes and goes but leaves you with vast painfree periods. Not so with silent pain: it is with you day and night, every moment. It encircles the self like a vise. It's like carrying around a broken arm, Annie said: "The pain never disappears; it's so intense that at times you have to run from it; nothing ever really heals; you feel as if everything inside you is always more or less broken, with the edges raw and exposed. Imagine your entire body, soul, spirit, like that broken arm." But, Annie continued:

> there is a real objective magic here. You feel it in the work crews, in walks up to the lake, in the mountains in the middle of winter, even in the silence. It's in the rocks and the history of the place. For many residents the ranch will be their last effort at making some sense out of their lives. If I were to tell you there is a spiritual meaning in cleaning up the barns or picking apples or hauling woods, you'd probably think I was crazy. But you have seen it; you've seen what it did for Billy; you've listened. It's not a

dramatic magic, rabbits jumping out of hats; the magic of the ranch is slow and subtle. It creeps up on you, and suddenly you see it; one morning when you stand in the cold and you look at those trees or you listen for the silence, that's when you begin to understand the magic and that's when the silent pain pulls away a bit. And for the first time in your life you're able to stand still and not have sheer hell pulling at your temples. It's quite a feeling; I don't know how else to describe it other than to speak of it as magic; at those times I'm out of myself, my own suffering, and my own sense of myself as an abysmal failure. For those moments, when that magic runs in and through you, you're free. You begin to sense what life is all about, and the silent pain disappears.

Try sitting all day in a hospital back ward, with people trying to slit their wrists or looking for the nearest piece of rope so they can hang themselves. Mental patients, when they want to kill themselves, are ingenious; they'll swallow perfume or mouthwash, eat poison, find the strangest places to strangle themselves. It's amazing how resourceful someone is who truly wants to kill himself. Yet you don't see that here; you don't see the suicidal impulses, the angry slashing; you don't see the silent pain as projects in physical mutilation. Silent pain eats away your soul; it takes your flesh and like a dull knife works its way in. That's torture; no matter how sympathetic the doctors or how caring the staff (and it's rare to find both), you're the only one in there, and silent pain drips through you like acid. All you can do is sit and stare and try to hope you won't be dead in the next few seconds. Or you try to avoid the grim images your mind ingeniously creates in its isolation and terror. I'll never go back to that, to those places. Even the most well-intentioned professionals can't protect you from silent pain, since this is the world where we crazy ones are truly sovereign. And even with all the information you give to your doctors, nurses, social workers, and mental health aides, they can never be there with you. It's an isolation that is indescribable. Silent pain isn't always king at Spring Lake Ranch. We fight it, with some humor, comradeship, and sympathy. We try to stay outside it, by trying to be a little bit free, by seeing what part of ourselves lies in the others around us, by working with our hands and producing something, by reminding ourselves that we are human.

Limitations on the General Will and Its Capacities

In this section I quote extensively from clinical languages, although I am not unaware of the forms in which a scientistic language may skew reality. To what extent are the psychiatric descriptions reliable? To what extent are they a summary of confusions and attributions that have plagued the patient throughout his or her life (or career) in and out of mental hospitals? It is obviously difficult to know. I have to assume a certain amount of descriptive accuracy in clinical evaluation. Residents I spoke with at Spring Lake Ranch exhibited states of mind (and being) that indicated serious dislocations in perception, feeling, the sense of time, reality, and relatedness. It is, then, a mistake to see in psychiatric language simply a case of labeling. It is also a mistake to read psychiatric evaluations as if their language contains indisputable truth based on the authority of a profession.

In my view, the usefulness of such language lies in the phenomenological description of a field of being from a specific point of view, in this case a psychiatric one. This is not to say that scientistic language supplants or more accurately describes states of mind and being than does narrative metaphor. In Ricoeur's (1977) terms, *imaginatio* and reason or science provide different pictures of experience that by its very nature is elusive and confounding. Another point of view at the ranch comes from entries in the residents' records by the many nonprofessional staff. What these often free-floating and spontaneous entries convey is a picture of emotional dislocation, selves struggling to locate boundaries and meaning, and often incapacitating and discouraging disturbances in relations with others. The entries from staff, while not couched in the same language as clinical psychiatric evaluations, nonetheless reveal similar pictures of persons in extreme emotional states overtaken by internal metaphors that remove consciousness from a historical and interpersonal world. What the records suggest is not so much selves distorted by a professional language (although that, at one time, may have been part of it) but human beings suffering from terrifying and debilitating inner perceptions.

Residents at Spring Lake frequently bring with them case histories that suggest poor prognoses. The ranch therefore finds itself housing persons whom the psychiatric world regards as chronic and basically untreatable. The histories of Rachel and Richard (persons suffering from both Phase 1 and Phase 2 delusions; see Chapter 8) are fairly typical of a significant proportion of residents. First, excerpts from Rachel's psychiatric review record:

Age 9: Learning difficulties, on the periphery of social group.

Age 14: Psychotherapy for declining academic performance, violent outbursts; beginning medication; leads to better performance in school.

Age 15: Ideas of reference and delusion that a character from a TV show actually comes to see her; two months later medications stopped; decompensation; admitted to mental hospital; for following year various medications tried, to no avail; overly psychotic, auditory hallucinations, paranoia, feels she may be thrown through window, suspicious, unable to concentrate.

From psychiatric evaluations during her hospitalization:

Therapeutic efforts focused on the patient's rageful outbursts, sexually provocative behavior, and difficulty structuring her time, all of which slowly responded to nursing intervention. She became more verbal in psychotherapy, was able to discuss her depression and suspiciousness and her awareness of the problems caused by her low frustration tolerance. . . . During this period the patient became grossly psychotic [when medications were reduced], again with auditory hallucinations mimicking those of another patient, paranoid tendencies, and on one occasion she put her arm through a glass window.

Rachel's psychiatric diagnosis on admission to the hospital was "schizophrenia, catatonic, subchronic with acute depression"; her diagnosis on discharge was "schizophrenia, residual, chronic." At age eighteen, Rachel came to Spring Lake with the classic symptoms of schizophrenia, a poor prognosis, and an inner world that inhibited her action in consensual reality. She appeared destined to lead the life of a chronic schizophrenic, falling in and out of psychosis. Traditional psychiatric interventions had for the most part failed.

The following excerpts from staff notes on Rachel's progress and integration in the life of the ranch were written by persons who dealt with Rachel on work crews, who supervised the house she lived in, who came in daily contact with her. They therefore provide a fairly accurate summary and description of her behavior. (I should add that these notes are open to residents; not only are they invited to read their own notes, but they are also free to make their own entries in the record—another example of the connection between the individual and the community.)

2/8: Rachel went skiing Friday and had a great time; she learned quickly and was a real trooper about trying new stuff. She even took a lesson even though she was nervous about it . . . has seemed happier, more cheerful recently.

4/19: Rachel was extremely paranoid, frightened she was going to be killed; refused her meds but later took them; wouldn't talk or eat a good part of the day.

5/15: Rachel came on the trip to ——. When we got there she was a bit upset because it didn't seem that anyone would take to her. She didn't think there would be anyone to hang with. . . . I went off to the horse farm with other folks. When I got back I found Rachel walking alone on the street. She was in really good spirits. *She'd spent the afternoon on her own* [my italics].

The fact that the ranch would even think of allowing Rachel to spend an afternoon on her own suggests a certain measure of integration. With her history, chronicity, and a diagnosis of schizophrenia, if this had been a day trip from a mental hospital, it is improbable that staff would even have taken her, let alone have allowed her to spend time by herself. Rachel's ability to be alone for one afternoon does not, of course, indicate full integration into a community, but it certainly suggests a measure of trust on both sides.

6/9: Rachel doing wonderfully with her diet. She has lost 18 lbs. She'll be going home this week for a week. She is looking forward to the time in ——. She is a bit down over her departure and the changes taking place around her.

7/16: Rachel very agitated last P.M.; anger and frustration regarding meds forcing her to remain out of the sun and to restrict her summer. Calmer this A.M. Went shopping in town, bummed by weight gain and difficulty in buying clothes . . . decided against ceasing thorazine today.

7/24: Rachel struggles with the ranch; at times she finds it the perfect place for her; at other times, she wants to "break from it" and return home. [In late July her parents visit, but Rachel] does not seem to have slipped back after her parents' visit. Thorazine has been reduced.

7/27: I spoke with Rachel the other night, and she's expressed fears of being vulnerable, possessive in friendships, and vaguely overpowered by authority figures. The arguments flowed easily under well-worn titles and labels as though she had spoken and thought of them often before. There was a pressing concern of hers, however, that is a problem with being antisocial. She is aware of her erratic and sporadic energy and would like to feel more in control of them rather than by them. She decided to make an effort to be more social, even though at times it is, obviously, not the easiest thing to do. She said she feels socially crippled at times because of not being able to "small talk."

Rachel survived and lived at the ranch in an environment where she experienced a certain degree of freedom and found herself contributing productively to shared, common purposes. By the end of her two years, not only was her medication level down from previous hospital levels; she also found herself able to sustain communal activity and the demands of work crews. For this former psychiatric patient, that must be considered a significant gain.

That Rachel was able to take the community of Spring Lake Ranch into herself is testimony to her own resiliency, intelligence, and willingness to struggle. But whatever demons dominate Rachel's internality, she found enough trust in the Spring Lake environment to attempt to deal with that confusion and pain through reliance on the community, by attempting to project the community as a therapeutic transference. If Rachel fails on the outside (and it is not at all clear that she will be able to adapt), it will not be because the ranch failed her or because she has lost what she internalized from the experience. Rather, failure would indicate that Rachel, like so many schizophrenics, has found the technocratic society impossible to deal with in instrumental terms. The world outside the ranch provides little in the way of asylum, and a person like Rachel, already beset by serious psychological difficulties, may be unable to sustain the regime of continued disappointments characteristic of a culture that overvalues certain skills to the exclusion of others. Nevertheless, the ranch gave Rachel an opportunity to refract her identity through a community, a way of "being" she had never known. The experience also appeared to show her that individuals can be trusted; that the self is capable of collaborative action; and that productivity as a human being engaged in work lies within her abilities and is a direct outgrowth of her energies.

Rachel's case demonstrates a hopeful outcome of community and work in facilitating integration and diminishing psychotic terror and immobility. Richard's case, on the other hand, sadly testifies that in some instances the self's public being, its capacity to work in common, lacks the tenacity to combat the power of delusion and the entropic pull of the self's internal reality. The following excerpt is from a psychiatric evaluation done two years prior to his admission to the ranch.

On examination [Richard] was severely retarded in the psychomotor areas, had suicidal ideation, and felt completely helpless and hopeless. He also withdraws himself into his room more frequently than usual and described his feeling as one of gloom. . . . He was found to have become more verbally paranoid, talked about hearing voices over the TV, and became more hostile to his parents. He also seemed to feel that his mother and his prayer group cast a spell on him. It was quite apparent that the patient presents a picture which either fulfills the criteria for a schizoid affective schizophrenia or a manic-depressive illness in a person with a paranoid personality.

Richard first stayed at Spring Lake for a few months in the spring of 1982, after which he returned home, but his condition failed to improve. His psychiatrist wrote to the ranch director:

Dr. —— and I agree that the present clinical picture is that of chronic schizophrenia. The only uncertain point is how long the condition has been going on, since the rather garbled history I have been able to assemble is much more suggestive of a series of depressions than of a schizophrenic process. However, the clinical picture at the moment is clearly schizophrenic in form. There are both auditory and visual hallucinations. Both seem to be reflections of thoughts or memories that are going through his mind. The voices are most often the voices of people in his immediate surroundings, such as his uncle or aunt. The "pictures" seem to be visual representations of memories of previous scenes which are

brought to his mind by some association. . . . He is certainly not dangerous enough that I can take charge of him as an involuntary patient. He
seems a very innocuous young man indeed. What frightens me is that his
condition may drag on and that he may skip from facility to facility without anyone ever being able to take total charge of what is going on. . . .
He seems at present to have the best relationship with yourselves, and I
hope that may be capitalized upon.

Richard returned for the second time to the ranch, and even though
he ultimately fought a losing battle with the introjects of his inner
world, an effort was undertaken by the staff to contain his fear and to
integrate his fragmented self with the larger community. The following
excerpts from the progress notes describing his second stay give some
indication of how difficult that became.

3/12: Richard arrived today. I spent the afternoon with Richard; I was
amazed to see the warm reactions that everyone had to seeing Rich
again. He seems glad to be back and was joking about now being
an "old resident" who has come back. He seems a little scared about
being here for four months—like that's a long time. But the more
we talked about what the ranch would be like in the summer, the
more enthusiastic he became. We didn't talk much about his goals
while here—but I would imagine that dealing with the voices will
be our major concern. He still believes that the voices are real
people in his head and laughed when he told me that his doctor
didn't believe him.

4/9: I've had several talks with Rich lately. . . . He is having a very
difficult time with voices and now visual pictures. He most definitely believes that people are intentionally speaking to him in his
head or creating pictures. The other day he said they were doing it
because they wanted to keep him, although I could never get the
logic of it straight.

4/23: Tonight Richard said he wanted to bring Joan [a resident] to grievance committee because she was talking to him in his head. I told
him that I didn't think it was appropriate or would help because I
didn't think it had anything to do with Joan. He said that if the staff
don't believe him, than he should leave. I told him to talk to Peter
[one of the senior staff] about it. Rich constantly thinks and speaks
of leaving. I think the ranch is a difficult place for him to be because
there are so many people to affect him.

4/24: I told Rich that he couldn't bring Joan to grievance committee because of voices. He didn't like it because he feels he should have the right to since he thinks she is doing something to him. . . . But he agreed not to.

5/8: Rich and I just had a long talk. He had made a list of when he heard people talking to him and when pictures came. Joan still figures prominently; sometimes he hears her voice, other times just hears her name. Once Ted [another resident] said "Joan" and then Rich saw a picture of Joan. From this he infers that we [residents and staff] also control the pictures. That's distressing to him. He doesn't seem set in this idea, though, as it didn't carry over into the rest of the conversation. Apparently a lot of the pictures are sexual in nature. That's why Rich finds them so objectionable. We talked a lot about fantasies and imagination, and Rich said he makes no distinction between pictures and fantasies. From this we talked about whether all people had "pictures" and if they were normal. Rich said he went through 22 years without them and was happier. Apparently some of the pictures [in his mind] are homosexual in nature. That bothered Rich and upset him some. We talked about it for a while, but I don't think I convinced him that it was normal.

Rich likes having women around as friends. Rich was relieved to hear that sex isn't a requirement for being part of the human race, but I get the feeling that he's more torn than he lets on. He admitted that the pictures [in his mind] make him more interested, but he doesn't want to be.

5/24: Rich came to talk to me this evening. Seeing pictures where he hurts others, extremely concerned about this. He's confident he won't actually do it but doesn't like the experience of picturing it. We talked about how nice he is, never expressing anger or frustration. Also, he's feeling more depressed and looks it, to me; at times his voice dropped so it was barely audible . . . hands shake some, too.

7/16: I have been quite bothered by the change I've seen in Rich over the past week to week and a half. Rich is withdrawn, quiet, closed, and seems to be experiencing more frequent, intense, or bothersome voices and pictures. He is now speaking of leaving mid-July. The voices seem to cover a wide range of people now [several residents and staff members are listed] . . . seem to hit most anyone. In review meeting of July 7, Rich was more open and frank about content of voices than ever before. We basically told Rich that there is reason to stay and work to do, but if he didn't think it [the ranch] and what it represents would work for him, then he should leave.

7/28: Rich continues to feel that the voices and pictures are put there by an outside force, probably the person or persons he hears or sees, but last week for the first time Rich said that he could understand that most people could not accept that explanation and would think it to be very strange indeed. I'll miss Rich when he leaves next week; he's been very pleasant to work with and around, and his desire to find answers has been inspirational.

Spring Lake's emphasis on collectivity and collaboration, on being-in-common—the basis of its public life—could not withstand the assaults of Richard's inner voices and demons. That he felt he had to leave suggests not that the ranch failed him but that the social structure out of which he came and his own psychopathology exerted a strong and ultimately successful counterpressure. Even though Richard showed signs of taking in, or internalizing, the ranch's productive environment, and even though he developed extensive friendships and relations, whatever ego resiliency he derived from those experiences proved ephemeral against the pull of the delusional voices and the knowledge that he would have to leave.

Possibly if Richard had had more time, if he had been encouraged to think of Spring Lake as his home, encouraged by his surrounding social and familial system, the outcome might have been different. For him as for Rachel, it will not be that the experience of the ranch dissipates; it will be that the external social and economic world decides whether or not such individuals can survive. In Richard's private world nameless people talk to him, but they do not speak out loud; he hears music when no one appears to be singing; he believes specific individuals live inside his head. What kind of place is there for people like Richard? What will society, his family, do with (or to) him? One thing is clear: Spring Lake Ranch provided Richard with at least some sense of place and belonging. It gave him a point of view and a set of images which, no matter where he is, he is unlikely to forget.

Spring Lake Ranch and Rousseau's Social Contract

Annie and Aaron spoke of themselves as if they were citizens of a polity. They regarded the collective, the community, with the same fervor that Rousseau (1950: 31) projected into the sovereignty: "Instead of a renunciation, they [the citizens] have made an advantageous exchange; instead of an uncertain and precarious way of living, they have got one that is better and more secure; instead of natural independence, they have got liberty; instead of the power to harm others [or in the case of the mental patient, to harm themselves], security for themselves." Citizens gain "a right which social union makes invincible."

Constant deliberation, discussion, meetings, activity, meal times: all clarify the meaning and nature of the general will. The ranch's purposes remain a matter of public debate; and Rousseau's argument (1950: 37) about the deliberations of the general will is reflected in similar assumptions governing generality at the ranch: "Of itself, the people wills always the good, but of itself it by no means always sees it. The general will is always in the right, but the judgment which guides it is not always enlightened. [In the context of the ranch, this involves decisions made on the basis of private interest and desire.] It [the people] must be got to see objects as they are, and sometimes as they ought to appear to it. It must be shown the good road it is in search of, secured from the seductive influences of individual wills." Voting, council representation, morning meetings, the right to bring grievances, forums allowing for the clash of particular wills are the instruments through which the general will expresses itself at Spring Lake. All such activities, including work crew, embody the ranch's public will and its daily transformations.

Admittedly, much of this is due to the community's size, its face-to-face relations; yet even within so microcosmic a representation of action and decision there lie assumptions that give this community the quality of a *res publica*. Debates in the public forums, in Rousseau's words (1950: 37) forge a "public enlightenment" that "leads to the union of understanding and will in the social body"; the community's will not only transcends individual wills but also transforms human nature by virtue of the individual's participation in what the community arrives at as general. And when one wills oneself into the community, the self's internal regime undergoes significant changes. Argument, debate, complaints, frustration, the experience of emotional pain all register in the community's public life, but the community returns to its individual members a sense of satisfaction in collaborative action which inevitably affects the self's hidden and private world. And with the work environment embedded in a *res publica*, internal emotional constellations find themselves connected with the affairs of the community.

Jacques Derrida (1977: 145) rightly points to the maternal function of nature in Rousseau's thought: "Thus presence, always natural, which for Rousseau more than for others means maternal, *ought to be* self sufficient. . . . Like Nature's love, 'there is no substitute for a mother's love,' says Emile." It is this maternal quality, what Winnicott terms "holding," that appears in Spring Lake's attitude toward the residents. It is not an idealized all-good or an all-bad mother that emerges in the maternal function. It is rather a synthesis of firmness and containment, holding and obligation to others, care and understanding together with an insistence on work and responsibility. Staff may, like a "bad" mother, occasionally show impatience, exasperation, and frustration toward residents. But it is expected that anger or frustration, whether in residents or staff, will be brought into the open and talked out. In this sense it is not a paternal model: dominion, domination, paternal fiat, and *rule* do not characterize the ranch's political matrix.

Consider Spring Lake Ranch to be in Rousseau's terms a kind of "state": "The first and most important deduction from the principles we have so far laid down is that the general will alone can direct the State according to the object for which it was instituted, i.e., the common good" (Rousseau 1950: 23). This phenomenon develops at Spring Lake; the common good, involving the survival of the ranch as a productive extension of its residents' energy, governs all decisions. These processes of decision (open review meetings, the council, the grievance committee, morning meetings) create a participatory environment in which the sense of what is right derives from decisions about what is *general*. That the general will always tends to be right governs action at the ranch, and a great deal of effort is put into making sure that "generality" represents the outcome of all activity maintaining production and survival. "It is," Rousseau argues, "solely on the basis of this common interest that every society should be governed." Commonality, therefore, takes precedence over the private. And what stands behind conceptions and practices of sovereignty at the ranch appears in commonality: the collectivity organizing itself around issues involving public dimensions of being. "I hold then that Sovereignty, being nothing less than the exercise of the General Will, can never be alienated." Spring Lake Ranch is not a place governed by competing centers of power; its people (residents and staff) share common purposes; they stand, in relation to each other, like Rousseau's collective being. Its purposes, therefore—its sovereignty—cannot be alienated without destroying the ranch's basic operating principles.

What represents Spring Lake Ranch is itself; it is the sovereign for staff and for residents. It is not an institution but a self-governing community maintaining a delicate balance between the needs of survival and the capacities of the residents. The pressure at the ranch is to move outward toward others, to participate in the common aims.

For Rousseau (1950: 23), sovereignty appears in the "exercise of the general will"; further, "the particular will tends, by its very nature, to partiality, while the general will tends to equality." This principle is embodied throughout Spring Lake Ranch's daily, practical activity: from the morning meeting and "reading" from the work book (the equality of work), to the residents' right to invite whomever they choose to their own review meetings (the equality of review), to the openness of staff reports (the equality of judgment), to the participation in grievance and council meetings (the equality of representation).

Never at Spring Lake Ranch did I hear complaints about unequal treatment, lack of rights, a sense of being inferior to staff. Since equality was never an issue, it appeared to be a working principle. Complaints were voiced about the pressure of the group will: the pressure to accept the work crews as a daily fact of life; the pressure to work to one's capacity; the pressure not to complain about working; the pressure to sign up occasionally for one of the paid chores; the pressure not to be too demanding. But all these pressures derived from the status of the general will, not from complaints about unequal treatment or rigid hierarchical definition of patient and doctor. Sovereignty at the ranch assures equality; whether in all instances that equality works to the private interests of everyone is not always clear. But then, at the ranch the private interest becomes secondary to the public imperative. What is resisted is the tendency to withdraw, to build private fortresses; to retreat into sleep rather than make morning meeting; to dwell on private psychological realities rather than confront the demands of work crew.

It should not be assumed that legitimate private complaints are overlooked; Spring Lake Ranch is not a marine boot camp. In deciding who will work where, efforts are made to take into account a resident's physical capacity and state of mind: obviously, someone with a bad back will not be put on wood haul; a resident undergoing a severe emotional reaction will not be asked to work. Further, the activity of a work crew never lasts beyond its scheduled two and a half hours. Nor is Spring Lake Ranch an outward bound experiment in wilderness living or a rigidly controlled work camp. It is, rather, a place where Rousseau's sovereignty defines what is general and right; and the group exercises psychological pressure to induce individuals who for so many years have lived in environments where the private was more important than the public to realize and internalize what the sovereignty projects as common.

When Annie commented on residents who sit at the end of the dining table, who act like "flies spinning off the flywheel," she represented the sovereignty; she was voicing what the sovereignty defines as the *general* will. It was not that Annie sought to force these individuals into action, although I believe she would regard that prospect as desirable and necessary to the resident's own psychic welfare. Rather, she hoped that residents who separated themselves from the community would become aware of the self-destructive aspects of their own isolation. In Rousseau's terms, to alienate oneself to the social compact is to find a measure of freedom; from Annie's perspective, to be alienated from that compact is to experience a despairing aloneness and solitude. There are times when residents at the ranch do reflect by themselves, when privacy is treasured and respected. But the kind of privacy that involves meditation and self-reflection is not withdrawal in favor of a partial interest; it is more like a moment of rest and peacefulness in the woods of Vermont, a noticeable if momentary solitude.

Consistent with Rousseau's philosophy is Spring Lake Ranch's insistence on resisting any imposition of illegitimate authority: that is, authority that does not derive from sovereignty. No leader imposes his or her will; senior staff coordinate, guide, and teach both junior staff and residents. The director of the ranch is one among equals; major decisions (involving finances, expansion, capital improvements, fund raising) are discussed collectively. Leadership is based on skill and function rather than on administrative prerogative or institutional power. "The moment a master exists," writes Rousseau (1950: 24), "there is no longer a sovereign, and from that moment the body politic has ceased to exist." Similarly with the ranch: Staff believe that the ranch would fail if it were organized according to a well-defined, hierarchy; that if it were to assume the trappings of a conventional power-oriented politics, its mission would be subverted and its sovereignty would collapse. I heard this expressed countless times; the absence of power relations was noticeable even to newly-arrived residents, who had great difficulty in figuring out the person in charge. What the resident comes to realize is that no one person but the "sovereignty" is "in charge." In this community, where office doors are left unlocked, it is the willingness to trust the sovereignty that maintains cohesiveness and collaboration.

Rousseau draws a distinction between the general will, which "is always right and tends to the public advantage," and the "deliberations of the people," which may be fallible and wrong. Further, we do not "always see what . . . our own good" is, and though "the people is never corrupted . . . it is often deceived" (1950: 26). It is true that occasionally decisions are made that are wrong (in Rousseauian terms, decisions or actions that contravene the general will), that work against the common interest. At Spring Lake, something may be decided in a public forum that works contrary to the interests of the ranch. For example, suppose a resident is having a particularly difficult time, and it is decided at a grievance committee to allow that resident to skip every other work crew. Such a decision may turn out to have been ill advised: it may lead to additional requests for such an arrangement; people may grumble about private arrangements and resent having to work while others lie in bed or lounge in the reading room beside the woodstove in the middle of the Vermont winter. Nevertheless, what is important, at least in Rousseauian terms, is that whatever decisions are made are ultimately reflected in the community's commitment to public and general purposes. If a decision undermines those purposes, then indeed the deliberations of the people may have been misconceived, and the community may be forced to act to rectify the mistake. Doing so may involve convening a meeting in which the resident involved discusses his or her feelings with other residents and staff. It may provoke informal conversations at meals, with questions being raised as to why that person feels it necessary to avoid work. To reach a sense of common interest, then, may require effort and struggle, may bring on resentment and feelings of being lied to or betrayed; yet at some point the interest of the whole will prevail over a decision that inadvertently supports the interests of the "private" and the "partial."

What Rousseau speaks of as the "will of all"—that is, the sum total of private wills—might be understood in the context of Spring Lake Ranch as Richard with his voices and pictures, Annie with her self-destructiveness and her need to flee and run away to alien environments, Rachel and her fragmented sense of what reality is and her confusion over her place in the social world. Each of these individual wills is really the private, internal self appearing as separation, delusion, and inner fragmentation. That these wills, often expressed in delusion, run up against the general or consensual purposes of the ranch is understandable; further, they exercise the same destructive impact that Rousseau sees in egoistic interests whose major commitment lies with self-aggrandizement and personal power and advantage. The assertion of private will for whatever reason, the withdrawal into private need, the force of egoism—no matter how it is expressed psychically or materially—endangers sovereignty. At Spring Lake the impulses behind privatization are not personal aggrandizement or material greed but primarily pressures inside the self that pull it away from the ranch's common aims. Privacy means succumbing to the voice of delusion, to one's own inner demons and conflicts.

It is in this respect that the "will of all," in Rousseau's words, is so dangerous to what the ranch represents as general and common. The "will of all" is a summation, the adding-up of private wills and private desires. Such wills drive the forces of separation, and because of their divisiveness these "wills" pull communities apart. The general will, however, may contradict the will of all because it represents only what is public and common. It is the true expression of what the community wills *as a community of free citizens*. Rousseau (1950: 26) writes: "There is often a great deal of difference between the will of all and the general will; the latter considers only the common interest, while the former takes private interest into account, and is no more than a sum of particular wills."

"It is therefore essential," says Rousseau, "if the general will is to be able to express itself, that there should be no partial society within the state" (1950: 27). It is this condition the ranch strives to attain: the "partial society" of the psychotherapeutic relation becomes a threat to day-to-day survival; the "partial society" of laziness induced by fractures in the ego's capacity to sustain action and relationship becomes a threat to collaborative effort; the "partial society" of wanting to be separate and alone undermines the capacity and ability of the group to provide containment and support.

It would not be understating the purposes of the ranch to suggest that much in its approach to the seriously disturbed human being reflects the spirit behind Rousseau's observation: "Every man being born free and his own master, no one, under any pretext whatsoever, can make any man subject without his consent. To decide that the son of a slave is born a slave is to decide that he is not born a man" (1950: 105). And Spring Lake Ranch's philosophy would agree with the following: "All institutions that set man in contradiction to himself are worthless" (1950: 134).

Take, for example, the factor of size in determining the structure of relationship (and the public) at Spring Lake. Derrida (1977: 137) writes that in Claude Lévi-Strauss's view of native communities in central Brazil, "the criterion of authenticity" appears in the "neighborliness" of these small communities where "everyone knows everyone else." Derrida sees as coming from Rousseau this conception of the "natural" community (a universe set apart from culture, particularly from writing) and of what community means as an extension of nature: "This model of a small community with a 'crystalline' structure, completely self-present, assembled in its own neighborhood, is undoubtedly Rousseauistic."[1] What Lévi-Strauss finds as the fluid and authentic processes of community among the Indians, then, possesses (in Derrida's view) a Rousseauian origin or significance. To discover authenticity and neighborliness in face-to-face encounters, in a public realm where speech encloses self, is to experience community from a perspective that echoes arguments in Rousseau's *Discourse on the Origin and Foundation of Inequality among Men* and *Essay on the Origin of Language*.

Derrida speaks of these Rousseauistic qualities as "self-presence, transparent proximity in the face-to-face of countenances, and the immediate range of the voice" (1977, 138). These qualities, I suggest, emerge persistently in the day-to-day life of Spring Lake Ranch: "self-presence" in the constant meetings and encounters between persons, the reality of participation being indistinguishable from the reality of self; "transparent proximity in the face-to-face of countenances" in the work crews, in discussions during meals and morning meetings, and in the immediacy of decision-making around the matters of the farm and its administration; "the immediate range of the voice" in the sense that speech and decision appear concurrently—that is, the governing of the ranch takes place in *public* spaces filled with speech, argument, and persuasion. Staff and residents are actively engaged in a field of speech; speech becomes the currency of governance; it defines citizenship.

Derrida (1977: 139) quotes from Rousseau's essay on language: "The subjects must be kept apart . . . that is the first maxim of modern politics." Rousseau in *The Social Contract* finds this maxim reprehensible: separation provokes corruption and venality and contributes to the disintegration of the civic virtue; it discourages citizenship and action; it encourages domination and tyranny; it pushes the polity toward a model of rulership based on paternal dominion. It manifests itself in the pursuit of private interest and in the fragmentation of what is general and common. The extent to which this Rousseauistic percept, the argument *against* separation, is embodied and realized at Spring Lake is remarkable: the greatest danger to the community, I heard repeatedly, comes from separation. The observation peppers Annie's commentary; it is a view of the community's process and significance constantly on the minds of staff. Separation is seen as the greatest threat; therefore, daily activity is organized according to the proposition that separation creates divisiveness and fosters privatization of will. If residents occasionally chafe at this incessant public scrutiny of action and decision, the great majority I talked to believed that the movement away from separation, the ranch's consistent effort to keep residents focused on *community,* brought considerable benefit. It increased self-esteem; it developed a sense of purpose and commonality; it diminished inner anguish and terror. In this sense, the public life of the ranch produced a therapeutic effect.

Finally, at Spring Lake Ranch what Rousseau calls a "civil religion" exercises a tremendous influence. It is built around work and constitutes the community's fundamental therapeutic orientation. Civil religion defines the nature of belief and purpose at the ranch. In Rousseau's words: "There is therefore a purely civil profession of faith of which the Sovereign should fix the articles, not exactly as religious dogmas, but as social sentiments without which a man cannot be a good citizen or a faithful subject. While it can compel no one to believe them, it can banish from the State whoever does not believe them—it can banish him, not for impiety, but as an anti-social being incapable of truly loving the laws and justice, and of sacrificing, at need, his life to his duty" (1950: 139).

Now while the civil religion at Spring Lake Ranch does not require the sacrifice of "life" for "duty," it still holds critical assumptions about work crews and their purposes. A resident who persistently refuses to work not only becomes an affront to the general will but violates the community's sense of justice. Banishment is not explicit, but the non-working resident soon comes to see that inactivity leads to a psychological and social banishment from the group; that it increases isolation, the obvious disapproval of peers, and the impatience of staff. If the civil religion is not internalized or accepted as the ranch's governing set of principles, it is humanly impossible for any resident to maintain connection with the sovereignty. Refusal of the civil religion, then, is tantamount to refusal of the community itself.

Yet this is not as harsh as it sounds; it involves no overt coercion or effort to persuade or induce the reluctant resident into some civil acknowledgment of the ranch's overriding principle. It is rather something of a sentiment and a recognition that for the resident who chooses both to listen to the sentiment and to act on it, there can be salutary and rewarding consequences. There is, then, no public enforcement of work; it is only that the resident who decides not to work will eventually leave the ranch, simply because the self has no emotional or spiritual place within it. It would be futile to remain, purposeless.

The civil religion of the ranch does not work against the interests of the self. If anything, collaboration is, in Rousseau's terms, a "profession of faith" whose ultimate objective is the restoration of the self, the recovery of a measure of self-respect and, through common endeavor, an awareness of what it means to be a sentient, alive, and productive individual within a community of human beings. Spring Lake Ranch not only restores community; it restores hope. It is not an exercise in force or any program other than the acknowledgment that if the self succeeds in attaining dignity, part of the reason will be its effectiveness in action-in-common.

11 /

The Politics of Exclusion
and the Concept of Place

I have been speaking about the importance of narrative, taking literally Lacan's observation (1978b: 1025) that "it is always at the juncture of speech . . . that the manifestation of desire is produced." I have attempted to show how language, the language of persons excluded by the society, produces a symbology that comments on such political concepts as community, citizenship, and participation; on the obsession with death and self-mutilation, disintegration and regression; on the nature of the self's alienation and the power of delusion in eroding human connections. I have suggested that what these patients speak reveals a politics of the self, as that politics appears in a discourse existing on or beyond the borders of association, the world experienced in the language of exclusion and denial. And I have argued that the language of metaphor, as it appears in narrative storytelling, may be a revealing political language, a source of political knowledge, and a commentary on the structure of rationality. Billy and Chuck and David (in his manias) live and exist outside the borders; Annie, Julia, and Ruth occupy or have occupied a position on the border, knowing themselves and the conditions of their lives to be places of exile and torment. Lacan's understanding of *Oedipus at Colonus,* the tragedy of aloneness and bitterness, appears as a mythology, a language of tragedy, which embodies or enacts the modern plight of emotional and physical exclusion and the terror of its loneliness, isolation, and rage.

Persons like Chuck, Billy, and Richard—and, to a lesser extent, Annie and David—become the long-term victims both of their inner monologues and of society's incapacity to tolerate or integrate those whose speech and frames of reference seriously disturb prevailing linguistic and behavioral norms. Ruth and Julia are now back in society. Each leads what passes for a normal life: Ruth has resumed full-time work and in the evening attends classes at a local community college; Julia attends the state university and has a part-time job. Each, once alienated from community, has established ongoing emotional relationships; each seems firmly entrenched in association. Each appears to function with knowledge systems firmly grounded in the world of culture. David still struggles with the demons or sirens of his unconscious world. He has for two short periods been readmitted to the hospital; on the outside he lives and works in a local halfway house. But it is important to distinguish the affective and linguistic positions of former patients who like Ruth and Julia now live in the Aristotelian world of ends and purposes from the chronically debilitating states of mind and being that are represented by Chuck and, to a lesser extent, Annie (though Annie makes strenuous efforts at living in a world of others).

Chuck remains at Sheppard-Pratt, still delusional, hearing voices, caught up in inner symbolizations that he keeps tightly guarded; he adapts to whatever treatment innovation he faces. It is the tragedy of the schizophrenic. He often appears to be a caricature of Kierkegaard's knight of infinite resignation; he believes he will outlast all humankind and live for a billion years, only to wake up and be utterly alone. He admits that he feels, even now, an extraordinary tiredness and wonders how he carries the burdens of his life. Yet Chuck plays at being the good patient, dutifully following his behavioral regimen and taking his medications in a tightly organized and highly structured unit reserved for the chronic schizophrenic. Each of these long-term outcasts, the silent wanderers, remains trapped by a delusional knowledge that has no audience and begins from a deeply hermetic logic sealed off from the historical and social world (Glass, 1985).

This closing chapter, then, addresses some of the problems that face the chronically mentally ill and psychotic, the ones the society regards as hopeless, incurable, and ultimately (in Foucault's terms) invisible. To speak with such patients for any period of time, to encounter the madness of a Billy or a Chuck, is to be convinced of the very real presence of a self that is ill, in which sickness defines the field between self and other. To participate in that dialogue is to come away with the recognition that mental illness is hardly a myth; it is real fact embodied in persons caught up in the exclusionary dynamics of the society and the tyranny of their inner voices.[1]

Outside and Inside: Problems in Being a Former Patient

A growing body of evidence suggests that the chronic mental patient drifts from a halfway house to a boarding-house in the rundown sections of some large city, and frequently ends up back in the hospital (the "revolving door syndrome"). Deinstitutionalization, while emptying some of the more flagrant back wards of mental hospitals and replacing incarceration with management through medication and community-based facilities, has created a host of new problems centering on the former patient's ability and need to discover a sense of place and community.[2] While deinstitutionalization is to be preferred to the locked back ward, it is not a movement that has responded to the relation between the self's sense of its own *public* effectiveness and collaborative aspects of working in common (its being with others). What has emerged in the drearier areas of large cities is something akin to a psychological proletariat, living and (rarely) working in a social universe noticeably short on sympathy and empathy.[3]

Deinstitutionalization involves more than an ideological position or view of mental health and hospitals.[4] It has become a very real social fact on the level of community: how to provide community, how to prevent the isolation of the homeless, how to contain the very real alienation that such persons experience.[5] While it is true that many patients return to the outside world and lead productive lives, the great majority find themselves trapped from two directions: from inside, confusion and self-doubt, intensified by lack of a sense of place; from outside, the suspiciousness of a social world that regards mental disorders with fear and anxiety. Former patients who are successful in rein-

tegrating possess skills relevant to the complex technological society
and also have access to effective support services. The least successful in
adapting, on an economic level, are those whose labor is regarded as
peripheral to any specific job-related activity and who, because of in-
sufficient training and low skill levels, find it difficult to sustain a long-
term work relation with the surrounding community. It is no exag-
geration to say that the latter form the vast majority of the chronically
mentally ill, particularly in economically disadvantaged populations.[6]

Even the halfway house becomes a transition point for unhappy
individuals whose connection with reality is not only tenuous but also
threatened by an unresponsive and hostile competitive world.[7] Many
regard the halfway house as "halfway to nowhere," a depressing way
station that offers little help. If the former patient is to have any kind of
life outside the hospital, both private and public aspects of being require attention. Since it is not a primary function of the medical model
to inquire into the relation between the private and the public self, the
psychological impact of work, and the absence of community, these
issues are generally not systematically explored as part of hospital treatment. This is a real limitation in what the medical model offers in the
way of orienting the self toward the *public* demands of civil society.
What emerges as a compelling fact in conversations with patients and
former patients is the difficulty in formulating a sense of community
that can be sustained in the face of overwhelming pressure and demand
for *performance* from the outside civil society.

The Private and the Public: Efforts to Bridge the Gap

Part of the task of restoring the self's sense of place is to create environments where the expression of self, as a peculiar and idiosyncratic way
of framing reality, is not regarded as evidence of some supposed
second-class humanity or citizenship. The chronically mentally ill have
performed usefully in sheltered workshops, in jobs that require cooperation and mutuality, work that involves some form of being in public,
consensual actions. It is therefore not a foregone conclusion that the
chronically disturbed can be expected to perform only at some menial
or subhuman level; even the regressed schizophrenic may possess un-

usual and surprising capacities, depending on how those capacities are organized and the specific tasks the self is taught to master.

Yet the whole issue of work and collaboration for the chronic mental patient is a thorny one. It is handled variously, depending on the social and cultural context. Whatever the cultural environment, the issue of the relation between the private and public self remains critical. Consider two widely divergent cultural backdrops that shed light on this dialectic between the private and public: the dispersal of chronic patients within the town limits of Geel, in northeastern Belgium, and the treatment of chronic schizophrenics in Israel.[8]

Geel has a long history (dating back to the thirteenth century) of accommodating the mad and, even more important, of demonstrating sensitivity to the public needs of the chronic patient. The town's foster care program has a unique reputation in the history of the treatment of the mentally disturbed; accounts of Geel in American psychiatry, for example, can be found as far back as the mid-nineteenth century: Pliny Earle (1887), superintendent of the Northhampton [Massachusetts] Lunatic Asylum, wrote somewhat critically in his annual report for 1879 that the system of treatment in Geel, because of its effort to assimilate the mad to the way of life of the normal society through boarding in local homes and providing work on the farms, would be unsuitable to the American environment.

Geel is a place, then, which has had an enormous impact on theories of foster care and of ways to integrate the chronic patient into an ongoing community. It was therefore with some excitement that I anticipated my visit. In Israel I hoped to find data on the integration of the chronic patient by visiting kibbutzim and interviewing schizophrenics who had been members. Further, I thought that the Israeli emphasis on the collective (the talent of the kibbutzim for creating and sustaining vital collectivist organizations) would illuminate the particular difficulties of persons as private as schizophrenics in dealing with formal modes of organization and collective types of work.

In both countries I met with mental health practitioners and administrators; I visited hospitals, community care centers, sheltered workshops, residential care houses; I spoke at some length with patients and residents (in all kinds of mental health facilities) both with and without the aid of translators. In Geel, economic reality and technological advance appeared to be endangering this centuries-old tradition and radically altering the attitudes of the townspeople. In addition, the *practice* of care—the *laissez-faire* approach to psychosis through the absence of confinement—had come under attack from mental health professionals in other districts in Belgium, particularly in the south. Several people in Israel mentioned the need for a kibbutz for the chronically disturbed, staffed and organized by professionals and paraprofessionals committed to working with this population. Yet no one had a shred of hope that the idea would ever be accepted, much less funded, by the state, although there is a kibbutz for the mentally retarded.

Neither in Geel nor in Israel did I see treatment programs that offered any startling innovations, but the dedication of persons connected with these programs and their efforts to work in environments that were significantly underfunded and understaffed were enormously impressive. Ingenuity, adaptation, persistence, and making virtues of necessities consistently distinguished the commitment of these workers. The following observations may shed some light on the broader issue of the relation between the private and the public self.

The Geel program consisted primarily of four interrelated areas: a central hospital handling acute and severe long-term cases; the foster care program for which Geel is primarily noted, in which residents are boarded in homes throughout the city; sheltered workshops and activities programs both at the central hospital and in buildings located elsewhere in town; and the general acceptance of the idea that the residents are free to wander about the town as long as their behavior conforms to general canons of civility. The presence of foster care residents among the townspeople created no major problems. Historically, the residents had been assimilated into what had been a rural, farming economy. With Geel's increasing prominence as a center for high-tech industry, however, opportunities for their integration into the town's labor force have significantly declined. Except for a few sheltered workshops, housed primarily within the environs of the central hospital, work (or seeing the chronic patient as a complex factor in a political economy) did not figure significantly in Geel's therapeutic regimen. The consensus of those connected with the program seemed to be that the tolerance of the Geel citizenry had declined, largely because of an influx of outsiders for whom the tradition of coexisting with the mentally ill was either unknown (and a rude shock) or a vague and somewhat distasteful part of Geel's history.

Though the number consistently declines, in 1985 there were 900 foster care residents, mostly elderly persons living in homes scattered throughout the city. The median age of the residents was fifty-eight years; some were as old as seventy. Criticism comes primarily from Belgian psychiatrists who regard treatment on the Geel model as unscientific, anachronistic, out of step with the times. Geel is also thought to be unresponsive to the needs of young chronic patients, who are becoming the largest segment of the chronically disturbed population.

The foster care program (the per diem cost in 1985 was $6.00) is among the least expensive forms of care in Belgium. The financial arrangement for sheltered workshops is an interesting one as well. The state pays, directly to the hospital, 60 percent of the cost; the private industries for whom the work is done—usually "piecework" of various kinds—supports the remaining 40 percent. The hospital administers the workshops; patients or residents are paid on an hourly basis. Though such a system could obviously be open to abuse, it has not in Geel led to either financial chicanery or administrative corruption. It is justified and defended in the language of coproduction: not only do the workshops diminish the costs of mental health care through the contribution of private industry, but they also provide income for persons who otherwise would be wards of the state and virtually penniless. At least 90 percent of foster care residents and hospitalized patients have been abandoned by their families or have virtually no family life and receive no financial support from outside. The relation between the hospital and private industry raises, of course, the important question of potential exploitation, but both administrators and workers in these mini-factories feel that the financial arrangements are, given the circumstances, fair.

Proponents of these programs argue that in mental hospitals, 80 percent of a patient's contact time is with other patients; in Geel, given the dispersal of patients throughout the town, 80 percent of contact time is with normal society. In this respect, community is a central aspect of treatment combined with the salutary effects of natural or noninstitutional environments. And the importance to the chronic patient of having a public space is considered a vital aspect of psychological well-being. The content of that public space is primarily defined as the right of the residents to walk about the town, frequent its bars and restaurants, and sit in the public squares; still, even this much public life is far better than wandering the corridors of a mental hospital, since the resident's experience is open to the community and occurs within its boundaries. Further, it is argued, keeping the chronic patient in the community allows the self to become something more than an object to be managed by science; rather, the self's human ecology constitutes the primary focus of treatment, although the foster care program does rely on science in using medications and making provision for their administration.

Two examples I found in Israel spoke compellingly to the relation between public and private. First, in a small factory near Haifa, work—particularly working in common—was an essential part of treatment. Second, the status of schizophrenics on the kibbutzim pointed up both the dilemmas of collectivist organizations in confronting the radical withdrawal of the schizophrenic, and the peculiar loneliness and isolation of the schizophrenic within the kibbutz environment.

The factory, the Kirit Ata Workshop for Mental Patients in the Haifa Area, was quite remarkable: 60 percent of the workers were chronic; each would be considered schizophrenic. Yet each was participating in a complex production line that involved the reconditioning of used telephones, performing difficult and often intricate labor that required both training and a certain level of skill. The factory occupied two large buildings in an industrial section of a Haifa suburb. According to its manager, the operation served as a vital structure in the workers' sense of what community entailed: its responsibilities and the pride in maintaining a community centered on work. To be at the factory, to work with others within this kind of social environment, became for many the link to a hopeful future and to actions that gave meaning to the sheer demands of day-to-day survival. In the manager's words:

The workers would frequently show up two hours before their shift and sit outside waiting for their work assignments. It wasn't that they were confused about the time. When I asked them why they were there so early, they said it just made them feel good to sit outside the place where they felt they were making and contributing something useful to society and for themselves.

I visited the Kirit Ata Workshop in 1985; run by a local branch of the B'nai B'rith under the supervision of the local social welfare agency, it is still in operation, providing significant work experience for the chronic patient.

It was a different situation altogether on the kibbutzim. Resident schizophrenics generally refused to adhere to the group's conception of work and participation, and those who had been sent to residential care facilities in the city were very reluctant, if not adamantly opposed, to returning to a kibbutz. They preferred the anonymity of the city, its hetereogeneity, and its opportunities to find places to hide. Their problems on the kibbutzim were compounded by the facts of collective and group behavior: the feeling and sensation that all eyes were directed toward the self, the sense of being exposed and vulnerable, the impatience of the group with crazy thoughts and ideas, the premium on normality.

The schizophrenic, because of withdrawal to an inner world, fears highly public environments; thus, the collaborative structure of a kibbutz takes on frightening properties, whereas the family-oriented systems of kibbutzim depend on conformity, normality, and public cooperation as *forms* of security. Further, a significant proportion of schizophrenics are children of Holocaust survivors; the kibbutzim therefore find themselves in the difficult position of feeling a moral obligation to care for these persons (relative to other sectors of Israeli society, the kibbutzim spend a great deal of money on mental health care) yet also express impatience with their unwillingness to work on a regular and consistent basis. This is a real problem on agricultural kibbutzim during times of harvest.

The kibbutz speaks to the issue of collective behavior and action; it represents a homogeneous society acting collectively to attain shared goals. It also, like Spring Lake, possesses qualities that may be likened to what Rousseau described as the general will, and like Spring Lake the kibbutz can exercise a powerful sense of the group need, as opposed to the individual interest. The kibbutz, as a place to live and be, graphically demonstrates the intricate and often delicate process of tying the individual into the group. It is in some respects a place that symbolizes both the possibilities of that relation and its dangers. The feeling of being absorbed into a demanding group will accounts for something of the fear that schizophrenics expressed about returning to their kibbutzim.

At Spring Lake, Annie might say that such persons have not grasped the meaning of what is common. And I heard variations of Annie's criticism of the retreat to privacy from several regular kibbutz members. To paraphrase their comments: "We feel torn about how to deal with any of our members who become mentally ill; we of course offer them the best in care and treatment. But we still do feel resentment. You have to understand our position: at the harvest, as just one example of what we need to do, it is essential to pick the grapefruit, to pack it, to ship it. If the work is not being done, if a person refuses to leave his room because of imaginary conversations or depression or whatever, it means one less worker in the field, possibly longer hours for everyone else, and so on. Do you see? The group will here means survival. If the work is not finished, we will wither; if the meals are not cooked, we starve; if the guard is not posted, we may be infiltrated by terrorists—and so it goes. Sometimes our members who are mentally ill simply are incapable of grasping these very real facts of survival. If every one of us here were to sink into our private worlds, the kibbutz would disintegrate."

It is not that the kibbutz is hostile to the individual. Quite the contrary: it shows extraordinary tolerance (at times) and forebearance. What develops within the kibbutz is an intense competition between the interests of the individual and the common welfare of the group. A schizophrenic, for example, speaking with voices or caught up in an endless succession of hallucinations, becomes for this kind of group both an impediment and a threat because the psychologically impaired member reminds the entire group of its vulnerability not only to outside forces but to the pressures of internal emotional conflict.

Whether or not the general will becomes oppressive depends on perspective and the position of the self. At Spring Lake it lifts the schizophrenic from a total and absolute focus on the internal, on inner voices and imaginary dialogues. It provides a context, an environment that situates the self in a social and work relation with others, with the hope that this kind of public life may have some healing effect. To be schizophrenic in a kibbutz, however, may be a terrifying psychological experience that reinforces the sense of aloneness and separateness. For persons suffering this intense alienation, the general will may in fact appear to be tyrannical and unjust. For both the kibbutz and the therapeutic community, though there are significant differences in structure, the community's definition of what is general and common frames action and relationship. In the kibbutz that interest represents members who psychologically inhabit prevailing notions of consensuality and normality; at Spring Lake the general will works in the interests of those whom society has excluded from its consensual foundations, those it names as psychologically unfit, ill, or dysfunctional.

It would be difficult to find, in a social context, a more dramatic example of eccentric action than that of the schizophrenic, even though that eccentricity is not motivated by a calculated, instrumental reason. It is a form of behavior and thought that by its very nature sets the individual away from the group; to be schizophrenic is to be separate, different. That sense of separation and exclusion finds itself intensified within the collective refraction of the kibbutz environment. It is understandable that schizophrenics are terrified of eating in huge dining halls, sometimes holding as many as a thousand people. To be so exposed is to be destroyed, annihilated by a self-consciousness induced by an infinitude of others. As one former kibbutznik, living in a residential treatment facility in Jerusalem, put it: "I was the promise of my kibbutz, one of its shining lights; and then I got sick. It was terrible; everyone was so kind, but I knew I had fallen in their eyes. I never want to go back; I hate that place." In the competition between the interests of the individual and those of the group, the schizophrenic inevitably fares poorly.

Nevertheless, what I saw in Israel and to a limited extent in Geel parallels a sentiment expressed particularly by those associated with sheltered workshops in the United States: that the chronic patient possesses the capacity to act on specific (if not circumscribed) social and economic imperatives. In other words, the level of psychological and emotional impairment need not *necessarily* lead to an unproductive and miserable life. The strictly clinical environment, however, the world that ministers *only* to the internal in the form of treatment and/or management, is not set up either to accommodate or to focus on the relation between political economy and chronic mental states.

The medical model, frequently insensitive to the demands of the public self, utilizes a theory of power as therapeutic intervention which moves toward the amelioration of psychological pain, not the construction of an alternative view of being and action. It is not a function of the medical paradigm to think of diminishing psychic pain as a product of the links between public, collaborative participation and underlying emotional conflict. The place of the self in political economy is often ignored or is seen as having no therapeutic significance. Yet is not work, with the collective and public quality of its basic action, a source of self-respect and esteem?

Therapy of whatever kind becomes, in the medical approach, an escape from pain, a view consistent with much in the classical liberal position that regards the flight from pain as the critical psychological dynamic in the maintenance of relationships. Gardening, woodwork, social skills, art, dance, recreation: all *hospital* therapies find themselves compartmentalized as moments in an activities program. It was precisely this kind of compartmentalization and its negative effects that motivated social workers in Haifa to found a factory operated for the most part by chronic mental patients. Therapy in the medical model is action geared to what is seen as a passive object, the self's psychological body—a phenomenon that has become even more pronounced with the increasing reliance on antipsychotic medications to treat what are often regarded as the organic or biochemical origins of illness. In the Haifa model, therapy *also* consists in encouraging the *expression* of self through *public* forms of participation.

While the psychotherapeutic treatment of the chronic patient is a humane and sincere effort to respond to unbearable pain, the governing paradigm avoids an equally important issue: the connection between the inner life and the place or space that might facilitate the self's integration with a public sense of its own worthiness. It is frequently an overwhelming task for the chronically disturbed to find tolerant places, particularly in the area of work, that involve collaboration between "normals" and "chronics." In Geel, for example, barriers to local employment for the mentally disturbed came not from local employers—who expressed an interest in working with the central hospital and the foster care program—but from town workers on the production lines, especially new workers who had recently moved to Geel and who objected to working side by side with "loonies." Contrast this to the factory in Haifa, where "normals" and "chronics" were working side by side, with equal demands placed on both. It is a sad story, Geel's decline in tolerance, not only because of the demise of what in the past was a humane form of treating madness but because of what the town and its central hospital meant in times of political crisis: the values of tolerance were part of Geel's political *culture*. For example, after the invasion of Belgium by the Nazis, the Geelians resisted in a way peculiar to their own tradition: the townspeople hid Jews among the patient population of the central hospital and, to a lesser extent, in their own homes as foster "patients."

The medical paradigm moves to contain the internal; it intervenes in precisely those areas seen to be skewed in terms of prevailing social conceptions of normality and acceptability. But what gives the self a consciousness of its public identity lies for the most part outside the objectives and sense of purpose of the mental hospital (the agent of the medical paradigm). Since therapy labors on different parts of the self, since it is disconnected from the broader concerns of the self's public being, it is understandable that patients often feel confined, worked upon, and frightened of what faces them in the outside world (most of the foster care residents I spoke with in Geel, by contrast, did not feel confined or hemmed in by the system). And on the outside, local jurisdictions simply do not have the funding or resources to provide for the self's productive being. Whatever resources do exist are expended on necessities (food, shelter) and, if possible, therapies (usually group therapy) that will keep the self (client) in some kind of contact with mental health professionals.

Power and the Medical Gaze: Limitation in Self-Definition

For Michel Foucault (1977: 201), the self as it is worked on by the professions is a victim of power. While much in Foucault's critique illuminates the nexus of social relations in which the self is enmeshed, I do not accept the larger implication that therapy may be harmful precisely *because* it is an agent of social power. Nevertheless, Foucault does highlight the importance of giving some consideration to the constituents of the self in its *public* mode of being.

A more limited and, I believe, realistic (as opposed to ideological) use of Foucault would be to suggest that even though the disturbed self finds itself enmeshed in relations of power, those relations do not necessarily have to be harmful. To correct the imbalance in power relations (the private self monitored by the therapies), it may be necessary to provide the self with some sense of its place in a public world, to respond to the need for work in common, an existence involved in being with others—again, a sentiment that in Israel lay behind the view (although not the majority view) that the interests of the chronically disturbed may best be served by integration into collective forms of organization and action.

In the modern mental hospital, what Foucault (1977) calls the scrutinizing or "panopticon" mentality[9] (the Benthamite model of control) has been transferred to a variety of methods: behavioral conditioning (token economies), medication and electroshock therapy, therapies that move to normalize behavior, expressive and social therapies pursued in isolation one from the other (the self seen as a series of pieces to be administered, whether in the form of language, art, dance, family relationships, or group dynamics). The light that Jeremy Bentham so effectively proposed as a substitute for the dungeon now appears as a technology of power that holds psychosis through a variety of interventions into the internal or hidden self, psychopharmacology being the most recent and technological of the modern treatments. Physical constraint is no longer necessary, except in rare instances of disruptive or assaultive behavior, since the power of the panopticon extends, through medication, to specific synapses and sites in brain cells. A Foucauldian analysis, however, does ignore the very real fact that for the patients the therapies diminish psychological pain, and medications alleviate some of the more frightening symptoms in severe mental illness.

Even with the modern panopticon, in its form as power containing the internal self, patients experience intense anxiety over the prospect of discharge. Returning to the world means losing the security of the ever present therapeutic gaze. While Foucault conceives professional intervention as an exercise of power (domination), the patient may demand it in the frantic search for relief from pain and for acknowledgment that the pain is real and terrifying. In the words of Eve, at Sheppard-Pratt:

Here I am speaking to you about my feelings and thoughts; and when I'm discharged, I'll have to be tremendously careful about who I speak to. . . . At least here there are any number of people who will listen. But outside the hospital, who is there? Maybe my boy-friend? But even he is frightened of what I am. . . . I often think about my discharge, where I will be put, who they'll put me with. . . . Do I have to go back home or to a halfway house? It's so confusing because I feel so homeless, without any place to go, or maybe nowhere is a place. I just don't know. It makes me so sad; my life, I think, is like a leaf.

She was describing something of the despair patients suffer in their effort to come to grips with the feeling that they are not part of any community, that they are grist for the mill of an institution in which they are dependent clients. However, while she could be quite bitter about what she perceived as real inequalities, Eve also acknowledged and respected what the hospital offered as containment for her own feelings of disintegration. In spite of her anger at inequality, she was grateful for the relief:

Why would I want to leave? So I can go back home and live in a little room or listen to the prattle of roommates who really care about nothing but getting ahead? At least here people want to understand all parts of who you are. Even though I hate being on a locked ward, I still feel a sense of unity with many of the patients, even the sickest.

Eve's observations are fairly typical. Such patients come to respect and even feel comfortable within the hospital's therapeutic world. Yet the feeling of placelessness, of being nowhere; the dread of returning to previous lives they know will be unresponsive, of not having jobs or not believing that they even deserve one—this fear of the future accounts for much of their pessimism and cynicism. As Andrew (also at Sheppard-Pratt) put it:

What makes it so difficult is that no one cares about the world we have to go back to. . . . the therapists and nurses speak to us about discharge and we make "plans," but no one really asks questions about what we are going back to. They assume that's what we want or should want. Yet if you're psychologically different, out there, it can be deadly. They'll kill you for it, either with phony kindness or solicitousness or with disdain and hostility. Either way you lose and end up being a parasite. The hospital, even with all its activities, is still a place to be sick, not a place to go to work.

The experience here has helped, although I was a bit concerned that few people cared about what my illness meant. I don't want to think it was all for nothing, or that my delusions only told me I was sick. I would hope there was at least some meaning in my craziness. . . . On balance, you ask, did the hospital help me? Sure; I opened up here; I felt safe . . . I didn't have to rationalize my behavior or explain my feelings if I chose not to. . . . No one judged me, and there were a few moments when I felt good, peaceful inside.

Confinement cuts both ways. It encircles the self in definition; it names internal worlds in the language of illness; in some respects it dominates the self through infantilization. But it also provides comfort, containment, and the place to express, represent, and work through often unbearable psychological pain.

This was Andrew's second hospitalization; after his previous discharge, he had lived for a few months at a local halfway house:

I hated it . . . I disliked most of the other residents; they were all so into themselves. And we didn't communicate very much, only over trivial stuff like washing dishes or keeping the halls clean or making our beds. It was like being in camp all over again, except instead of counselors we had aides who treated us like children. My parents' lack of concern made it even more difficult because I sensed in them relief that I hadn't come home. My friends treated me like some animal from outer space. I began to see dead ends, no way out; here I was in a halfway house that was notable only for the antiseptic smell of its halls, and the need for residents to stay glued to the TV every morning. I would go to my job, yet my colleagues would stay clear of me or treat me like a fragile piece of china. My supervisor reviewed my work, and I think he had some

doubts that an "ex-patient" could really do the [computer] programs. But my life had no meaning; I got up in the morning,
caught the bus to work, came home. It was depressing, and the
residents were more depressed than I was. At some point, I don't
know why—maybe a bad day at work or I was turned down by a
girl I wanted to date, whatever—I decided to cut my wrists. I
think, looking back on it, I wanted back in [the hospital], and that
was the only way I knew how to ask.

The Invisible Self: On Countervailing Forces to Elimination

In an interview in *Telos* regarding prisons, Foucault (1974: 155) argued that once the inmate enters prison, he becomes a nonperson to
society. A process is initiated that excludes the convict (generally for
years if not the rest of his life) from a political, social, and economic
sense of place. Prison therefore serves as a mechanism to break down
the convict, to render him invisible to the social order, without hope
for a viable social future. While this is not true in all cases, it is a
direction that confinement reinforces. The inmate begins a career that
effectively shuts him out of a productive social life. "Society eliminates
by sending to prison people whom prison breaks up, crushes, physically eliminates."

Obviously, the conditions are not so harsh in humane psychiatric
hospitals (although many state and veterans' hospitals certainly now
and in the past have treated patients like inmates or criminals). Even
so, treatment invariably remains isolated from the self's public being,
from its collaborative potential as a person who works and produces.
Constraint is still present, not as an external force that works on the
physical body but as a set of internalized moral regulations defining the
self's structures of perception. The mental patient as a disruptive social
influence is eliminated through therapeutic controls.

It is not as brutal a phenomenon as what Foucault sees as the crush-
ing of prisoners—"Once they have been broken up, the prison eliminates them by 'freeing' them and sending them back to society"—but
like the prisoner, the former patient, even with the ever present social
gaze defining reentry and adaptation, faces enormous troubles. In

Geel, for example, therapy now primarily involves weekly visits to the foster home by a social worker, and whatever the resident receives from contact with others at various workshops and activities programs (including a social club) scattered throughout town. The activities programs perform a useful function in allowing the residents some social dimension to what are, for the most part, hidden and dreary lives. The exclusion practiced by family, friends, and employers, however, never completely disappears; and the label "ex-patient" is a powerful one in this society. Many find themselves desperate, alone; they think about life as simply a matter of survival, feeling that little exists for them in the surrounding community. Attempted suicide, incapacitating symptoms, intolerable delusions may force the former patient's caretakers—whether family, halfway house, or friends—to place the person back in the hospital.

Some hospitals are more efficient and brutal than others in the process of elimination; yet no matter how benign the hospital setting, social interest dictates the masking of what society defines as mental illness. How that eliminative process works for the discharged patient, how the self fares in it, depends on the extent of medical health coverage, the willingness of families to sustain the cost of decent treatment, the luck of having been in a progressive mental institution or therapeutic community, the support of friends, and so on. It is obviously a phenomenon that should be distinguished from the treatment of former prisoners or from the kind of confinement Goffman (1961) speaks about in his analysis of total institutions. But at what point does the mental patient become a prisoner? What is the line or boundary that separates prisoner from patient? And—a question Foucault (1974: 161) raises in connection with prisoners—to what extent does social interest dictate the severity and extent of the exclusionary process?

In addition to exclusion for social or political reasons (from rights, responsibilities, jobs, adequate living conditions), many former patients—and this is especially true for the chronically mentally ill—suffer from a way of looking at the world that in important respects differs from the prevailing social orientation. If the former patient has been schizophrenic (putting aside for a moment the many different manifestations of this state of mind), it is more than likely that the self's theory of knowledge will involve delusional definition and reference. A delusional reading of reality, nonconsensual and often fantastic, is typical of schizophrenic persons. What this means is that the self's theory of knowledge refuses to allow it to participate in conventional rituals, since those rituals and assumptions lack the necessary perspective and tolerance to accommodate the schizophrenic's world view. Any kind of life for the schizophrenic outside the hospital not only involves a series of existential compromises and frequent disappointments but also means living with thoughts and ideas that others find bizarre, weird, or downright crazy, even though the crazy thoughts may be harmless and not interfere with social obligations.

For the chronic patient who is capable of living and functioning (more or less) outside a hospital setting, delusions may not necessarily disrupt daily tasks and activities. But they may create conflict and misunderstanding in environments insensitive to these representations of thought. In the words of Ned, a resident of a halfway house, "I still have strange thoughts. Sometimes they come out, and people look at me as if I were a man from Mars." Even though the former patient may have a number of options—day care centers, sheltered workshops, halfway houses, support groups, and so on—it is still necessary to survive and deal with so-called normal people who have a discouragingly low tolerance for the peculiarities even of nonthreatening "crazy" imagery and behavior. One of the great strengths of Geel, at least in the past, lay in the fact that the foster care residents were treated as persons who deserved to be and live in the town, not separated from it.

With very few exceptions, existence as schizophrenic or chronic means falling into nonperson status in Foucault's sense, a state of invisibility that involves a lot of drifting and confusion. Support systems are often inadequate; those I saw in Israel, for example, were frequently improvised with almost no financial backing from the state. The effort to rejoin society, especially in economic contexts, usually fails; activity suffers, and mistrust and disappointment pull consciousness away from any relation to public values, whether in work or in social activity. What the schizophrenic self trusts are delusions; and the more stressful life becomes on the outside, the more the delusion functions as a source of refuge and self-definition—unless it is counterbalanced by a community or work*place* that functions as a holding or containing environment. As one former patient put it: "When things start to fall in around me, the crazy thoughts come back." When delusion invades consciousness, the self loses its social connections, its relations to social time and space. Delusional time and space replace the self's rootedness and identity in interpersonal and social situations; the result is a loss of the self's public being, a reversion to private knowledge systems, and most important, a complete loss of the sense of community.

Personhood and Self: On the Recovery of Place

What, then, might be a way out of the impasse, the limitation in the medical model's view of the *public* self? On the one hand, the medical paradigm focuses treatment primarily on the inner self; power encircles and inhibits action. On the other, community-based resources in the postdischarge world are limited; the former patient faces hostility from economic forces and internal impediments in the form of social impairments, low skill levels, inability to master complex technologies, and so on. If the rapid rise in homelessness is any indication, not enough is being done to minister to the public self of the chronically disturbed, not to mention the persistent psychological torment and fear that constitutes a large part of waking life for such an individual.

It is necessary, then, to rethink the concept of place and what it means for the chronically mentally ill. A humane psychiatric environment makes a serious effort to recover the human in the depersonalized, delusional self. Its effort, however, is limited by the failure to think through completely the relation between psychotherapy, work, and an identity grounded in some sense of a life in common. Further, delusional patients resist attempts to root perception psychically in what Harry Stack Sullivan (1953) called "consensual reality." It is therefore quite difficult for the chronic mental patient to struggle toward personhood, given the strength and tenacity of delusional defenses. The struggle is complicated even more by the impact of what to the former patient are socially noxious and objectifying dynamics in political society. If reentry into society serves to prolong the self's alienation and aggravate feelings of worthlessness and despair, it might be useful to rethink place as a synthesis of the public and private, an environment that defuses the impact of internal alien objects and creates an awareness of work with the objective of enhancing the feeling of efficacy and the public recognition of community or ends-in-common.

It is not at all clear that even the most progressive mental hospitals succeed in recovering on a long-term basis the humane and productive potential of the self who, for whatever reason, has withdrawn from social life. If even now, former patients find themselves shunted to undesirable labor within society, if they see themselves on the margins of the economic marketplace, if employers are hesitant to consider them for employment or fellow employees refuse to work with them, if all these things are part of the contemporary economic landscape, it seems unlikely that prospects will improve in the near future. The economy has become increasingly dependent on complex rational skills, on computer and information services and technologies that require extensive education and adaptation to prevailing social and cultural standards. It is therefore essential to look toward new ideas in the very serious problem of keeping the homeless, the placeless, within the bounds of the social order and not creating an underclass of alienated who remain permanently excluded from the social system.

What E. E. Schumacher (1973) has argued about economics on a human scale may provide an alternative way of looking at the connection between community and production, what might be called the functions of "place," as place relates to the chronic patient.[10] Schumacher's humanism, his emphasis on collaborative activity, his discussion of scale and technology, and his respect for nature and production hold values that offer an alternative to the instrumental and highly complex institutions that become so perplexing and unnavigable for the chronically mentally ill. It might even be useful in this regard to reexamine the historical Geel, to explore the possibility of coproduction within manageable limits, to develop innovative organizational techniques and approaches in both rural and urban environments, to encourage and fund small-scale enterprises that might be able to harness the *limited* but very real productive potential of the chronic patient.[11] Such persons are *not* completely dysfunctional or untreatable. If the chronic patient is to have any kind of productive life, it is doubtful that such a life will, on a long-term basis, be found in bureaucratic centers of power and in technologies that confound the self's perceptual capacities. Much of the solution to homelessness may depend on society's being able to encourage a productivity and a *relation* to production that enhances self-respect and contributes to self-esteem. To solve the problem of place, understood as both productivity and community—what Schumacher calls the self's productive "habitat"— is to go a long way toward solving the psychological alienation of the homeless.

This is not to say that hospitals fail to provide useful and important services. I am not arguing against concrete and humane actions to alleviate the inner terror of the self—a problem, for example, in much of the French critique of psychiatry; to couch the argument only in terms of ideology is to obscure and minimize the very real suffering of persons with mental illness. I do suggest that there are structural limitations to the functions of the hospital precisely because it refuses to treat the connection, or lack of it, between the self's private being and its public requirements.[12]

I do not question the premises of psychotherapy or the expressive therapies (art, dance, recreation, social skills, and so on). Sensitivity to the self's internal needs is essential, and patients respond to concerned and committed therapists. I cannot emphasize too strongly that symptomatic relief of pain, which the psychotherapies offer, is better than no relief; and it is no easy task to defuse the delusional bases of knowledge and identity in the more psychotic patients. But it might be productive to think of place in a political language—the language of community and civility, productive activity and collaboration—and not only in medical language and the paradigm of disease and hospitalization. If what is lacking in the chronic mental patient is a belief in the efficacy of some form of public life—life shared with others not in silent wonderment or, at the other end, paralyzing fear but in expressive work and discourse—then such efficacy might be stimulated by allowing the self to conceive of its own future in a place where productive activity is infused with participation.

The language of disease, the medical language that exercises such a powerful hold over the patient's sense of identity and liberty, reinforces the self's knowledge of its own separateness, its essential and abiding alienation from the species, from *community;* in this respect, the staff of Spring Lake Ranch has developed a powerful critique. It is just such alienation and its persistence that form the real threat not only to the displaced, the homeless, but to the very society that because of its neglect and willed blindness bears considerable responsibility for the tragedy of this situation.

Finally, the concept of treatment, under this view, would be more open to thinking about the relation between public and private, between the self's productive being and the self's internal world and its alienation from consensual reality. In most psychological and psychiatric theories the private or hidden, whether inside the unconscious or in the brain or in behavioral and chemical dysfunctions, becomes the object of therapeutic intervention. But it is also the self's being in public, its work, its interpersonal relations, and the inevitable politics of persons, institutions, and bureaucracies that drive troubled individuals into feelings of failure and hopelessness, particularly if those individuals have already been funneled through mental hospitals and the professional mental health care network. After such a journey the self experiences itself as so sick that even to think of itself as healthy and worthwhile requires an almost heroic movement from pessimism and dejection to at least some belief in the possibility of transformation. It is the feeling of fragmentation, placelessness, and loss of rights that the chronic patient strives to escape. Yet it is precisely these feelings that the self encounters when it faces the competition, complexity, and instrumentalism so characteristic of modern society.

Much of the political issue here is how to create a viable sense of individuality yet still maintain a productive contact with society. Even the most alienated require a sense of self and self-integrity in order to live and survive as persons, much less citizens. To be an individual is a vital need for the person who has suffered from debilitating internal images, whether those images were the delusional systems of schizophrenics or the universe of dread and sense of imminent fragmentation that plague the borderline self. In closing, then, I return to Kohut's remarks on individuality as a way of situating the imperatives of being an individual within the *empathic* need of identifying with community.

Individuality and Self-Fragmentation: The Issue of Cohesion

Kohut's ideals of individuality focus on the private self; he is not concerned with individuality in any strictly political sense, although his essay "On Courage" examine instances of courageous action, political resistance, and self-cohesion in the face of tragedy. Clearly, he admires persons who resist tyranny and oppression; he also sees in tragic art the

opportunity for the "spectator . . . to experience in temporary identification with the tragic hero, the unfolding, expansion and triumph of
his own nuclear self." And "paradoxically, the spectator, participating
in the ultimate self-realization of the tragic hero, experiences his own
self as more vigorous and cohesive than he ever can in his real life"
(Kohut 1985: 39).

Yet Kohut distinguishes, I believe, between ideals of individuality
that appear as self-enhancing actions within the context of identifying
with others, and conceptions of action that require a certain kind of
individual. He admires the hero, the tragic actor, the exceptional human being; certainly such figures act as models, he argues, for the best
(persons with a firm sense of their *nuclear* selves) in human motive,
commitment, and conviction. As a psychoanalyst, however, Kohut
addresses himself primarily to what it means to live as a person, an
individual, in a shared world of others, facing the requirements of the
day-to-day. It is the individual in community that preoccupies him:
how the self relates to others; how the environment affects emotional
identification, the relation between internal images, and responses
from others surrounding the self.

Kohut does not see himself as defending the heroic, lonely individu-
alism of a Nietzsche or a Kierkegaard, the self standing alone against
the sentiments of the mass and the coercive power of social values,
reaching for a transcendent, revelatory meaning. He rejects liberalism's
possessive individualist (as an ideal). He would not support the severe
anticommunitarianism exemplified in the work of such modern novel-
ists as William Burroughs, Jerzy Kosinski, Robert Stone, Martin Amis,
and Joan Didion. Nor is he concerned with idealizing the Freudian ego
desperately seeking the aims of the pleasure principle against the interests and wishes of an often antagonistic, hostile culture (which forms
much of the position of the Frankfurt school). As I have argued, his
psychoanalytic assumptions reflect a Rousseauist preoccupation with
the effect of community on the self. He returns consistently to the
commonplace and interpersonal, to images drawn from ordinary day-
to-day labors, the sentiments of tolerance and understanding, the affirmation of the intersubjective connection between persons, the private
realm where the drama of life is played out.

He examines, then, two orders of individuality: there are his
periodic reflections on heroic action in both art and politics; and his
considerably broader focus on and detailed discussion of the ordinary,

the existential, the relation between individuality and self-cohesion, the importance of cooperation and community, and the construction of values that support interdependencies and autonomy. In the last chapter of *The Analysis of the Self* (1971) he speaks of different factors bringing about changes in the narcissistic personality. Each of these changes increases and expands the reality of what it means to be an individual: progressive and integrative developments within the narcissistic realm (diminishing the impact of the grandiose self); de-idealizing the omnipotent object; constructing value systems that acknowledge reciprocity (workable, community-oriented ideals); an increase in empathy; and enhancement of creativity, humanity, and wisdom.

While heroic action is possible and commendable, it is not in Kohut's view necessarily realistic for all persons; the "realization of the nuclear self" may take different forms, although the nuclear self and its firmness sustain life and action during periods of personal and political tragedy. The lonely hero asserting truth against the oppression of politics and culture, the political actor undertaking enormous odds (facing death and execution) in resisting tyranny, the embattled drive-dominated ego fighting the raging unconscious currents of desire, passion, and revenge (Captain Ahab) all become in Kohut's view dramatic representations of the power of the nuclear self. Hamlet, Michael Kollhaus, Captain Ahab, Prince Myshkin: each of these figures reveals, in Kohut's terms, "certain deeply anchored, even idiosyncratic, psychic configurations" (1985: 49); each fulfils the patterns of the nuclear self; all attain "firmness and permanence as they live through their tortured lives" (1985: 41); each expresses an individuality that, no matter how unique, refracts the human edges of action and choice. Yet such creations of *art* reside in a hyperreflective universe whose concerns reach levels that are simply beyond the immediate needs of the modern self who struggles in daily life for coherence, for internal structure; who suffers silently, like Julia, against the ever present threat of disintegration; or who, like Billy, find themselves locked into a silent, inner universe. To contain and repair states of terrified distraction, immobilizing thoughts, horrifying sensations of breaking apart: that is the core of the connection Kohut draws between psychoanalysis as an activity of self-understanding (and as a *therapy*) and the imperatives of a realistic sense of community and individuality.

It is not Kohut's view that hard choices are absent from politics, or that individuals lack heroic capacity, or that art should avoid mirroring human suffering and possibility. Nor does he believe that it is impossible for persons to reach into the patterns of their nuclear selves for inspiration and value. Quite the contrary: art reveals the greatest of human passions and actions; it demonstrates vital psychological and emotional realities, choices that encompass the individual's fate in tragic encounters with unconscious drives, primitive political forces, injustices of the most devastating kind. Art portrays the sheer will involved in keeping the self together, in assimilating and transcending both internal and external sources of disintegration and decay. And it is art that indirectly comments on such persons as Chuck, Ruth, David, and Julia—society's unrecorded, unwitnessed disintegrations—who demonstrate how fragile individuality is in contemporary society, how susceptible the self is to entropy and its debilitating consequences.

To conclude: in Kohut's view, psychoanalysis addresses (or should address) itself to "the loss of the secure feeling of being a unit in space, a continuum in time and a center for the initiation of actions and for the reception of impressions" (1977: 155–56). This Winnicottian notion of the "discontinuity of the self," which Kohut finds eloquently described in the literature of Marcel Proust and Franz Kafka and the art of Picasso, motivates his concerns as a therapist, about individuality. Kohut's aim is to restore cohesion, the central structure of both individuality and community, to the "diseased unmirrored self." Further, this concern motivates his critique of classical psychoanalytic drive theory which, in its Hobbesian preoccupation with instinctual energy, ignores the centrality of fragmentation.[13] "Classical theory cannot illuminate the essence of fractured, enfeebled, discontinuous human existence: it cannot explain the essence of the schizophrenic's fragmentation, the struggle of the patient who suffers from a narcissistic personality disorder to reassemble himself, the despair—the guiltless despair, I stress—of those who in late middle age discover that the basic patterns of their self as laid down in their nuclear ambitions and ideals have not been realized. Dynamic-structural metapsychology does not do justice to these problems of man, cannot encompass the problems of Tragic Man" (1977: 238).

Finally Kohut looks to art and metaphor to describe, to witness, what disintegration as a human event means; to provide images for reflecting parables of the nonhuman, the alienated, the lost self, the fragmented and schizophrenic aspects of human existence. But the contemporary mirrors lie not in the great hero standing alone against instinct and culture but in the disconnected, dissociative screams of a Gregor Samsa, in the faceless and dead universes of a painter such as Réné Magritte, and, I would add, in the distorted images of persons like Billy, Chuck, and Annie.

"Just as it is the understimulated child, the insufficiently responded-to child, the daughter deprived of an idealizable mother, the son deprived of an idealizable father, that has now become paradigmatic for man's central problem in our Western world, so it is the crumbling, decomposing, fragmenting, enfeebled self of this child and later the fragile, vulnerable, empty self of the adult that the great artists of the day describe—through tone and word, on canvas and in stone—and that they try to heal." It is threats to individuality, the breakup of the nuclear self, the nihilism of experience that become subjects of a textual language composed of image, metaphor, and symbol. "The musician of disordered sound, the poet of decomposed language, the painter and sculptor of the fragmented visual and tactile world: they all portray the breakup of the self and, through the reassemblage and rearrangement of the fragments, try to create new structures that possess wholeness, perfection, new meaning. . . . Gregor Samsa, the cockroach of Kafka's *Metamorphosis,* may serve here as an example. He is the child whose presence in the world had not been blessed by the empathic welcome of self-objects—he is the child of whom his parents speak impersonally, in the third person singular; and now he is a nonhuman monstrosity, even in his own eyes" (1977: 286–87).

In the words of Eugene O'Neill: "Man is born broken. He lives by mending. The grace of God is glue."[14] It is in this sense that the situation of so many patients described in this book takes on tragic properties and impels the self to exist and survive on or beyond the borders of civil society.

Notes

1 Metaphor as Political Knowledge

1. For a fascinating discussion delineating the relation between storytelling and narrative function, see Ricoeur's analysis (1984: 149–55) of "following a story."

2. Lacan (1968) also speaks of the symbolic dimension, the world of social rules and language that tie the self into civil society. Sherry Turkle (1980: 157–58), in her article on French antipsychiatry, has some interesting observations: "For Lacan, madness is not the negation of normality with normality defined as bad and madness as privileged or as an 'absolute' good [Laing's (1968) position, for example, in *The Politics of Experience*]. Madness is quite simply a kind of communication or expressed demand. Because the psychotic has not fully acceded to communication, the Symbolic dimension [what Harry Stack Sullivan (1953) calls 'consensual reality'], the order of language and society, his communications are difficult to decipher. . . . For Lacan, the resolution of the Oedipal crisis marks the entrance of the subject into the discourse of language and society which he refers to as the Symbolic dimension. We enter the Symbolic dimension by accepting our father's rules and interdictions and, through him, we accept social laws and social language which begin to live within us as presences."

For a fascinating analysis that weaves interconnections between psychotic and borderline states and the institutional-symbolic framework of capitalist values, see also Kovel 1981.

3. There is considerable dispute over the relation between chemistry, physiology, and states of mind; there is even dispute in medicine over the nature of physiological causality itself: is schizophrenia, for example, caused by a virus, by chemical imbalances

in the brain, by abnormal neurovascular structures? It seems to me that Grotstein's effort (1986: 55–56) to relate biology to psychology is a reasonable one and leaves open the possibility of taking a position on one side or the other, depending on the nature of the case, its phenomenology, and the kind of history available from the patient and his or her family: "I wish to emphasize my belief in the capacity of states of mind to alter the neurophysiology and the anatomy of the central nervous system, either temporarily or permanently, and therefore predispose the latter to become the unfortunate but inexplorable substrate for psychotic vulnerability." However, Grotstein raises the additional question of the impact of psychological trauma on the functioning of the nervous system itself: the relation between biology and psychology may be so delicate (and intricate) that the nervous system responds to overwhelming trauma by literal alteration in its chemical functioning and neurophysiological wiring. "The schizophrenic and the borderline patient have undergone an infantile catastrophe predisposing them to an infantile psychosis rather than to an infantile neurosis. The consequences of this [including biology] are the inconsequentialization of the experience itself, with a permanent alteration of the psyche in a manner that predisposes it to be unknowing of the significance and depth of human experience, or, when this experience is inescapable, to inevitable disorganization and fragmentation." And "whether the inability of the schizophrenic personality, born as it is in the ashes of an ancient infantile castastrophe [Grotstein's view of major causality, given his perspective as a psychoanalyst], has any bearing on the predisposition of schizophrenics toward brain damage and alterations of brain lateralization is a matter for speculation." (Contrariwise, a biological psychiatrist might argue that Grotstein's presuppositions about "infantile catastrophe" are "matters of speculation.")

4. Plato (1964) writes: "Then the mimetic art is far removed from truth, and this, it seems, is the reason why it can produce everything, because it touches or lays hold of only a small part of the object and that a phantom. . . . All the poetic tribe, beginning with Homer, are imitators of images of excellence and of the other things that they 'create' and do not lay hold on truth. . . . The imitator will neither know nor opine rightly concerning the beauty or the badness of his imitations" (10.598bc, 600e, 602a).

5. What the Greeks conceived of as public tragedy appears in different forms in the privacy and hiddenness of the mental hospital: the woman who kills her children; the man or woman who feels so overwhelmed by guilt that the effort is made to tear out the eyes; the self driven to murderous distraction by feelings of betrayal and passion. What I found unusual, however, if not outright bizarre, was the language of psychiatry in describing what Sophocles regarded as heinous crimes against humanity and self. It would take us too far afield here, both legally and philosophically, but it might be interesting to compare how the language of psychiatry encloses, for example, "Medea," and how the tragic poet describes the same act. What does it mean, for example, to speak of therapy for a woman (one who spent considerable time in a mental institution by court order) who has brutally murdered her two small children? What is the role of society in prescribing treatment for an action so horrendous? Is a clinical language sufficient to name and relate the psychological, historical, and existential components of the murder of one's own children? What is the responsibility of psychiatry in this regard, and what kind of meaning can treatment have in the context of a crime so unspeakable?

6. James (1971: 113) writes: "Thought and reality are made of one and the same stuff, which is the stuff of experience in general. . . . That which is outside of us and that which is inside, that which has extension and that which does not, blend into one another in an indissoluble marriage. This reminds me of those circular panoramas in which real objects, rocks, plants, broken chariots, etc., which occupy the foreground, are so ingeniously tied in with the painted background depicting a battle or a spacious landscape, that one can no longer distinguish the objects from the painting. The seams and the joints are imperceptible. Would this be possible if the object and the idea were absolutely dissimilar in nature?"

7. Derrida (1981: 105) quotes Nietzsche in this regard: "Let us renounce the notions of 'subject' and 'object,' and then the notion of 'substance,' and consequently all of its diverse modifications, for example, 'matter,' 'spirit,' and the other hypothetical beings, 'eternity,' and the 'immutability of matter,' etc. Thus we also get rid of materiality."

2 The Struggle between Delusion and Intersubjectivity

1. Mental patients and residents of therapeutic communities are subject to rules, restrictions, predefined policies, and administrative fiat. It makes little sense to maintain that mental patients, persons enclosed by institutions, given diagnoses by medical authority, are as free and equal as staff, psychiatrists, psychologists, administrators, nurses, and mental health workers. The professions, as Michel Foucault (1954) has argued, define and classify; they constitute regimes of power; psychiatry draws boundaries around appropriate and inappropriate speech and action. Therefore, inequality exists in the operation of institutional environments. But the politics of institutions is not the focus of this book. It is not my intent to belabor what has already been carefully argued in treatises on what Erving Goffman (1961) called "total institutions."

2. "In psychosis," writes Grotstein (1986: 41), the self "may deteriorate to the zero dimension of nullity or infinity in which the walls and dimensions of the space-time continuum collapse, leaving fragmentation and dissolution." Consciousness "may restitute pathologically in the negative first dimension of autistic reconstruction in which a makeshift world, a mock-up copy of the external world, seems to be secretly purloined from the real world and taken into the inner labyrinth of the autistic world." Yet even in this copied world, in the radical form of what Plato called "semblance," the self still lives and remains very much alive, although "delusionally self-sufficient and logically consistent." It is, however, a life that keeps the self empty and depleted, unattached and alone, a rote object carrying out ritualized actions.

Notice how Foucault (1954: 51, 48–49) describes this state of being: "The schizophrenic's time is also subject to interruption but this occurs through the imminence of the Sudden and the Terrifying, which the patient can escape only through the myth of an empty eternity; the schizophrenic's temporality is thus divided between the fragmented time of anxiety and the formless, contentless eternity of delusion"; "The most consistent delusion appears to the patient just as real as reality itself."

3. For some classic studies on manic-depression (and its psychological components), see K. Abraham (1911), "Notes on the Psychoanalytical Investigation and Treatment of

Manic-Depressive Insanity and Allied Conditions," in *Selected Papers of Karl Abraham* (London: Hogarth Press, 1949), pp. 137–56; H. Deutsch (1951), in "Panel on Mania and Hypomania," *Bull. Amer. Psychoanal. Assn.* 7:265–76; S. Freud (1917), *Mourning and Melancholia,* Standard Edition, 14:237–60 (London: Hogarth Press, 1961); E. Jacobson (1953), "Contribution to the Metapsychology of Cyclothymic Depression," in *Affective Disorders,* ed. P. Greenacre (New York: International Universities Press); M. Klein (1935), "A Contribution to Psychogenesis of Manic-Depressive States," in Klein 1948; B. D. Lewin (1959), "Some Psychoanalytic Ideas Applied to Elation and Depression," *Amer. J. Psychia.* 116:38–43; M. S. Mahler (1966), "Notes on Development of Basic Moods—The Depressive Affect," in *Psychoanalysis—A General Psychology,* ed. R. B. Loewenstein et al. (New York: International Universities Press); P. N. Pao (1968), "On Manic-Depressive Psychosis: A Study of the Transition of States," *Amer. J. Psychoanal.* 16:809–832. For a biological approach, see D. Rosenthal (1975), "The Spectrum Concept in Schizophrenic and Manic-Depressive Diseases," in *Biology and Major Psychoses,* ed. D. X. Freedman (New York: Raven Press).

4. From earlier psychiatric notes:

The patient is admitted to —— because of the emergence of another attack of the manic type. He is greatly overactive, overtalkative, unable to sleep and constantly on the run, so much so that he undertook tremendous runs . . . and [excursions]. . . . David is readmitted to —— at his own request, caused by a marked intensification of a manic and distraught state which had been developing while he was studying at —— University and which we have been unable to control adequately on an out-patient basis. He has been overactive, losing weight and not eating well. He is up at all hours, talking endlessly and is quite literally running too hard. . . . The day before admission he ran frantically to Kennedy's grave in order to put a compass on the perpetual flame. [He said he did this] to give a new direction to the country. Then he ran to the Lincoln Memorial to kill a Lincoln penny. There is some grandiosity from time to time in that he writes poetry and thinks of himself as one of the great poets, and sends his writings to prominent public figures.

On admission, his mood is very high. He is elated, furious and perhaps delusional, although he did not express these clearly, but his whole manner is grandiose. His sensorium is quite clear. There is a fair amount of cooperation, but rather poor control of his behavior. He is restless, pacing, wolfing his food, and is unable to relax. [He] will scream at night. He loses his temper, smokes all the time, and when he runs out of cigarettes, takes other patients' and ransacks the drawers of another patient's furniture, and turns over flowerpots, and in a temper tantrum sets fire to a paperback in the middle of his floor accidentally. This causes a serious smoke problem, because of the composition of the flooring. . . . David [formulates] grandiose ideas about life and its meaning and [has constructed] the symbolism of a mandala for the entire world.

5. Even with his preoccupations, his fantasy life, and his flights into mania (delusion), David often appeared sane and coherent, as noted in psychiatric reevaluation several weeks after his admission to Sheppard-Pratt:

A neatly, though casually dressed, clean-cut looking young man walked in, sat down and was generally cooperative. He seemed to be in good contact with the interviewer and had a very personable, ingenuous charm about him. There was some degree of anxiety and obvious inner conflict, but not to say inappropriate or unseemly affect. His presentation was quite likeable. His speech was clear, coherent, relevant and logical, though at times he hesitated, paused and was silent for very short periods of time. There were no abnormalities in word usage. His mood seemed mildly depressed with a blunted though appropriate affect. There was no evidence of hallucinations, delusions or suicidal thinking, though specific questions were not asked about this.

6. Fantasies, which defended David from the terror of community, worked in the following way. David would meet someone, usually a woman; then he would fantasize a relationship as the meeting developed. The fantasy, unknown to the other person, played out ambitious projects: marriage, successful career, children, life in a mansion, scenes of happiness and fun (particularly hiking, sailing, canoeing), elaborate plans for the future. The actual meeting would last only a short time; it might be a chance encounter with no meaning beyond a bit of small talk, but while it continued, David built imaginative scenarios that he kept hidden—scenarios that had nothing to do with the reality of the event itself. When the other person (inevitably) went away, David would experience intense disappointment and despair, feelings bordering on death or imminent disintegration. A few hours later the relationship was dead and finished, as if it had never taken place. David may even have believed that the other person had died. From the woman's point of view, the meeting was often terribly awkward, filled with long periods of silence, lots of staring, and serious looks. She might feel uncomfortable but be unable to explain why. She would cut the meeting short and leave, thinking of David as a shy, nervous young man to be avoided.

Such fantasy was critical in David's difficulties with intimacy and closeness; it should, however, be distinguished from delusion, because fantasy was David's effort to contact real others and real situations. It provided an inner place where David "tested," as he put it, or perceived different permutations within a given context. While it served emotionally protective functions, fantasy never removed David psychically (as had delusion) from the intersubjective world; rather, it brought him face to face, particularly in his therapy, with the interpenetration of imagination (and the reasons he relied on fantasy) and reality. It was a source of often great pain but also of self-awareness, since David could distance himself from such a fantasy, talk about it, and reflect on its meaning and cause.

7. The seductiveness of the Sirens' song draws Ulysses, but even though it is "melodious," it disguises the real madness and viciousness of their intention. "'Come this way, most admirable Odysseus, glory of the nation: stay your ship, and listen to our voice! No man ever yet sailed past this place, without first listening to the voice which sounds from our lips sweet as honey! No, he has a great treat and goes home a wiser man.' . . . So they sang in lovely tones. From the bottom of my heart I longed to listen, and I ordered the men to set me free, nodding my head and working my brows; but they simply went on pulling with a good swing" (Homer 1937: 141–42). Circe, however, earlier had warned Ulysses to watch out for the Sirens' seduction: "First you will come to the Sirens, who bewitch every one who comes near them. If any man draws near in his innocence and listens to their voice, he never sees home again, never again will wife and little children run to greet him with joy; but the Sirens bewitch him with their melodious song. There in a meadow they sit, and all round is a great heap of bones, mouldering bodies and withering skins" (1937: 138). Similarly, delusion entices the self; it isolates consciousness. It pulls being away from the social world. It entraps and seduces. And it represents a viciousness as terrifying and dangerous as the Sirens' fatal call.

After his bouts with psychosis, David reminded himself that once again he had avoided the fate of the Sirens' victims: a catastrophe that had turned them into a pile of "mouldering" bones and "withering skins." Ulysses' being bound to the mast, exhorting his crew not to untie him, insisting they plug their ears: all this for David constituted real parallels to his psychological situation. David endured voices and delusions; he fought with his own inner Sirens. But he also knew that when he found himself in his own "straits of the Sirens," in the midst of a manic episode, he would not destroy himself. The environment, he knew, would respond with holding and protection. In his madness he would be kept from killing himself.

8. David periodically referred to his fate as being caught up in the whirlpool of Charybdis: "The other cliff is lower, as you will see, Odysseus. They are not far from one another; you could shoot an arrow across. There is a wild fig-tree growing from it, a tall tree covered with leaves; and Charybdis underneath swallows down the black water. Three times a day she spouts it out, three times a day she swallows it down: she is a terror—don't you be there when she swallows! No one could save you from destruction, not Earthshaker [Zeus] himself!" (Homer 1937: 140).

9. The imagery of forging a passage, struggling against the sea and the crazy tides of Charybdis, appears in David's poem "Logs":

> In transcience of thought
> I saw the mermaids cross my bow
> Staving off the albatross
> Pounding swells as salt spray
> Hit my face
> Flotsam of coffin pine woods
> In my wake.
> Barnacles of remembrance
> Tear through the waters of my passage
> and leeward to the coast
> Rock shore of country lost in wilderness
> Through the wrath of storming nightfall
> Towards the lighthouse bound.

3 Psychotic Terror

1. In many respects, David's psychotic regressions illustrate Grotstein's observation (1986: 31): "The patient has entered into what appears to be an alien world that is strange, bizarre, eerie, uncanny, and/or weird. . . . The space-time domain of psychosis is not that of the third dimension of boundaries, limitations and ordered sequences"; it approaches instead "the zero dimension [certainly indicated in David's altered states in LDS] where there are no boundaries and no sequences, only infinity and dissolution" (for example, David's becoming a particle). In the "restitutive phase" (analogous to David's reemergence from the mania), the images or delusions are not as extreme, as cosmic, but belong rather to the negative first dimension, the autistic world of reversals, of eerie imitations of the real world, of exaggerations, and more" (something akin to David's struggle up the "twenty-one levels" of reality).

What could be seen and heard of David's experience in LDS, the language and behavior of his delusional wilderness, was recorded in nursing notes taken every fifteen minutes. A few selections demonstrate the distance of his experience from the gaze of sympathetic observers. Very little of David's symbolic world appeared in these notes; his delusions remained so intensely private that they emerged only sporadically with no hint of their vast systems and cataclysmic transformations.

—Pt. [patient] was yelling and stated he wanted to kill himself; he was trying to scratch his wrist with his nails.
—Sporadic banging of door . . . banging on wall.
—Pt. on hands and knees on mat; continues to laugh bizarrely and makes loose connections, disorganized.
—Pt. acknowledged "hearing voices"; appears frightened and says he can't "tolerate the pressure, pressure to achieve greatness," yelling female peer's name, scratching at door.
—Pt. stated he was lonely and needy . . . banging on door, continues to say he is lonely and needs someone to hold him.
—Pt. screaming quite loudly, states he's claustrophobic and wants to be let out . . . banging on door saying he "can't take much more of this." [This entry occurred toward the end of David's stay in seclusion; it would place him, in his own journey, somewhere around "level fifteen or sixteen." He found it a "little easier" to contain himself, and he began to experience seclusion as "tight, confining, four walls closing in on me." It was, according to David, a sign that the mania was fading.]
—Pt. reported several times "it's going to be a hell of a night" [David experienced himself here as a prostitute in a hotel room]. Most of what he says does not make much sense [to the observer] such as, "I am a woman and I wonder why I'm not having my period." Later talked about "menstrual cycles" and has worn a blanket over his head while wandering around quiet room.
—Pt. yelling, banging, screaming, "Help, help, help."

David's emergence from psychosis went back and forth, but the direction always lay towards reintegration, and each day brought him closer to the world of persons, to intersubjectivity. It would be a mistake to underplay the role of an experiential dialectic (engagement with others) in diminishing the terror of delusional states and their hold on his organization of knowledge. Even with medication, otherness finally drew him back into the human world:

> In seclusion, I constantly talked to God, but as I came back, God disappeared from my mind; other people seemed more interesting. It's not that I forgot the delusions. I recalled them as bad dreams, horrible nightmares, and hallucinations. Eventually the quiet room became distasteful to me, and I looked forward to recesses, which became long and more involved with other patients. That suited me. It was like waking up from a monstrous horror show. The terror and panic subside; and the quiet room becomes simply four walls, a bare mattress, nothing much more, a place of bad memory.

4 Withdrawal from the Public World

1. The term "borderline" has a number of different meanings and a somewhat complex history. Its modern psychiatric debut can be traced to Knight (1953), although Stern (1938) apparently was the first to use the term. Its psychoanalytic lineage may be

found in Deutsch's (1942) classic study of the "as if" personality, Zilboorg's (1941) analysis of ambulatory schizophrenia, and Federn's (1952) discussion of latent schizophrenia. Gunderson and Singer (1975) provide an interesting discussion of what borderline signifies and whether the term means patient, state, personality organization, character, pattern, or syndrome.

Some of the most important *psychoanalytic* approaches include those of Kernberg and Masterson. Kernberg (1967: 10–11) looks for "descriptive symptoms" as "presumptive evidence." For example, he lists "Anxiety; Polysymptomatic neurosis [e.g., multiple phobias, bizarre conversion symptoms, dissociating reactions, hypochondriasis]; Polymorphous perverse sexual trends; 'Classical' prepsychotic personality structures [e.g., paranoid personality, schizoid personality, hypomanic personality]; Impulse neurosis and addictions; 'Lower level' character disorders." Kernberg (1967: 12–24) also points to the importance of identity diffusion and the role of primitive defense mechanisms such as splitting, primitive idealization, projection, projective identification, denial, omnipotence and devaluation, and lack of superego integration.

Masterson (1976: 29) argues that "separation for the borderline patients does not evolve as a normal development experience but, on the contrary, entails such intense feelings as abandonment that it is experienced as truly a rendezvous with death." The patient "thus fails to progress through the normal developmental stages of separation-individuation to autonomy." Many commentators (e.g., Boyer and Giovacchini 1967) argue that while patients with borderline personality disorder suffer complex and difficult object relations and significant feelings of emptiness, and may in fact act out a great deal, they still do not fall within the sphere of psychotic illness. For a good review of the characteristics of the borderline personality, see Barley et al. (1986). To be "borderline" is to exist in a terribly disruptive emotional state, but it is not to be insane. "If we think of the neurotic dilemma in terms of excursions of a pendulum, we might say that the excursions of the pendulum in the psychological world of the borderline patient cover an infinitely wider amplitude than in the world of the neurotic" (Masterson 1976: 17).

Masterson's work has been greatly influenced by Mahler (1975) and her theory of phases of development, particularly the relation she draws between the role of the mother (or the person performing the mothering function) and the child's efforts at separation and individuation. This theme has been extended and amplified by the observations of Schulz (1980) on the "all or nothing" position of the borderline. Kohut (1977: 114) takes a considerably different perspective and speaks about the violence of borderline types as a consequence of failures in the early empathic relation. While he does not use the borderline category (or diagnosis), many of his narcissistic patients do possess what are generally regarded (especially in more traditional psychoanalytical approaches) as borderline symptoms. His patients' "destructiveness," he argues, should be seen "not as the manifestation of a primary drive that is gradually unveiled by the analytic process, but as a disintegration product, which, while it is primitive, is not psychologically primal." Winnicott (1965: 233), who in many respects shares affinities with Kohut, speaks of the primitive quality of the individual's relationship to objects; such relations "include a splitting of the object, so that ambivalence is avoided, and also splitting in the personality itself to match the splitting of the object." This situation gives rise to "crude talion fears, which make the individual withdraw from relating to objects." See also Modell (1963). For the historical line of thinking that sees what

Kernberg calls "borderline personality organization" as a function of disturbance in object relations, see Deutsch 1942, Fairbairn 1952, Jacobson 1964, Kernberg 1975, and Klein 1946. For a comprehensive review of object relations theory, see Greenberg and Mitchell (1986).

2. According to the definition of "Borderline Personality Disorder," in *Diagnostic and Statistical Manual of Mental Disorders III*, 3d ed. (Washington, D.C.: American Psychiatric Association, 1980, 322–23), at least five of the following are required:

(1) impulsivity or unpredictability in at least two areas that are potentially self-damaging, e.g., spending, sex, gambling, substance abuse, shoplifting, overeating, physically self-damaging acts;

(2) a pattern of unstable and intense interpersonal relationships, e.g., marked shifts of attitude, idealization, devaluation, manipulation (consistently using others for one's own ends);

(3) inappropriate, intense anger or lack of control of anger, e.g., frequent displays of temper, constant anger;

(4) identity disturbance manifested by uncertainty about several issues relating to identity such as self-image, gender identity, long-term goals or career choice, friendship patterns, values and loyalties, e.g., "Who am I," "I feel like I am my sister when I am good";

(5) affective instability: marked shifts from normal mood to depression, irritability, or anxiety, usually lasting a few hours and only rarely more than a few days, with a return to normal mood;

(6) intolerance of being alone, e.g., frantic efforts to avoid being alone, depressed when alone;

(7) physically self-damaging acts, e.g., suicidal gestures, self-mutilation, recurrent accidents or physical fights;

(8) chronic feelings of emptiness or boredom.

This definition misses the peculiar permeability between delusion and consensual reality. In my experience it was quite common to find delusional forms of identification in borderline patients, particularly during periods of intense stress. Personality disorders have enormous influence on epistemology.

6 Return to the Human Text

1. Examples of Ruth's openness and willingness to reflect on her experience appear in the following excerpts from her activities therapy chart.

May 30: There has been a profound shift in her, in her sense of self (rudimentary but growing) and self esteem, and in her sense of what she wants in her life (divorce, children, school, etc.), and in her ability to work with other people constructively rather than in her old, frustrating, yes/no pattern. She continues to need work, particularly on developing her sense of self, liking her body and ego boundaries.

June 22: In Art Therapy, her images focus on the victim role lately and more on relationship with others. In sessions she is moody and showing more aggressiveness, sarcasm, and energy. In Interpersonal Skills, Ruth continues to consolidate earlier gains. She projects a more confident posture and is more open in facial expression, shows a broader range of affect, all indicative of a balanced self esteem.

June 26: The psychodynamic thrust of her work [in Dance Therapy] now is autonomy, the ability to stand on her own two feet. Her legs are important to her as is her strength, her ability to say and do what needs to be done, to sort out her old life and to build a new one, her ability to represent herself and her needs accurately, appropriately, and sensitively in relationship to others without feeling put down, undeserving, or in need of a false front. In the Dance Therapy group she takes on the role of the rebellious adolescent with skilled pleasure, fully conscious of exploring this role. She is feeling a new freedom to move. In individual work, the work also involves all manner of aggressive play, push, pull, drag, sock, grab, etc. She remains concerned, however, that others feel intimidated by her, afraid of her, and she will be working on this particularly over the next few weeks, exploring this fear in movement as in verbal sharing.

July 12: Ruth has made significant progress in her sense of self and in her capacity for self-observation and reflection. She is excited by her self-discovery, almost as though she is for the first time discovering who she is apart from her earlier relationships and their familiar expectations. She is giving and receiving much feedback and is more risk-taking and seems to have a real desire to understand rather than her former aggressive defensive responses. In Art Therapy, she has criticized the group for the lack of self-disclosure, but it is interesting to note that *in her scorn she seemed to forget that she was the same way six or eight months earlier* [my italics].

2. For an incisive and thorough intellectual biography of Melanie Klein, see Grosskurth 1987; for an approach to the philosophic and political implications of Klein's theory, see Alford (forthcoming).

3. In Kohut's view, the psychoanalytic relation allows for the representation or re-creation of early infantile distortions; it restores, through the different transferences, the course of "gradual modification" to the "grandiose self"—a process "traumatically in-terrupted in childhood" (1971: 108). It enables the self to refract its injuries, to visual-ize their structure (partly through the activation of fantasy), to assimilate infantile sensations of entitlement, unexplainable anxieties, and frustrations.

7 The Wish for Nonbeing

1. It is not that the borderline self *is* the political world; it is rather that the *breakdown* of self provides insight into extremes that may present danger to the cohesion of the polity. E.g., when Plato (1964: Book IX) speaks of the decline of the ideal city, he ties that decline (and fragmentation) to the destruction of character; the structure of the self reflects the structure of the state. The self becomes a microcosmic representation for broader tendencies and failures in structures governing the polity. For Aristotle (1978), that breakdown entails the regime of the "mean": the capacity to rule and be ruled, to achieve balance and moderation, to control desire and its power of separation and isolation.

2. For the borderline self, the violence of the inner world defines all properties of the external world. This is particularly striking in the case of Alexandra, a twenty-year-old patient who spent less than a year at Sheppard-Pratt. Extremely abusive and violent, constantly in quiet room, vomiting, defecating, urinating, tearing up foam mattresses, Alexandra nonetheless possessed an extraordinary artistic ability. During one episode she ripped up a foam mattress and constructed soft sculptures of staff in different stages of being hung, strangled, and mutilated. She drew similar pictures on the quiet-room

walls, even more gruesome than the foam sculptures. Death, mutilation, annihilation: these were Alexandra's world as represented in art. From all accounts her spontaneous action-artwork was horrifying, and the nooses drawn on the walls were eloquent testimony to the extent of her alienation and rage against the human world and anyone's efforts to come close to her. Throughout her hospitalization Alexandra remained isolated, unpredictable in her outbursts; she had little knowledge of a shared community of ends.

3. For interesting treatments of this theme, see Bloch 1978 and Miller 1986.

4. Shoshana Felman (1983: 1031) emphasizes the power of the death instinct symbology in Lacan's interpretation: "At the same time that *Oedipus at Colonus* dramatizes the 'eternization' of the Oedipal desire through its narrative symbolization, that is, Oedipus' birth into his symbolic *life,* into his historical, mythic *survival,* the later play also embodies something of the order of an Oedipal *death instinct,* since Oedipus, himself the victim of a curse and of a consequent parental rejection, pronounces, in his turn, a mortal curse against his sons. Oedipus' destiny is thus marked by a repetition-compulsion, illustrating and rejoining, in Lacan's eyes, Freud's tragic intuition in *Beyond the Pleasure Principle.*"

5. Felman (1983) argues that the myth of Oedipus at Colonus motivated Lacan's own self-identification in the psychoanalytic movement and as a practitioner of psychoanalysis (the "doing" of the theory). In addition, she suggests, Lacan interpreted Freud's formulation of a death instinct in *Beyond the Pleasure Principle* (a position discounted or ignored by the psychoanalytic establishment) as a kind of primary masochism, and he emphasized the importance of the presence of death in the language of the unconscious and the self's own historical context. Felman draws striking parallels between the project and drama of Oedipus and Freud's and Lacan's own relation to Sophocles' representations.

6. A number of articles deal with the function of the transitional object in the borderline's world. Gunderson, Morris, and Zanarini (1985) provide a review of the empirical and psychoanalytic literature and also suggest guidelines for further research that takes into account both empirical and psychoanalytic formulations. Arkema (1981: 23) argues that the borderline utilizes the transitional object "in a passive regressive perceptual mode that has the qualities of a first transitional object." Gaddini and Gaddini (1970) stress its cultural and symbolic features, an argument that bears certain parallels to Greenacre's (1969) view that the transitional object is a stage in the individuation process. Also see Brody 1980, Coppolillo 1967, Feinsilver 1983, and Kahane 1967.

7. Aristotle (1978) speaks of citizenship in a very practical sense, defining the citizen by one criterion as "a man who shares in the administration of justice and in the holding of office" (3.1274b32). It would be difficult to attribute to the patients discussed in this book, including Julia, citizenship in the strict sense of the formal requirements that Aristotle describes in the *Politics*. But the Aristotelian view, broadly understood, applies if citizenship for these persons is interpreted for what it is in a realistic way, given capacity and situation: a terribly difficult project of embracing, through tentative efforts, the public world and its insistence on engagement and organization. In the small face-to-face places of collaborative therapeutic interaction, there is an opportunity to practice a form or style of citizenship. And this practice of citizenship (even though

when it does appear in action it may be rudimentary) is, in terms of its foundations and ethics, *Aristotelian* in principle.

8. The Aristotelian approach to citizenship, the play of excellence, moral equality, and a willingness to understand self in the context of moral standards, involves relations among others that enhance the aims of community. Christopher Lasch (1984: 254) writes: "The highest form of practice, for Aristotle and his followers, is politics, which seeks to promote the good life by conferring equal rights on all citizens and by establishing rules and conventions designed not so much to solve the problems of social living as to encourage citizens to test themselves against demanding standards of moral excellence. . . . The Aristotelian conception of practice has more in common with play than with activities defined as practical in the modern sense. Practices in the Aristotelian sense have nothing to do, as such, with the production of useful objects or with satisfying material needs."

Aristotelian practices certainly presumed a respect for self and others and an unyielding commitment to the community and what it represents ethically. In this sense, practical reason (*phronesis*) and its political context may be thought of in the context of the view of play described by Winnicott (1971: 51–52): "There is a direct development from transitional phenomena to playing, and from playing to shared playing, and from this to cultural experiences. . . . Playing implies trust. . . . Playing is essentially satisfying. . . . Playing can be said to reach its own saturation point, which refers to the capacity to contain experience." I am not suggesting that Winnicott's view of play is a direct analogue to the Aristotelian notion of cooperation, but it may be a psychological underpinning or framework for a more comprehensive sense of public "play."

8 "Mama, Make Me Dead"

1. Freud (1900: 261–63) reads the drama of *Oedipus the King* as a commentary on willful but unconscious intentionality; at Colonus, however, the crime and its aftermath, far from being a childhood fantasy, bring down upon Oedipus a historical fate that destroys his virtue (*arete*) and banishes him to the world of the "heartless." In Aristotelian terms, Oedipus's actions have taken him perilously close to the "uncivil," the world of "beasts," the self without goodness or polity. Blinded, an outcast, caught up in his own horror and pain, no longer the good ruler or the good man, Oedipus endures his anguish and, even more grimly, directs his hatred at his own sons. The regime of guilt continues to destroy and perpetuate itself.

at first
My mind was a boiling cauldron, nothing so sweet
As death, death by stoning, could have been given me;
Yet no one there would grant me that desire.
It was only later, when my madness cooled,
And I had begun to think my rage excessive,
My punishment too great for what I had done;
Then it was that the city—in its good time!—
Decided to be harsh, and drove me out . . .
Out I went, like a beggar, to wander forever!

[Sophocles 1960 2.433–41, 445]

2. It might be interesting to think of Ruth's voice as a delusional transitional object that allowed her to make her journey from the futility and sadism inside (the void of her depression) to outside, reestablishing the patterns of her historical self.

10 Boundaries of a Public Selfhood

1. Derrida sees Lévi-Strauss as a modern Rousseauian who finds in the central Brazilian Indians the kind of innocence and uncorrupted naturalness that Rousseau attributed to the "state of nature." Further, Derrida argues that the Rousseauian critique of writing (as a form of domination and enslavement) also appears in Lévi-Strauss's formulations regarding the nature of the Indians and the extent to which their civilization has remained uncorrupted or unpolluted by Western values (writing as a form of keeping track of slaves, counting, political economy, and so on). Derrida (1977: 133) quotes from Rousseau's *Emile*—a sentiment, he adds, that can be found with equal fervor in Lévi-Strauss's *Tristes tropiques*—"O man . . . behold your history, such as I have thought to read it, not in books written by your fellow creatures, who are liars, but in nature, which never lies." If, along these same lines, it is nature (a state of mind and being that represents little in the way of culture or socialization) which emerges when one listens to those the society calls mad, then the utterance (like the rituals and myths of primitive societies) contains a significance, a resonance that moves in different directions from reason or rationality (the Hobbesian "reckoning of consequences"). Rousseau may be seen as a critic of this kind of rationality, just as Lévi-Strauss launches an attack against traditional anthropology for its overly ethnocentric and rationalistic approach to primitive tribes. Further, the utterance of the mad (or, better, the psychically homeless) may be considered Rousseauian in the sense that it is the language of the heart (the self unmediated by social forms), a linguistic place that constitutes a view or commentary on the structures of civil society and its values.

For the seriously mentally ill to attain, much less establish, a faith in community is a transformation as compelling as for Rousseau's natural man to leave nature for the moral benefits and interdependencies of political association. The argument for the civilizing and moral effects of culture also appears in the Aristotelian concept of association. Existence outside of community or association is no existence at all.

For a fascinating analysis that shows the parallelism between the theories of Lévi-Strauss and Rousseau, see Derrida's "Nature, Culture, Writing" (1978: 97–118; see esp. 101–6 for a general discussion of the nature/culture opposition and its relation to Rousseau's thought).

11 The Politics of Exclusion

1. It makes little sense to confront schizophrenics with an ideological-political critique of their illness if, while you are constructing a political position, they feel themselves being picked apart by an ax or burned alive by the fires of Hell. Nor does it make much sense to attribute causality to a *strictly* historical-capitalistic-economic matrix when the actual family histories of so many schizophrenics (as Laing, e.g., demon-

strates) are horrendous and when there is overwhelming evidence suggesting either intrapsychic or interpersonal or biological causes.

Deleuze and Guattari (1983), Foucault (1979), Laing (1968), and Szasz (1974) exercise important critical functions in reminding psychiatry and psychiatrists of their too frequent neglect of public, political, and economic factors in the definition, diagnosis, and causality of mental illness. It is a mistake, therefore, to dismiss these theories and the entire antipsychiatry position or not to listen to its criticism. But when theory becomes overly ideological, the patient tends to disappear and the critique dominates the discussion. I urge that the primary focus, from whatever vantage, should be *what the self speaks,* the utterance of estrangement or madness and the meaning it conveys about self and world.

2. For an analysis of this phenomenon, see H. R. Lamb (1980: 1224–28); and Bachrach (1978: 573–78). Bachrach calls for a "reassessment" of the plight of those persons who have "largely been lost to the service delivery system" (p. 575). Also see Bachrach 1980.

The federal government has sponsored a number of studies; one of the best is "Report of the Last Panel on Deinstitutionalization, Rehabilitation, and Long-Term Care," in *Task Panel Reports Submitted to the President's Commission on Mental Health,* vol. 1 (Washington, D.C., 1978), esp. pp. 356–75.

3. See R. F. Mollica (1983), "From Asylum to Community: The Threatened Disintegration of Public Psychiatry," *N. Engl. J. Med.* 308:367–73. Mollica points to the serious problems of treating lower-class patients, including the fact that "universal entitlement" for the mentally ill does not mean or translate into plentiful facilities. Also see H. Goldman and N. H. Adams (1983), "Deinstitutionalization: The Data Demythologized," *Hosp. and Comm. Psych.* 34:129–34.

4. The literature is copious on this theme; for general overviews, see Bachrach 1983; J. A. Talbott (1981), *Chronic Mental Patients: Treatment, Progress, Systems* (New York: Human Sciences Press); J. A. Talbott, ed. (1981), *The Chronic Mental Patient* (New York: Grune & Stratton).

5. An increasingly influential argument in the literature suggests that it may be time to rethink the role of the state hospital in caring for the chronically mentally ill. E.g., Leona Bachrach (1986) finds that 50 of every 100,000 people in the U.S. population reside as patients in state mental hospitals. Lamb (1984) points to the increasingly desperate situation of the homeless on the nation's streets and in urban centers. Several commentators note the utility of the state hospital as a place where "multiple functions" can be carried out humanely and with consideration of the welfare of the patient. The argument suggests novel forms of organizing services and programs within the state hospital physical setting: See H. H. Goldman, C. A. Taube, D. A. Reiger, et al. (1983), "The Multiple Functions of the State Mental Hospital," *Amer. J. Psychia.* 140:296–300. T. J. Craig and E. M. Laska (1983), "Deinstitutionalization and the Survival of the State Hospital," *Hosp. and Comm. Psych.* 34:616–22, call for "communitizing" the state hospital. For a discussion of "custodialism" versus "communitizing," see J. K. Wing (1981), "From Institutional to Community Care," *Psych. Quar.* 53:139–52. For a fascinating symposium on the *psychiatric* rehabilitation of chronic mental patients, see the NIMH publication *Schizophrenic Bulletin* 12, no. 4 (1986); cf. esp. John Strauss's rejoinder to the symposium, arguing that rehabilitation may in fact be considered a form of therapy. There has also been an extensive debate in Italy involving political

ideological arguments on both sides of the state hospital versus the "return to the community" issue; for a detailed examination of this debate, see *Hosp. and Comm. Psych.* 37 (August 1986).

6. For a discussion of this aspect of the plight of the homeless, see GAP 1982; D. A. Treffert (1977), "Sane Asylum: An Alternative to the Mental Hospital," *Curr. Psychiatr. Ther.* 17:309–14; E. Baxter and K. Hopper (1981), *Private Lives / Public Spaces: Homeless Adults on the Streets of New York City* (New York: Community Service Society of N.Y.); B. Pasamanick, F. R. Scarpitti, and S. Dinitz (1967), *Schizophrenia in the Community: An Experimental Study in the Prevention of Hospitalization* (New York: Appleton-Century-Crofts). The argument here is that conventional services are inadequate to the enormous demands and needs of the chronically ill. Also see M. E. Hombs and M. Snyder (1982), *Homelessness in America: A Forced March to Nowhere* (Washington, D.C.: Community for Creative Non-Violence).

7. Miller (1986) is considerably more sanguine than, e.g., Lamb (1984) regarding the capacity of community services to handle effectively the plight of the chronic mental patient. Also see J. E. Gudeman and M. F. Shore (1984), "Beyond Deinstitutionalization: A New Class of Facilities for the Mentally Ill," *N. Engl. J. Med.* 311:832–36; C. A. Kiesler (1982), "Mental Hospitals and Alternative Care," *Amer. Psychol.* 37:349–60; J. F. Borus (1981), "Deinstitutionalization of the Chronically Mentally Ill," *N. Engl. J. Med.* 305:339–42.

8. A number of persons generously contributed their time and effort in arranging this research. In Geel, I am indebted to Dr. H. Matheussen, medical director of the Central Psychiatric Hospital; to Dr. J. Schrijvers for his efforts in facilitating the visit and providing a translator; and to Frans Vaneynde, administrator of the hospital. In Israel, I am grateful to Dr. Michael Avrouskine of the Public Health Service for arranging interviews and setting up contacts; Dr. Yacov Naisberg of the Rambam Medical Center in Haifa for allowing me to accompany him on his rounds to local kibbutzim and serving as my interpreter at the Kirit Ata Workshop-Factory; Zalmon Sher, manager of the Kirit Ata shop; Muriel Dominitz, a social worker at Kibbutz Matsuva; Dr. Stanley Schneider, director of the Summit Institute in Jerusalem; Dr. Eric Moss, director of a community mental health center outside Tel Aviv; Toby and Judy Hammerman, social workers in a suburb of Tel Aviv; and Dr. Y. Bar-El, director of Kfar Shaul Mental Hospital in Jerusalem, who were all extremely helpful. Finally, I am much indebted to Dr. Uri Lowental for his kind hospitality and informative conversation.

9. For a critique of Foucault's conception of the hospital, particularly in terms of its function in providing a sense of place and constancy, see the discussion of the York retreat and of Samuel Tuke's conception of moral treatment in A. Rosenblatt (1985), "Concepts of the Asylum in the Care of the Mentally Ill," *Hosp. and Comm. Psych.* 35: 244–50.

10. Schumacher (1975) has had a profound influence on reassessing the relation between technology (its size and scale) and the sustenance and maintenance of human life. He has consistently argued for small-scale technologies adapted to place and need, and he sees a connection between such technologies (and their use) and the pursuit of community. Further, it is conceivable that his theory could be useful in thinking about the theory of community and its relation to the chronically mentally ill (with special emphasis on economic structure and technological implementation).

11. Rural Spring Lake Ranch in Cuttingsville, Vermont (Chapter 9, 10) and urban

Fountain House in New York City provide useful models for a workable and sensible theory of coproduction between an institution and chronically disturbed persons. Fountain House, providing post-hospital care, is a club run chiefly by former patients which serves meals and functions as a meeting place and community center. But it is known primarily for its success in training former mental patients for effective work relationships: its transitional employment program has been a model for more than 240 similar programs throughout the country and abroad. The paid staff is quite small; the work in the club, from housecleaning to meal preparation to office duties, is performed by the members. Further, an outreach program involves agreements with local employers whereby members may work in the club for a time, then be placed—generally for a six-month period—in an "outside" entry-level position. Currently, 600–700 members participate in the day programs, and some thirty local employers have agreed to employ 140 members part time. One member, who was a patient in a mental hospital for twenty years, says that the program has allowed her to "be with others" and, in her words, gives "you the pride of making your own money . . . being on your own." Fountain House, then, providing its members with training and the chance of gainful employment, is an alternative to long-term hospital care.

For a comprehensive approach to this question and an excellent review of a variety of modern programs, see Warner 1985.

12. For some pioneering studies of the effect of compartmentalization on treatment and relations within the hospital, see Caudill 1958; Greenblatt, Levinson, and Williams 1957; Stanton and Schwartz 1954. It should be mentioned that these works accept the hospital as a useful therapeutic environment and, unlike Goffman's (1961) global critique, each author accepts the fundamental and abiding legitimacy of the hospital as an institution.

13. Cf. Kohut's critique (1977: 247) of traditional interpretations of the Oedipus complex: "The dramatic, conflict-ridden Oedipus complex of classical analyses, with its perception of a child whose aspirations are crumbling under the impact of castration fear, is not a primary maturational necessity but only the frequent result of frequently occurring failures from the side of narcissistically disturbed parents."

14. From Eugene O'Neill, *The Great God Brown,* quoted in Kohut (1977: 287).

References

Alford, F. Forthcoming. *Melanie Klein and Critical Social Theory: An Account of Politics, Art, and Reason Based on Her Psychoanalytic Theory.* New Haven, Conn.: Yale University Press.

Arendt, H. 1958. *The Human Condition.* New York: Anchor, Doubleday.

Aristotle. 1978. *The Politics of Aristotle.* Trans. Ernest Barker. New York: Oxford University Press.

Arkema, P. H. 1981. "The Borderline Personality and Transitional Relatedness." *American Journal of Psychiatry* 138:172–77.

Bachrach, L. L. 1978. "A Conceptual Approach to Deinstitutionalization." *Hospital and Community Psychiatry* 29:573–78.

———. 1980. "Is the Least Restrictive Environment Always the Best? Sociological and Semantic Implications." *Hospital and Community Psychiatry* 31:97–103.

———. 1983. "An Overview of Deinstitutionalization." In *New Directions for Mental Health Services: Deinstitutionalization,* ed. L. L. Bachrach. San Francisco: Jossey-Bass.

———. 1986. "Deinstitutionalization: What Do the Numbers Mean?" and "The Future of the State Mental Hospital." *Hospital and Community Psychiatry* 37:118–221, 467–74.

Barley, W. D. et al. 1986. "Characteristics of Borderline Personality Disorder: Admissions to Private Psychiatric Hospitals." *Psychiatric Hospital* 17:195–99.

Bloch, D. 1978. *"So the Witch Won't Eat Me": Fantasy and the Child's Fear of Infanticide.* Boston: Houghton Mifflin.

Boyer, L. B., and P. L. Giovacchini. 1967. *Psychoanalytic Treatment of Characterological and Schizophrenic Disorder.* New York: Science Books.

Brody, S. 1980. "Transitional Objects: Idealization of a Phenomenon." *Psychoanalytic Quarterly* 49:561–605.

Bultmann, R. 1956. *Primitive Christianity in Its Contemporary Setting.* London: Thames & Hudson.

Caudill, W. Z. 1958. *The Psychiatric Hospital as a Small Society.* Cambridge, Mass.: Harvard University Press.

Coppolillo, H. P. 1967. "Maturational Aspects of the Transitional Phenomenon." *International Journal of Psychoanalysis* 48:237–46.

Deleuze, G., and F. Guattari. 1983. *Anti-Oedipus: Capitalism and Schizophrenia.* Minneapolis: University of Minnesota Press.

Derrida, J. 1978. *Of Grammatology.* Baltimore, Md.: Johns Hopkins University Press.

———. 1981. *Positions.* Chicago: University of Chicago Press.

———. 1982. "White Mythology: Metaphor in the Text of Philosophy." In J. Derrida, *Margins of Philosophy,* trans. Alan Bass. Chicago: University of Chicago Press.

———. 1984. "Mes chances." In *Taking Chances: Derrida, Psychoanalysis, and Literature,* ed. J. H. Smith and W. Kerrigan. Baltimore, Md.: Johns Hopkins University Press.

Deutsch, H. 1942. "Some Forms of Emotional Disturbance and Their Relationship to Schizophrenia." *Psychoanalytic Quarterly* 11:301–21.

Earle, P. 1887. *The Curability of Insanity.* Philadelphia: Lippincott; rpt. New York: Arno Press, 1972.

Ehrlich, R. 1985. "The Social Dimensions of Heinz Kohut's Psychology of the Self." *Psychoanalysis and Contemporary Thought* 8:333–54.

Fairbairn, W. R. D. 1952. *An Object Relations Theory of the Personality.* New York: Basic Books.

Fanon, F. 1968. *The Wretched of the Earth.* New York: Grove Press.

Federn, P. 1952. *Ego Psychology and the Psychoses.* New York: Basic Books.

Feinsilver, D. B. 1983. "Reality, Transitional Relatedness, and Containment in the Borderline." *Contemporary Psychoanalysis* 19:537–69.

Felman, S. 1983. "Beyond Oedipus: The Specimen Story of Psychoanalysis." In *Lacan and Narrative,* ed. R. C. David. Baltimore, Md.: Johns Hopkins University Press.

Foucault, M. 1954. *Mental Illness and Psychology.* New York: Harper & Row.

———. 1974. "On Attica: An Interview." *Telos* 19:154–62.

———. 1977. *Language, Counter-Memory, Practice: Selected Essays and Interviews.* Ed. D. F. Bouchard. Ithaca: Cornell University Press.

———. 1979. *Discipline and Punish.* New York: Vintage.

Freud, S. 1900. *The Interpretation of Dreams.* Standard Edition, vols. 4–5. London: Hogarth Press.

——. 1920. *Beyond the Pleasure Principles*. Standard Edition, vol. 18. London: Hogarth Press.

——. 1927. *The Future of an Illusion*. Standard Edition, vol. 21. London: Hogarth Press.

Gaddini, R., and E. Gaddini. 1970. "Transitional Objects and the Process of Individuation: A Study in Three Different Social Groups." *Journal of the American Academy of Child Psychiatry* 9:347–65.

GAP (Group for the Advancement of Psychiatry, Committee on Psychopathology). 1982. *Positive Aspects of Long-Term Hospitalizations in the Public Sector for Chronic Psychiatric Patients*. New York: Mental Health Materials Center.

Giovacchini, P. L. 1986. "Schizophrenia: Structural and Therapeutic Considerations." In *Comprehensive Model for Schizophrenic Disorders: Psychoanalytic Essays in Memory of Ping-Nie Pao, M.D.*, ed. D. B. Feinsilver. Hillsdale, N.J.: Analytic Press.

Glass, J. 1985. *Delusion: Internal Dimensions of Political Life*. Chicago: University of Chicago Press.

Goffman, E. 1961. *Asylums*. New York: Anchor Books.

Grade, C. 1976. *The Yeshiva*. New York: Bobbs-Merrill.

Greenacre, P. 1969. "The Fetish and the Transitional Object." *Psychoanalytic Study of the Child* 24:144–64.

Greenberg, J. R., and S. A. Mitchell. 1983. *Object Relations in Psychoanalytic Theory*. Cambridge, Mass.: Harvard University Press.

Greenblatt, M., D. J. Levinson, and R. H. Williams. 1957. *The Patient and the Mental Hospital*. Glencoe, Ill.: Free Press.

Grosskurth, P. 1987. *Melanie Klein: Her Work and Her World*. Cambridge, Mass.: Harvard University Press.

Grotstein, J. 1986. "Schizophrenic Personality Disorder: 'And If I Should Die before I Wake.'" In *Towards a Comprehensive Model for Schizophrenic Disorders: Psychoanalytic Essays in Memory of Ping-Nie Pao, M.D.*, ed. D. B. Feinsilver. Hillsdale, N.J.: Analytic Press.

Gunderson, J. G., H. Morris, and M. D. Zanarini. 1985. "Transitional Objects and Borderline Patients." In *The Borderline: Current Empirical Research*, ed. T. H. McGlashan. Washington, D.C.: American Psychiatric Press.

Gunderson, J., and M. Singer. 1975. "Defining Borderline Patients: An Overview." *American Journal of Psychiatry* 132 (January):1–10.

Hobbes, T. 1950. *Leviathan*. New York: Dutton.

Homer. 1937. *The Odyssey*. Trans. W. H. D. Rouse. New York: New American Library.

Jacobson, E. 1964. *The Self and the Object World*. New York: International Universities Press.

James, W. 1971. *Essays in Radical Empiricism and a Pluralistic Universe*. New York: Dutton.

Kafka, F. 1969. *The Trial*. New York: Vintage.

———. 1976. *Penal Colony: Stories and Short Pieces.* New York: Schocken.

Kahane, M. J. 1967. "On the Persistence of Transitional Phenomena into Adult Life." *International Journal of Psychoanalysis* 48:247–58.

Kernberg, O. 1967. *Severe Personality Disorders: Psychotherapeutic Strategies.* New Haven, Conn.: Yale University Press.

———. 1975. *Borderline Conditions and Pathological Narcissism.* New York: Jason Aronson.

Kierkegaard, S. 1954. *The Sickness unto Death.* Trans. W. Lourie. New York: Doubleday.

Klein, M. 1946. "Notes on Some Schizoid Mechanisms." In *Development in Psychoanalysis,* ed. J. Riviere. London: Hogarth Press, 1952.

———. 1948. *Contributions to Psychoanalysis: 1921–1945.* London: Hogarth Press.

Knight, R. 1953. "Borderline States." *Bulletin of the Menninger Clinic* 17:1–12.

Kohut, H. 1971. *The Analysis of the Self.* New York: International Universities Press.

———. 1977. *The Restoration of the Self.* New York: International Universities Press.

———. 1984. *How Does Analysis Cure?* Chicago: University of Chicago Press.

———. 1985. *Self Psychology and the Humanities.* New York: Norton.

Kovel, J. 1981. *The Age of Desire.* New York: Pantheon.

Lacan, J. 1968. *The Language of the Self.* New York: Delta.

———. 1977. *Ecrits: A Selection.* Trans. Alan Sheridan. New York: Norton.

———. 1978a. *The Four Fundamental Concepts of Psychoanalysis.* New York: Norton.

———. 1978b. *Le Seminaire, Livre II: Le moi dans le théorie de Freud et dans la technique psychoanalytique.* Paris: Seuil. Quoted in *Lacan and Narrative* (1983), ed. R. C. Davis. Baltimore, Md.: Johns Hopkins University Press.

Laing, R. D. 1968. *Politics of Experience.* New York: Ballantine.

Lamb, H. R. 1980. "Structure: The Neglected Ingredient of Community Treatment." *Archives of General Psychiatry* 37:1224–28.

———. 1984. "Deinstitutionalization and the Homeless Mentally Ill." *Hospital and Community Psychiatry* 35:899–907.

Lamb, H. R., and R. Peele. 1984. "The Need for Continuing Asylum in Sanctuary." *Hospital and Community Psychiatry* 35:798–802.

Lasch, C. 1984. *The Minimal Self.* New York: Norton.

Lévi-Strauss, C. 1969. *The Raw and the Cooked.* New York: Harper & Row.

———. 1973. *From Honey to Ashes.* New York: Harper & Row.

Mahler, Margaret S. 1975. *The Psychological Birth of the Human Infant.* New York: Basic Books.

Marx, K. 1964. *Early Writings.* New York: McGraw-Hill.

Masterson, J. F. 1976. *Psychotherapy of the Borderline Adult.* New York: Brunner/Mazel.

Miller, A. 1986. *For Your Own Good: Hidden Cruelty in Child-Rearing and the Roots of Violence.* New York: Farrar, Straus & Giroux.

Modell, A. H. 1963. "Primitive Object Relationships and the Predisposition to Schizophrenia." *International Journal of Psychoanalysis* 44:282–91.

Nietzsche, F. 1956. *The Birth of Tragedy and the Genealogy of Morals.* New York: Doubleday Anchor.

Pao, Ping-Nie. 1971. "Elation, Hypomania, and Mania." *Journal of the American Psychoanalytic Association* 19:787–98.

Plato. *The Republic.* 1964. Trans. P. Shorey. In *The Collected Dialogues of Plato,* ed. E. Hamilton and H. Cairns. New York: Bollingen Foundation.

Ricoeur, P. 1970. *Freud and Philosophy.* New Haven, Conn.: Yale University Press.

———. 1977. *The Rule of Metaphor.* Toronto: University of Toronto Press.

———. 1984. *Time and Narrative.* Chicago: University of Chicago Press.

Rousseau, J. J. 1950. *The Social Contract and Discourses.* New York: Dutton.

Sartre, J. P. 1949. *No Exit and Three Other Plays.* New York: Vantage.

Schulz, C. G. 1980. "The Contribution of the Concept of Self-Representation/-Object-Representation Differentiation to the Understanding of the Schizophrenias." In *The Course of Life: Psychoanalytic Contributions towards Understanding Personality Development,* vol. 1, *Infancy and Early Childhood,* ed. S. I. Greenspan and G. H. Pollock. Washington, D.C.: NIMH Publications.

Schumacher, E. F. 1975. *Small Is Beautiful: Economics as If People Mattered.* New York: Harper & Row.

Searle, J. 1969. *Speech Acts.* Cambridge: Cambridge University Press.

Searles, H. 1960. *The Non-Human Environment.* New York: International Universities Press.

Sophocles. 1960. *Oedipus at Colonus.* In *Greek Tragedies,* vol. 3, ed. D. Grene and R. Lattimore. Chicago: University of Chicago Press.

Stanton, A. H., and M. S. Schwartz. 1954. *The Mental Hospital: A Study of Institutional Participation in Psychiatric Illness and Treatment.* New York: Basic Books.

Stern, A. 1938. "Psychoanalytic Investigation of and Therapy in the Borderline Group of Neuroses." *Psychoanalytic Quarterly* 7:467–89.

Sullivan, H. S. 1953. *Conceptions of Modern Psychiatry.* New York: Norton.

Szasz, T. 1974. *The Myth of Mental Illness.* New York: Harper & Row.

Trilling, L. 1955. *The Opposing Self.* New York: Viking Press.

Turkle, S. 1980. "French Anti-Psychiatry." In *Critical Psychiatry, the Politics of Mental Health,* ed. D. Ingleby. New York: Pantheon.

Volkan, V. 1981. *Linking Objects and Linking Phenomena.* New York: International Universities Press.

Warner, R. 1985. *Recovery from Schizophrenia.* New York: Routledge & Kegan Paul.

Winnicott, D. W. 1958. *Collected Papers.* London: Tavistock.

———. 1965. *The Maturational Environment and the Facilitating Process.* New York: International Universities Press.

———. 1971. *Playing and Reality.* New York: Basic Books.

Zilboorg, G. 1941. "Ambulatory Schizophrenia." *Psychiatry* 4:149–55.

Index

References in italic refer to material in case studies.

"Aaron" (Spring Lake Ranch resident), 172–173
"Alexandra" (borderline patient), 230*n*2
"Andrew" (Sheppard-Pratt patient), 207–209
Anger
  in borderline patient, *63–65, 67*
  empathic absence in development and, 98–99
  self-mutilation and, 115
"Annie" (Spring Lake Ranch resident)
  background of, *168–169*
  current status of, 194
  desire for place and, *168–171*
  silent pain and, *174–175*
  on types of residents, 169, 187
Annihilation, fantasies of, *106–109, 143–147, 168.* See also Death; Suicide
Arendt, Hannah, 157–158
Aristotle
  citizenship and, 105–106, 230*n*1, 231*n*7, 232*n*8

eudaimonia and, 114
friendship and, 109
political view of self in, 1–2, 7, 115
Politics, 105
Association. *See also* Community; Public self
  Aristotelian pursuit of goodness and, 114
  basic need for, and psychotherapy, 162
  struggle toward, in storytelling, 14–15
Authenticity, and "natural" community, 190

Bachrach, L. L., 234*n*2
Bentham, Jeremy, 206
"Billy" (Spring Lake Ranch resident), 172–173, 194
Biological factors, 15, 23, 24, 221*n*3
Body-as-text, *114–118*
Borderline personality. *See also* "Julia"; "Ruth"

Borderline personality (*cont.*)
alienation of, 119
anger in, *63–65, 67*
community and, 119–120
confusion in, *63–65, 67*
consensual reality and, 56–57, 100–102, 119
delusion and, 56–58, *70, 86–88, 91, 95,* 127, *138–143*
emotional world of, 57–58, 230*n*2
empathic absence and, 98–101
as exile, 104–105
fascination with annihilation in, *106–109*
fear and, *118–122*
hallucination in, *70, 81–83, 93,* 109
hospitalization experience of, *60–71*
masochistic compulsion in, *113*
Oedipus at Colonus and, 103–104, 106, 112–113, 125, 193–194
pain and, *79, 90, 108, 136–137*
phenomenology of, 56–58
as political category, 120–121
psychotic states as regression and, 14–15
psychotic suffering by, *80–81*
relationships and, 105
self as poisonous and, 109–114
sense of worthlessness in, 104, *141, 145, 146*
transitional object and, 116, 231*n*6, 233*n*2
violence of inner world and, 230*n*2
wandering of consciousness in, 104–106, 112

Certification, effect of, on borderline patient, *89*
Charybdis, in imagery of manic-depressive patient, *226n8, 226n9*
Chemical factors, 15, 23, 24
Chronic mental patient
encouragement of productivity in, 213–214
problems facing, 195–198, 213
role of state hospital and, 234*n*5
"silent pain" of, *174–175*
state of invisibility and, 209–212
work and, 196–197, 203

"Chuck" (schizophrenic patient), 128–129, 193–194
Citizenship
community of the ward and, 50
as hard-won, *54, 55*
Civil religion, work as, 150, 191–192
Collectivist organizations. *See* Kibbutzim
Common will, 150, 167. *See also* Participative community
capacities of, *176–180*
communal deliberations and, 184–185
kibbutz and, 201–203
limitations of, *180–183*
privacy and, 159–166, 186–187, 189
purposes of hospital and, 165
as right, 184, 185, 188
at Spring Lake Ranch, 159–166, 184–190, 202–203
vs. will of all, 188–190
Community. *See also* Association; Intersubjectivity; Public self; Public space; Relationships; Therapeutic community
borderline self and, 119–120
drive for, 7
as holding environment, 94, 211–212
in mental hospital, 165
provision of, for former mental patients, 195–196
as refuge, 4
size of, and Rousseauian concept, 190–191
as therapeutic Other, 160
views of, among patients, 7, 14, 173
Compliance, and sense of self, *110–111*
Consciousness
participatory action and, 150
in Phase 3 delusion, 127
in Phase 4 delusion, 127
wandering of, in borderline self, 104–106, 112
Consensual reality
borderline patient and, 56–57, 100–102, 119
chronic mental patient and, 212
Phase 4 delusion and, 127–128
psychosis and, 56, 57
schizophrenic world view and, 210–212
unfree inner states and, 3

Control, illusion of, *115–118*
Coproduction, models of, 236*n*11. *See also* Kirit Ata Workshop
Crimes, heinous, and language of psychiatry, 222*n*5
Culture, illusion vs. delusion and, 16

"David" (manic-depressive patient)
  current status of, 194
  descent into mania, *35–42*
  effect of public space on intersubjectivity in, *29–55*
  "Logs" (poem), 226*n*9
  loneliness and, *31–34*
  overview of case, *29–31*
  Phase 3 delusion and, *131–132*
  untitled poem on isolation, *41–42*
Death. *See also* Annihilation; Suicide
  desire for, *113*
  fascination with, in borderline patient, 112
  narrative of borderline patient and, *108*
  narrative of schizophrenic patient and, *128–129*
  as way of life, 113
Deinstitutionalization, and need for community, 195–196
Delusion
  in borderline patient, 56–58, *70, 86–88, 91, 95, 138–143*
  characteristics of movement away from, *95*
  contrasted with illusion, 15–16, 122
  demystification of, *138–143*
  vs. fantasy, in manic-depressive patient, 225*n*6
  in narrative of borderline patient, *86–88*
  in narrative of manic-depressive patient, *131–132*
  participatory citizenship and, 2–4
  politics of, 3–5
  in psychotic vs. borderline categories, 56–58
  receding of, in resident of Spring Lake Ranch, 167–168
  reflexive distance and, *138–139*
  societal tolerance for, in chronic mental patients, 211
  as unnatural state, 2–4

Delusion typology, 125–128
  Phase 1, 125, 127, *128–129, 138–139*
  Phase 2, 127, *129–130*
  Phase 3, 127, 130, *131–132*
  Phase 4, 127–128, *132–143*
Demystification
  of delusion, *138–143*
  of fantasy, *143–147*
Depression
  lifting of, and transference relation, *139–143*
  masochism as a dynamic of, 135–143
  narrative of borderline patient and, 134
  as Phase 4 delusion, 132–134
Derrida, Jacques, 19–20, 23, 108, 185, 190, 191
Desire
  for death, *113*
  delusion as defense against, 52–53
  strength of, 20
Despair, in borderline patient, 103, *138*
Dewey, John, 100
Discharge from mental hospital, anxiety over, *206–209*
Disintegration anxiety, 98
Drive theory vs. Kohut's view of self, 99, 218
Dybbuk, 86–89, 93

Earle, Pliny, 197
"Ed" (Spring Lake Ranch resident), 172
Ehrlich, R., 97
Elimination from society, countervailing forces to, 209–212
Emotion. *See* Feelings
Emotional world, of borderline patient, 57–58
Empathy. *See also* Nonempathic world
  absence of, for borderline patient, 98–101
  Kohut definition of, 98
  as modulation of delusional terror, 94, 95
  political values and, 95, 100
Epistemological system, and typology of delusion, 131
Equality, 105, 150, 186
Etiology, 15

Eudaimonia, 114
"Eve" (Sheppard-Pratt patient), 206–207

Factory workplace. *See* Kirit Ata Workshop
Family, and borderline patient, *68–70, 110–111*
Fanon, Frantz, *The Wretched of the Earth*, 107
Fantasy
  about relationships, *225n6*
  in borderline patient, *143–147*
  vs. delusion, *225n6*
  demystification of, *143–147*
  in manic-depressive patient, *225n6*
  unconscious, *146–147*
Farming community. *See* Spring Lake Ranch
Father, and borderline patient, *65–66, 72–76, 136–137, 140–141, 143*
Fear, *118–122*. *See also* Terror
Feelings
  symbolic narrative and, 18–19
  talk about, at Spring Lake Ranch, 159–161
  thinking and, 23–24
Felman, Shoshana, 113
Foster care, and programs in Geel, Belguim, 197–200
Foucault, Michel, 34, 205–206, 211
Fountain House (New York City), 236n11
Freud, Sigmund, 11, 113, 121, 231n4, 232n1
Friendship, concept of, *109*

Geel, Belgium
  arguments in favor of foster care program in, 199–200
  criticism of foster care program in, 198, 199
  current treatment programs in, 197–200
  historic sensitivity to patient's public needs in, 197, 213
General will. *See* Common will
Giovaccini, P. L., 15

Grandiose self, in abnormal development, 97
Grotstein, J., 28

Haifa model. *See* Kirit Ata Workshop
Halfway house, 195, 196
  patient's view of, 208–209
Hall at Sheppard-Pratt. *See also* Quiet room at Sheppard-Pratt
  actions on, of patient slipping into psychosis, *40–41*
  community and, 26–27, *50–51, 53–54*, 148
Hallucination, in borderline patient, 70, *81–83, 93*, 109
Heinous crimes, and language of psychiatry, 222n5
Hierarchy, and Spring Lake Ranch, 153
Historical continuity
  impact of madness on, *37*
  shared illusion and, 122
Hobbes, Thomas, 7, 94, 99–100, 218
  self and, 99, 100, 118, 119
Holding environments, 94, 211–212
Holocaust
  borderline patient and, *63, 65, 69, 140, 145*
  schizophrenics on kibbutzim and, 201
  in self-description by borderline patient, *79–84*
Homelessness, 212
Homo faber, 158
Human development, fragmentation of self during, 96–100
Husband, and borderline patient, *75–78*

Illusion. *See also* Fantasy
  contrasted with delusion, 15–16, 122
  intersubjectivity and, 121
  shared, 117, 122
  transitional object for adult and, 116–117
  transitional space and, 16
Imaginary
  interpenetration of, with the Real, 6, 24–25
  as Real, *144–145*
Imaginatio, 176
  vs. *intellectio*, 23

Imitation, 17, 19
Individuality
  heroic action and, 216–218
  self-cohesion and, 217–219
  self-fragmentation and, 215–219
Individual will vs. general will
  on kibbutz, 201–203
  at Spring Lake Ranch, 159–166,
    186–187, 189
Inner world
  consensual reality and, 3
  terror in, 6, 94, 95
  violence of, 230n2
Interdependence. *See* Association;
  Community; Public self
Interpenetration of Imaginary with the
  Real, 6, 24–25
Intersubjectivity. *See also* Community;
  Relationships
  discovery of, in human community,
    49–55
  effect of public space on images of,
    26–28, *29–55*
  as form of community, 149
  in reemergence from mania, *50–55*
  in self-transformation, *50–55*
  terror of, *30–31*
Isolation. *See also* Loneliness
  emotional, 104
  in Phase 1 delusion, 125
  of schizophrenic in kibbutzim
    environment, 200
  sense of, in mental hospital patients,
    175
Israel
  collective emphasis in, 197
  programs for chronic mental patients
    in, 200–203

James, William, 24
"Julia" (borderline patient)
  body-as-text and, *114–118*
  current status of, 194
  disintegration of self and, *109*
  fascination with annihilation, *106–109*
  Phase 3 delusion and, *131*
Justice, hope for, 105

Kafka, Franz, 100, 104, 105, 108, 145,
  219
Kibbutzim, status of schizophrenics on,
  200–203
Kierkegaard, Søren, 120, 194
Kirit Ata Workshop (Haifa, Israel),
  200–201, 204, 205
Klein, Melanie, 99
Kohut, Heinz, 57, 58, 94, 119, 120
  The Analysis of the Self, 217
  individual in community and, 215–219
  "On Courage," 215-216
  theoretical concepts of, 96–100

Labor, in Arendt's theory, 157–158. *See also* Work
Lacan, Jacques, 6, 20, 34, 52, 125
  language and, 12–14, 18–19, 193–194
  Oedipus at Colonus and, 112–113,
    231n4, 231n5
Language
  and demystification of unconscious
    fantasies, *146–147*
  images of historical vs. symbolic truth
    in, *142–143*
  of metaphor, 21–25, 193, 218–219
  in psychoanalytic experience, 12–13
  sense of place and, *34*
Language of madness
  content of narratives and, 12–15
  interpenetration of Imaginary with the
    Real and, 6, 24–25
  as source of political knowledge, 7,
    19–21
  volatility of, 16
Language of psychiatry, 176
  heinous crimes and, 222n5
  metaphor and, 21, 23
  patient's sense of separateness and, 214
Lasch, Christopher, 232n8
LDS. *See* Locked-door seclusion
Lévi-Strauss, Claude, 14, 190
Life, death as way of, 113
Locked-door seclusion (LDS), at
  Sheppard-Pratt, 42–43
  manic-depressive patient in, *44–49*,
    226n1

Loneliness
patient's description of, *31–34*
wish for community and, 7
Loss, and manic defense, 51
"Louis" (Spring Lake Ranch resident),
167–168

Machiavelli, Niccoló, 21
Magritte, Réné, 219
Mania
characterization of, 50–51
descriptions of descent into, *35–42*
descriptions of reemergence from, *47–
49, 226n1*
intersubjectivity in reemergence from,
50–55
Manic-depressive personality. *See also*
"David"
delusion in narrative of, *131–132*
effects of public space on images of
intersubjectivity and, *29–55*
staff description of apparent coherence
in, *224n5*
Marx, Karl, 157
Masks, *66–67*, 130
Masochism
in borderline patient, *113*
as a dynamic of depression, *135–143*
Maternal function, at Spring Lake
Ranch, 185
Medical model. *See also* Language of
psychiatry; Mental hospital;
Psychotherapy
psychiatric diagnosis and, 176, *234n1*
and public self, 165, 203–205, 214–
215
Memory, destruction of, in psychosis, *37*
Mental hospital. *See also* Medical model;
Psychotherapy; Sheppard and
Enoch Pratt Hospital
as community, 148
elimination of patient from society
and, 209–210
patient anxiety over discharge from,
206–209
power relations and, 205–206
purposes of, and public self, 165, 205
relief from pain and, 206

role of patienthood at, 161–162,
164–165
ward in, as public realm, 6–7
Mental patients, view of, by borderline
patient, *79*, 202
Metaphor
language of, 21–25, 193, 218–219
reality and, 15–21
Mollica, R. F., *234n3*
Moral values, and interdependence, 51,
96
Mother, and borderline patient, *74–75,
144*
Mother-infant relation, and community
at Spring Lake Ranch, 172, 185
Musar movement, 87*n*
Mythos. See Metaphor

Narratives of mental patients. *See*
Language of madness; *specific
patients*
Narrative structure of therapeutic
community, 5
Nazi delusions, in borderline patient,
81–85, 93
Neighborliness, 190
Nietzsche, Friedrich, 15
Nonempathic world. *See also* Empathy
effects of, in development, 98
Kafkaesque figures and, 100
violence in borderline patient and,
119
Nonrational phenomena. *See also*
Metaphor
human nature and, 18–21
importance of, 23–24

Object relations, 160
Oedipus at Colonus, 103–104, 106,
112–113, 125, 193–194
O'Neill, Eugene, 219
Other
language and, 12–13
psychotherapy as truth-encounter
with, 113–114
therapeutic community as, 160

Pain
  as affirmation, *108*
  borderline patient and, *79, 90, 108,*
    136–137
  schizophrenic patient and, *128–129*
  "silent," in former mental patients,
    174–175
  therapy as relief from, 204, 206–207,
    214
"Panopticon" mentality, 206
Pao, Ning-Pie, 50–51
"Partial society," 189-190
Participative community, 167. *See also*
    Common will
  act of taking and, 170
  consciousness and, 150
  delusion and, 2–4
  views of Spring Lake Ranch residents
    on, 170–173
Passion. *See* Desire
Passivity
  psychotherapy and, 161–165, 204
  residents of Spring Lake Ranch and,
    169–170
Philosophy, Plato's view of, 17, 19
Pitié. See Empathy
Place, as synthesis of public and private,
    212–215. *See also* Public space
Plato, 16–17, 19, 230*n*1
Play, and delusion, 122
Poetry, and narratives of mental
    patients, 16–20, 22
Political culture, psychological
    foundations of, 122
Power relations, and patient's public
    self, 206
Primordial masochism, 113
Prisoners vs. mental patients, 209–210
Privacy. *See* Common will; Individual
    will vs. general will
Productivity, encouragement of, in
    chronic mental patients, 213–214.
    See also Work
Psychiatric diagnosis, 176, 234*n*1
Psychosis. *See also* Borderline
    personality; Manic-depressive
    personality; Schizophrenic patient

consensual reality and, 56, 57, 210–
    212
  destruction of memory in, *37*
  Imaginary vs. Real in, *34–36*
  process of slipping into, *35–39*
  separation and extinction in, 52
  terror in, *38–39*
Psychotherapy. *See also* Language of
    psychiatry; Medical model;
    Transference relation
  absence of, at Spring Lake Ranch,
    154, 159–166
  critique of, 161–165
  demystification of annihilation fantasy
    by, *143–147*
  and inner vs. public self, 214
  language in, 12–13
  lifting of depression in borderline
    patient and, *139–143*
  patient's identification with sickness
    and, 161–164
  relational capacities of self and, 99
  as relief from pain, 204, 206–207,
    214
  symbolic vs. historic truth and, *142*
  as truth-encounter with Other, 113–
    114
Public self. *See also* Association;
    Community; Intersubjectivity;
    Public space; Relationships; Sense
    of place
  limitations on power of, in
    schizophrenic patient, *180–183*
  medical model and, 165, 203–205,
    209–210, 214–215
  need for attention to, and chronic
    mental patients, 199–200, 212
  privacy and, 159–161
  vs. private, for delusional self, 28–31,
    53–54
  as of therapeutic and political
    significance, 150
  work and, 157–159
Public space. *See also* Community;
    Public self; Sense of place
  for chronic mental patients, 199–200
  citizenship as discovery of, 49–55

Public space (*cont.*)
  function of, 2, 26–28
  as political, 51–55

Quiet room at Sheppard-Pratt
  borderline patient and, *80*, *89*, *90*
  description of, 42
  manic-depressive patient and, *43*, *44*

"Rachel" (Spring Lake Ranch resident)
  hopeful outcome of community and,
    177–180
  psychiatric evaluations of, *177*
  staff description of progress of, *177–179*
Rage. *See* Anger
Razor, as transitional object, *115–118*,
  121
Reality. *See also* Consensual reality;
  Imaginary; Truth
  and metaphor, 15–21
Relationships. *See also* Community;
  Intersubjectivity
  borderline self and, 105, *107*, *109*
  in delusion, 52
  fantasy constructions about, *225n6*
  sense of self and, *30*
  torture in, *107*
Religious belief
  in narrative of borderline patient, *75–77*, *84*
  as shared illusion, 121, 122
Res publica, 158, 184–185. *See also*
  Public self
"Revolving door syndrome," 195
"Richard" (Spring Lake Ranch
  resident), 194
  limitations on power of public self in,
    180–183
  psychiatric evaluations of, *180–181*
  staff description of progress of, *181–183*
Ricoeur, Paul, 13–14, 21–25, 176
Rousseau, Jean-Jacques
  *Discourse on the Origin and Foundation
    of Inequality among Men*, 98, 233n1
  empathy and, 121
  Essay on the Origin of Language, 190
  interdependent existence and, 14

natural man and, 173
The Social Contract, 149, 159, 191
Rousseauian conception of community,
  94, 96
  Spring Lake Ranch and, 148–166,
    172–174, 183–192
Routine, and psychosis, *36*
"Ruth" (borderline patient)
  background on, *58–61*
  current status of, 194
  demystification of masochistic
    delusion by, *138–143*
  demystification of sacrifice and
    annihilation fantasy by, *143–147*
  disintegration of self and, *61–71*
  Phase 2 delusion in, *129–130*
  Phase 4 delusion in, *132–143*
  regression toward psychosis in, *72–85*
  return to humanity by, *86–102*
  self-description, *61–81*, *134*
  staff description of, at second
    hospitalization, *133–134*, *229n1*

Sacrifice, fantasy of suicide as, *143–147*
Sanity mask, 130
Sartre, Jean-Paul, *No Exit*, 107
Schizophrenic patient. *See also* "Chuck"
  consensual reality and, 56, 57, 210–212
  hopeful outcome of community and,
    177–180
  independence in, 173–174
  limitations on power of public self in,
    180–183
  pain and, *128–129*
  physiological causality and, 221n3
  Rousseauian community and, *172–174*
  status of, on kibbutzim, 200–203
Schumacher, E. F., 214
Scientific language. *See* Language of
  psychiatry
Searles, H., 15
Self. *See also* Public self
  and civil religion of Spring Lake
    Ranch, 192
  disintegration of, *61–71*, *109*
  fragmentation of, in development,
    96–100

Self (*cont.*)
  Hobbesian view of, 99, 100, 118, 119
  intersubjectivity of, 26
  as narrative text, 21–25
  as poisonous, 109–114
  as political, 1–5
  politics of, 3–5
  private, and psychotherapy, 159–166
  public vs. private, for delusional self, 28–31, *53–54*
  search for sense of, *31, 33*
Self-esteem, and public life, 191
Selfishness, 169
Self-mutilation
  anger and, 115
  nonempathic world and, *119*
  spiritual annihilation and, *106–107*
Self-objects
  archaic, 101
  defined, 97
  empathy-absent environments and, 97–98
  infant's relationship with, 97–98
Self-transformation, intersubjectivity in, *50–55*
Sense of place
  acts of speech and, *34*
  importance of, 2
  lack of, and deinstitutionalization, 195–196
  loss of, in borderline patient, 100–102
  prison inmates and, 209
Separation
  as life threatening, 14–15
  Rousseauian argument against, 191
Shared illusion, 117, 122
Sheltered workshops, and chronic mental patients, 196–197, 203
Sheppard, Moses, 27
Sheppard and Enoch Pratt Hospital
  background on, 27–28
  Hall at, 26–27, *50–51, 53–54,* 148
  locked-door seclusion at, 42–43, *44–49,* 226*n*1
  patients at. *See* "Alexandra"; "Andrew"; "Chuck"; "David"; "Eve"; "Julia"; "Ruth"
  quiet room at, 42, *43, 44, 80, 89, 90*

Sickness, patient's identification with, 161–164
"Silent pain," of former mental patients, *174–175*
Singer, Isaac Bashevis, 86*n*
Sirens' song, and delusion, *225n7*
Social contract. *See also* Rousseauian conception of community
  Spring Lake Ranch and, 149–150, 174, 183–192
Sophocles, *Oedipus at Colonus,* 103, 104
Sovereignty, at Spring Lake Ranch, 185–186
Space-time continuum, in psychosis, 223*n*2, 226*n*3
Split-off self, and development, 97
Spring Lake Ranch. *See also* Staff, at Spring Lake Ranch
  administration at, 154–155
  authority at, 187
  bureaucracy and, 153–155
  common will at, 159–166, 184–190, 202–203
  as model of coproduction, 235*n*11
  overview of, 148–150
  as political community, 158–159
  private concerns at, 186–187
  resident composition at, *1983-1984,* 152
  residents at. *See* "Aaron"; "Annie"; "Billy"; "Ed"; "Louis"; "Rachel"; "Richard"
  Rousseauian conception of community and, 148–166, *172–174,* 183–192
  setting and context at, 151–159
  sovereignty and, 185–186
  therapeutic function of work at, 155–159, 191–192
  types of residents at, in view of resident, 169
  work as civil religion at, 150, 191–192
  work crews at, 151, 155, 157, 159, 167
Staff, at Spring Lake Ranch
  critique of psychotherapy by, 161–165

Staff, at Spring Lake Ranch (*cont.*)
divisions of, 153–154
and relations to residents, 151, 155, *171–172*, 185
Staff, in narrative by borderline patient, *63*, *87*, *91*
State hospital, and chronic mental patient, 234*n*5
Storytelling, in psychoanalysis, 13–14
Suicide. *See also* Annihilation; Death
in narrative of borderline patient, *61–63*, *69–71*, *88–89*
resourcefulness of mental patients and, 175
in staff-description of borderline patient, *60–61*
Symbol. *See also* Delusion; Fantasy; Illusion
razor as, for borderline patient, 115
as real, in consciousness, 12–13
shared illusion and, 51, 122
Symbolization, in narrative
importance of, 15–21
orders of, 15–16

Technological society, and chronic mental patients, 179–180, 195–198, 213
Terror
delusional, empathy as modulation of, 94, 95
of inner world, 6
of intersubjectivity, *30–31*
in psychosis, *38–39*
Therapeutic community
inequality in, 223*n*1
narrative structure of, 5
as public realm, 6–7
Spring Lake environment as, 150
Theseus, 104
Thinking, process of, and nonrational dynamics, 23–24
Tolerance
chronic mental patients and, 211
in political culture, 197, 205, 213
Torture, in fantasy, *107*, *144*

Transference relation. *See also* Psychotherapy
depression in borderline patient and, *139–143*
functions of, in community, 160
Transitional object
for adult, 116–117
borderline self and, 116, 231*n*6, 233*n*2
consent to be in society and, 122
illusory quality of, 121
for infant, 116–117
isolation and, 94–95
psychotic, 116
razor as, *115–118*, *121*
Transitional space, and illusion, 16
Trust
affective significance of, 101
delusion and, 122
public activity and, 162
Truth. *See also* Reality
notion of, 24
symbolic vs. historic, *142–143*
Turkle, Sherry, 221*n*2
Tyranny of delusional self, 5

Unconscious, as discourse, 12

Voices, experienced by mental patients, *78*, *128–129*, *135*, *138–139*, *181–183*
Voodoo, in narrative of schizophrenic patient, *128–129*

Weight gain and loss, function of, *106–107*, *111–112*
Will of all vs. general will, 188–190
Will-to-be, *53*, *54*
Winnicott, D. W., 16, 94–95, 107, 109, 110, 119, 185
as Rousseauian, 121–122
transitional object and, 116–117
Work
chronic mental patient and, 196–197, 199, 200, 211–212
as civil religion, 150, 191–192
foster care program in Geel, Belguim and, 199

Work (*cont.*)
  programs in Israel and, 200
  recognition of innate productivity
    and, 163, 164
  at Spring Lake Ranch, 151, 155–159,
    191–192
  theoretical perspective on, 157–158

therapeutic function of, 155–159,
  191–192
Work crews, at Spring Lake Ranch,
  151, 155, 157, 159, 167
Worthlessness, sense of, 104, *141*, *145*,
  146

Library of Congress Cataloging-in-Publication Data

Glass, James M.
  Private terror/public life : psychosis and the politics of
community / James M. Glass.
      p.   cm.
    Bibliography: p.
    Includes index.
    ISBN 0-8014-2300-7
    1. Delusions—Social aspects.   2. Delusions—Social aspects—Case
studies.   3. Self-perception.   4. Social interaction—Psychological
aspects.   5. Alienation (Social psychology)   6. Psychiatric hospital
patients.   I. Title.
RC553.D34G54   1989
616.89—dc20   89-31059